D1520234

Psychiatric Practice Under Fire

*The Influence of Government, the Media,
and Special Interests on Somatic Therapies*

ISSUES IN
PSYCHIATRY

Joseph D. Bloom, M.D.
Series Editor

Psychiatric Practice Under Fire

The Influence of Government, the Media, and Special Interests on Somatic Therapies

Edited by

Harold I. Schwartz, M.D.
Associate Professor and Associate Chairman
Department of Psychiatry
University of Connecticut School of Medicine
Farmington, Connecticut

Vice President, Clinical Affairs
and Medical Director
The Institute of Living
Hartford Hospital's Mental Health Network
Hartford, Connecticut

Washington, DC
London, England

Note: The authors have worked to ensure that all information in this book concerning drug dosages, schedules, and routes of administration is accurate as of the time of publication and consistent with standards set by the U.S. Food and Drug Administration and the general medical community. As medical research and practice advance, however, therapeutic standards may change. For this reason and because human and mechanical errors sometimes occur, we recommend that readers follow the advice of a physician who is directly involved in their care or the care of a member of their family.

Books published by the American Psychiatric Press, Inc., represent the views and opinions of the individual authors and do not necessarily represent the policies and opinions of the Press or the American Psychiatric Association.

Copyright © 1994 American Psychiatric Press, Inc.
ALL RIGHTS RESERVED
Manufactured in the United States of America on acid-free paper
97 96 95 94   4 3 2 1
First Edition
American Psychiatric Press, Inc.
1400 K Street, N.W., Washington, DC 20005

Library of Congress Cataloging-in-Publication Data
Psychiatric practice under fire : the influence of government, the
    media, and special interests on somatic therapies / edited by Harold
    I. Schwartz. — 1st ed.
        p. cm. — (Issues in psychiatry)
    Includes bibliographical references and index.
    ISBN 0-88048-479-9
    1. Biological psychiatry—United States. 2. Psychiatry in the
press—United States. 3. Biological psychiatry—Social aspects—
United States. 4. Biological psychiatry—Government policy—United
States. 5. Psychotropic drugs—Law and legislation—United States.
I. Schwartz, Harold I. II. Series.
    [DNLM: 1. Mental Disorders—drug therapy—United States—
legislation. 2. Psychotropic Drugs—therapeutic use—United
States—legislation. 3. Public Policy—United States. 4. Mass
Media. WM 33 AA1 P85 1994]
RC343.P88 1994
616.89—dc20
DNLM/DLC
for Library of Congress   94-26327
                                                                       CIP

British Library Cataloguing in Publication Data
A CIP record is available from the British Library.

*To Karen, Daniel,
and Jonathan*

Contents

The Influence of Special Interests, the Media, and the Courts on Psychotropic Drugs and Electroconvulsive Therapy

CHAPTER ONE

CHAPTER TWO

CHAPTER THREE

CHAPTER FOUR

Cost Containment: At the Cost
of Quality and Access?

Regulation of Controlled Substances
and New Drug Development: Law and
Scientific Practice at the Crossroads

Contributors

Robert T. Angarola, J.D.
Former General Counsel
White House Office of Drug Abuse Policy
Director
U.S. Cancer Pain Committee
Hyman, Phelps and McNamara
Washington, D.C.

Harold Bursztajn, M.D.
Associate Professor of Psychiatry and Codirector
Program in Psychiatry and Law
Harvard Medical School Department of Psychiatry at the
  Massachusetts Mental Health Center
Boston, Massachusetts

Alex A. Cardoni, M.S. Pharm.
Associate Professor of Clinical Pharmacy and
  Assistant Clinical Professor of Psychiatry
University of Connecticut
Storrs and Farmington
Clinical Psychopharmacology Consultant
Department of Psychiatry
Hartford Hospital
Hartford, Connecticut

James R. Cooper, M.D.
Chief
Medical Affairs Branch
Division of Clinical Research
National Institute on Drug Abuse
Rockville, Maryland

Dorynne J. Czechowicz, M.D.
Associate Director for Medical and Professional Affairs
Medical Affairs Branch
Division of Clinical Research
National Institute on Drug Abuse
Rockville, Maryland

Rodney Deaton, M.D., J.D.
Assistant Clinical Professor of Psychiatry
Indiana University School of Medicine, Indianapolis
Private practice, forensic psychiatry
Indianapolis, Indiana

Aaron Gilson, M.S.
Assistant for Policy Research
Pain Research Group
University of Wisconsin Medical School
Madison, Wisconsin

David J. Greenblatt, M.D.
Professor of Pharmacology and Experimental Therapeutics,
  Psychiatry, and Medicine
Tufts University School of Medicine
Boston, Massachusetts
Division of Clinical Pharmacology
New England Medical Center Hospital
Boston, Massachusetts

Edward Hanin, M.D.
Clinical Professor of Psychiatry
New York Medical College, Valhalla
Associate Chairman for Training and Research
Department of Psychiatry
St. Vincent's Hospital and Medical Center of New York
New York, New York

C. Stratton Hill, Jr., M.D.
Professor of Medicine
University of Texas
M. D. Anderson Cancer Center
Houston, Texas

David E. Joranson, M.S.S.W.
Associate Scientist and Director
Policy Studies
Pain Research Group
University of Wisconsin Medical School
Madison, Wisconsin

Richard B. Karel
Assistant Editor and Reporter
Psychiatric News
American Psychiatric Association
Washington, D.C.

Alan G. Minsk, J.D.
Attorney
Hyman, Phelps and McNamara
Washington, D.C.

Glen N. Peterson, M.D.
Private practice of general psychiatry
Oakland, California
ECT Consultant to California Psychiatric Association
Past Executive Director
Association for Convulsive Therapy

Jerrold F. Rosenbaum, M.D.
Associate Professor of Psychiatry
Harvard Medical School
Boston, Massachusetts
Director, Outpatient Psychiatry and Chief
Clinical Psychopharmacology Unit
Massachusetts General Hospital
Boston, Massachusetts

Harold I. Schwartz, M.D.
Associate Professor and Associate Chairman
Department of Psychiatry
University of Connecticut School of Medicine
Farmington, Connecticut
Vice President, Clinical Affairs and Medical Director
The Institute of Living
Hartford Hospital's Mental Health Network
Hartford, Connecticut

Introduction

The delivery of health care in America is a huge enterprise that is said to account for one-seventh of our gross national product. Health care has many parts: the training, licensing, and professional practice of physicians, nurses, and hosts of allied health care professionals; the hospital, nursing home, health care systems, and insurance industries; the pharmaceutical and medical technology industries; and the basic science and clinical research enterprise. The points of intersection between these many (and other) parts are nearly infinite; the complexity of the enterprise is virtually unparalleled; and the requirements for a safe, effective, and now cost-effective quality product are defining. It would be difficult to imagine that such an enterprise would not be heavily regulated. Indeed, the regulation of medical/health care practice in America has become such an industry in itself that a reduction in paperwork has become one of the goals of President Clinton's health care reform proposals.

Regulation is of course critical to the delivery of safe and effective health care. The courts, legislatures, and executive branches (through administrative law) at all levels, along with professional institutions and organizations, have had responsibility for critical functions such as regulating education, licensing practitioners and institutions, establishing and enforcing standards of practice and care, overseeing pharmaceutical and other product development, and regulating insurance, reimbursement, and access issues. Regulation in each of these areas is unquestionably vital for maintaining standards and uncovering lapses in practice. At the same time, as the complexity of health care has grown, the regulatory process has expanded in scope and depth, and, for the clinician, administrator, or executive in health care, meeting regulatory requirements sometimes seems to have displaced patient care as the focus of our attention. Health care reform will further revolutionize the delivery of health care through a host of regulations bearing on insurance, the structure of health care systems, and access to care.

Perhaps no medical specialty has experienced the impact of regulation to quite the degree as has psychiatry. Indeed, concerns about abuses possible in psychiatric institutions, the liberty interests of involuntarily treated patients, the possible overlap of treatment, and "behavior control," along with the seemingly unscientific nature of the psychotherapeutic enterprise, have all contributed to the regulation of psychiatric practice. Psychiatry is clearly at the forefront of those specialty practices most subject to cost-control regulation, perhaps because of a persistent skepticism on the part of the public and policymakers regarding the disease model of mental illness and a reluctance to acknowledge the efficaciousness of psychiatric treatments.

It is the premise of this book that the regulation of psychiatric practice is growing rapidly despite the rapid growth of a scientific neurobiology at the foundation of that practice. In fact, the practice of biological psychiatry appears increasingly to be besieged by forces seeking to control the interaction between doctor and patient. To make this argument, the authors of the 12 chapters contained in this book have culled from their own experience and research efforts or from the professional and lay literatures the most compelling examples of regulation gone awry or of regulatory-like influences that deleteriously affect sound clinical care. Although their views are strong, I am comfortable in allowing the material to speak for itself. This book should not be taken as an argument for an unregulated health care industry but rather as a warning that the goals of health care regulation may be confused by the goals of competing public policy or special interests and that the scientific basis of sound regulation may too easily be eroded.

The confusion of public policy goals is seen, for example, when federal and state legislation aimed at controlling substance abuse has the effect of interfering with the legitimate use of controlled substances in medical practice. Indeed, the treatment of severe and persistent pain in America is now acknowledged to be in crisis, in large part due to questionable drug control policies that contribute to massive underprescribing of opioids. Controlled substance regulation intended for opioids may be extended to classes of psychotropic medications such as benzodiazepines at considerable risk to patient care. The legitimate medical use of benzodiazepines declined with unfortunate consequences for patients, when New York State, in 1989, extended its triplicate prescription program to this class of medication.

The courts constitute another formal regulatory mechanism that threatens to dictate the shape of somatic psychiatric practice. In establishing the right to refuse treatment, courts have demonstrated a willingness to supplant medical judgments with legal ones, for example when making such fundamentally clinical judgments as the determination of the need for treatment and the appropriateness of particular treatment courses in individual cases. Administrative codes are another form of regulation that may further irrationally restrict practice, as in the strict codes that inhibit the use of electroconvulsive therapy (ECT) in California and elsewhere.

Although regulatory law, in its various manifestations, has generally attempted to balance various public policy goals (e.g., the need to control the diversion of illicit substances and the need to make controlled substances available for legitimate medical purposes), an implicit underlying principle in the regulation of medical practice has been that, at least in theory, regulations would be guided by scientifically determined standards of practice, or at least, that empirically determined clinical standards would not be sacrificed to other public policy objectives. Today, although most formal regulation of somatic psychiatry remains clinically sensible, the premise that formal regulation and less formal regulatory-like influences are driven by clinical science is being dangerously eroded. When quality of care was the only consideration, standards of quality formulated by clinical science were the unchallenged determinants of standards of practice. Now quality and cost containment are spoken in one breath. The imposition of managed care practices has had a huge regulatory-like impact on the use of somatic therapies (e.g., on the length of antidepressant drug trials that psychiatric inpatients may receive before a drug change or augmentation is imposed, perhaps prematurely). Managed care is, in fact, an experiment, the outcome of which is judged primarily by its impact on cost and secondarily by its impact on the quality of care. Were this a biological therapy with promise of equivalent impact, it would be carefully studied in select populations (who gave informed consent) before its use could be generalized to the public.

Perhaps most striking is the regulatory-like influence that special interest groups are exerting through the media and the courts. One study documented the deplorable decline in the legitimate use of methylphenidate for children with attention-deficit hyperactivity disorder in the Baltimore area following a negative media campaign and a spate of lawsuits believed to have been fomented by the Church of Scientology (Safer and Krager 1992). The children who went untreated suffered demonstrable declines in school performance as a result. Such negative media campaigns have labeled fluoxetine (Prozac) a "killer drug." But perhaps no therapeutic modality has been as much the victim of media vilification and inappropriate regulation as ECT. ECT has long been a target of the antipsychiatry movement and has been inappropriately constrained by the courts, local and state statutes, and administrative law. It is almost incredible to think that a municipal government (Berkeley, California) could by referendum ban, even temporarily, a vital therapeutic modality whose efficacy and safety are overwhelmingly documented in the world literature.

Physicians (and patients) are losing their autonomy in medical care delivery at an alarming rate. The regulation of practice seems increasingly to be driven by nonscientific objectives and to reflect public policy goals such as cost containment, the prevention of illicit drug diversion, or the influence of special interest groups, often at the expense of appropriate psychiatric treatment. That such developments can occur in formal regulatory bodies reflects a larger trend in American society and culture, the devaluation of the scientific process and the erosion of professional authority. We must now contend with the regulatory influence of *Geraldo, Oprah, Donahue,* and other tabloid vehicles, which compound the organized antipsychiatry efforts of disaffected ex-patient groups, Scientology, and other special interests by debasing the level of discussion about ECT, antidepressants "that kill," psychostimulants, and other valuable treatment modalities.

These developments are not occurring in a vacuum. They reflect anti-intellectual, unscientific, and antipsychiatric sentiments that are growing throughout our society. The outcome is regulation or regulatory-like influences that are controversial at best, unscientific and even irrational at worst. These themes need to be identified, examined, and recognized as the threat to patient care that they represent. To that end, this book is devoted.

Reference

Safer DJ, Krager JM: Effects of a media blitz and a threatened lawsuit on stimulant treatment. JAMA 268:1004–1007, 1992

Acknowledgments

I wish to acknowledge Stephen B. Soumerai, Sc.D., and Karen Blank, M.D., for their review of portions of the manuscript. I wish especially to acknowledge my administrative assistant, Carrol Mallory, for her invaluable help in all aspects of manuscript preparation.

The Influence of Special Interests, the Media, and the Courts on Psychotropic Drugs and Electroconvulsive Therapy

CHAPTER ONE

Clinical Trial by Media: The Prozac Story

Jerrold F. Rosenbaum, M.D.

Every psychiatrist knows, by training and experience, that powerful emotions are generally shadowed by their opposites. Experienced therapists are vigilant when idealized by patients, knowing that this initial "therapeutic honeymoon" heralds a rocky therapeutic road ahead. The higher the pedestal, the harder the fall. Perhaps it was this insight, derived from having spent so much time around psychiatrists, that explained the initial response by Dista (Lilly) Prozac (fluoxetine) sales representatives to the cover stories in *New York* magazine (Schumer 1989) and *Newsweek* (Cowley 1990) that heralded their antidepressant as either a "wonder drug" or a "breakthrough drug." Rather than reacting with enthusiasm to what seemed like priceless free publicity, company representatives appeared to cringe at the hype and idealization as reflected in true, but atypical, stories of miraculous transformation from treatment.

Because the overall efficacy in unselected populations of depressed patients appeared to be the same for this newer agent, fluoxetine, as for older ones, perhaps the feared reactive devaluation to this idealization would derive from the unmet expectations of unhappy consumers, enthusiastically seeking the same miracle response to the wonder drug. Other constituencies also might be perturbed by this focus on a single antidepressant agent—for example, psychotherapists averse to the use of pharmacotherapies, or rival pharmaceutical manufacturers attempting to redress imbalance. Perhaps, as would later turn out to be the case, groups antagonistic to psychiatric treatments in general would seize the moment to counterattack. But at that time, in early 1990, the real threat was probably celebrity status; Prozac was "news." Prozac was news because the stories suggested that pain, anguish, suffering, drug abuse, and a variety of ailments might yield to the taking of a pill. Prozac was news because 3 million members of our society had already tried this new agent. And news meant that news writers had a place to search for stories, and the quest for a story meant the need to generate reader and viewer interest, to find material that was exciting, alarming, and that would sell copy or airtime. The concern and anticipation of backlash was, as it turned out, appropriate; within a year of featuring in large letters the word "Prozac" on its cover along with a transcendent, floating fluoxetine pulvule, *Newsweek* headlined a vividly illustrated piece with the title "A Prozac Backlash" (Cowley 1991).

The media frenzy was extraordinary in its intensity and duration. By the time the national and local newspapers, magazines, television reports and specials were subsiding, Prozac had achieved a name recognition among the American public usually reserved for such national figures as presidents and vice presidents. By then, even good news and balanced reporting were perceived by the public as negative. Any statement about the drug, whatever its valence, sent jitters through current patients, prospective patients, and ultimately prescribers. These media events changed delivery of antidepressant treatment for patients, altered prescribing practices by physicians, and undoubtedly resulted in untreated depression and discontinued treatment of depression, with attendant costs to individuals and society in social and work impairment, personal and family suffering, and lives lost to suicide. All of this took place despite the overwhelming message from systematically ascertained data that this new agent, fluoxetine, compared with other treatments or compared with no treatment, was as safe or safer with respect to the emergence of suicidal ideation or behavior and far safer in terms of overdose toxicity. This course of events also raised questions about the ability of scientific medicine to stand up to the media and about the role of professional medical or psychiatric organizations to act to maintain balance with respect to educating the public. In the following sections, I present an overview of this story of Prozac and the media.

Prozac: The Drug

The original recognition, in the 1950s, that certain drugs could treat depression was revolutionary. The observation that a weak antitubercular drug, iproniazid, could elevate mood preceded the observation that drugs that inhibited the enzyme monoamine oxidase would be effective in depression. In the late 1950s, certain tricyclic agents were also observed to be able to relieve depression. That these were miracle drugs for those who could tolerate their side effects sufficiently to achieve an adequate dose and an adequate duration of treatment was indisputable. On the other hand, because of an array of side effects and other risks, substantial numbers of patients were unable to tolerate treatment; others, including responders to treatment, were burdened over time by annoying and occasionally dangerous effects. Clinicians worried also about fatal consequences ranging from drug-drug and dietary interactions with monoamine oxidase inhibitors or fatal over-doses with tricyclic antidepressants (TCAs) or monoamine oxidase inhibitors. The focus of new drug development was on improving the tolerability of treatment, initially with promotion of more tolerable TCAs (such as the secondary amine compounds, desipramine and nortriptyline) to a variety of strategies to counter unwanted adverse effects (Pollack and Rosenbaum 1987). It seemed likely that many of the adverse effects of these older agents derived from pharmacological properties that were not pertinent or specific to their antidepressant efficacy. Although TCAs had a variety of effects on acetylcholine, histamine, and α-adrenergic and other neurotransmitter receptors, investigations of the mechanism of action pointed to effects in the central norepinephrine and serotonin systems.

In the late 1960s and early 1970s, scientists at Eli Lilly and Company, particularly Ray W. Fuller, Ph.D., and David T. Wong, Ph.D., began to consider more seriously the question of a deficiency of serotonin linked to the pathophysiology of depression as well as the mechanism of action of antidepressants. Relatively low levels of serotonin had been reported in the central nervous system of depressed patients who had committed suicide (Bourne et al. 1968). The recognition by other investigators (Snyder and Coyle 1969) that specific neuronal uptake mechanisms for serotonin were present in the nervous system suggested a target site for antidepressant treatment development; inhibition of serotonin uptake could augment the effect of serotonin on its postsynaptic receptors. By early 1972, the technology existed to screen for molecules that could selectively inhibit serotonin uptake, and hundreds of new compounds were screened, including 57 phenoxyphenyl-propanamine derivatives, the class from which fluoxetine would come. From these compounds, fluoxetine was discovered in May of 1972 and was shown to have specific and enduring inhibition of serotonin uptake in rat synaptosomes. Tests on animals revealed that this effect occurred in vivo, and the first scientific publications on fluoxetine were presented in the spring of 1974 (Wong et al. 1974). The first human studies of fluoxetine in nondepressed volunteers began in May of 1976 and revealed that the drug was well tolerated up to 80 mg/day. The first fluoxetine phase 2 studies began in March of 1978, followed by phase 3 clinical trials beginning in January of 1981. The new drug application was submitted to the Food and Drug Administration (FDA) in the fall of 1983; it received a recommendation of approvability from the Advisory Committee in October of 1985 and was eventually approved for release on December 29, 1987, more than 4 years after the submission. By the beginning of 1993, more than 3,000 scientific articles had been published on fluoxetine. Within a few years of its introduction, Prozac, estimated to be generating a half a million new prescriptions a month, had become the most frequently prescribed antidepressant in the United States and was on its way to becoming one of the most successful drugs of all time.

What accounted for this early success? The expected side-effect advantages of this relatively selective new agent were apparent in clinical trials where approximately twice the number of patients on comparator agents (mainly TCAs) discontinued treatment because of side effects compared with fluoxetine. Lacking anticholinergic, antihistaminergic, and α-adrenergic blocking proprieties, fluoxetine spared patients the array of side effects consequent to these pharmacological properties, including dry mouth, blurry vision, constipation, cognitive impairment, tachycardia, sedation, weight gain, and postural hypotension; further, absent Type 1A antiarrhythmic (quinidine-like) effects, fluoxetine was not associated with intracardiac conduction delay and serious cardiac toxicity in overdose. Except for its greater cost when compared with older, generic antidepressants, and assuming comparable efficacy across subtypes of depression, the new agent was a clear advance over its predecessors.

Comparability of efficacy with respect to depressive subtypes remained a question for research. For example, some clinicians stood by with the older tricyclic agents for more severely depressed, hospitalized melancholic patients despite the absence of evidence that either melancholia or severity distinguished a group of tricyclic as opposed to fluoxetine responders. At the same time, many clinicians believed, and emerging data appear to support, the possibility that fluoxetine had a broader spectrum of efficacy, including superior efficacy for the chronic and milder depression subtypes, including atypical depressive, dysthymic, and other patients whose depressed mood and dysphoria had generally led to DSM-III-R (American Psychiatric Association 1987) Axis II diagnostic formulations. Fluoxetine also offered superior antibulimic and anti–obsessive-compulsive disorder effects.

Fluoxetine's lowest available dose, usually tolerated, was an adequate dose for most patients. This offered clear public health benefits, since most depressed patients are initially seen and treated by nonpsychiatric physicians, where antidepressant prescribing is generally avoided or administered with inadequate dose or duration. The availability of a low-risk, easy-to-prescribe, and easy-to-dose antidepressant promised to deliver adequate antidepressant pharmacotherapy to a much broader population. Fluoxetine, however, was not without side effects. Its side effects generally derived from the same mechanism of action that accounted for its therapeutic effects, in contrast with the older agents, whose adverse effects, in part, reflected properties unrelated to antidepressant mechanisms of action. In particular, fluoxetine was associated with side effects typical of the emerging class of selective serotonin reuptake inhibitors (SSRIs), including nausea, nervousness and anxiety, insomnia, and some increase in headaches. In only a small percentage of patients in clinical trials, however, were these side effects a reason for discontinuation. Some patients not able to tolerate the initial 20-mg dose because of nausea or anxiety were able to initiate therapy with lower doses, and clinicians learned to reformulate the agent by mixing capsule contents in water or juice and administering a 5- or 10-mg dose.

Wonder Drug

With its generally benign side-effect profile, ease of administration, and broad spectrum of efficacy, fluoxetine offered the possibility that treatment of depression, other than for treatment-resistant or complicated cases, was now safe and straightforward enough to be handled by primary care physicians. Psychopharmacologists would lightheartedly speculate about the implications of this possibility for the survival of their guild. Within 2 years of its release, however, fluoxetine would be the focus of a controversy that would render this concern premature.

During this time, systematic study of the longitudinal course of depression indicated that, for the majority of patients, treatment was not short term; for those with three or more prior episodes, with chronic symptoms before recovery, or with later onset of depression, the maintenance treatment of depression to prevent relapse would require long-term intervention. Long-term maintenance treatment meant the multiplying of short-term side effects over time, and increased the relative advantages of an agent that for many was not only extremely tolerable but for a significant number was indistinguishable from placebo.

On March 26, 1990, the cover of *Newsweek* featured, in letters larger than the name of the magazine itself, the word "PROZAC" with the subheading "A Breakthrough Drug for Depression." Beneath those words, floating ethereally in the clouds over a mountainous landscape was a 20-mg capsule of Prozac. Page 3 of the magazine featured a pill bottle with the words "The Power of Prozac" and a teaser paragraph with the title "A Promising New Weapon Against Depression." Partly in response to a previous feature story in *New York* magazine (Schumer 1989), the *Newsweek* article (Cowley 1990) posed the question "But is it really a wonder drug?" Beginning with the story of a middle-aged woman with a history of depression, bulimia, drug and alcohol abuse, and suicide attempts who had failed to tolerate a TCA the article noted that within a month of beginning Prozac, the patient had given up psychotherapy in favor of school and a full-time job, had quit tranquilizers and street drugs, no longer had murderous rages, and had made her marriage five times better while her well-being had improved "1,000%." Alongside such dramatic accounts, this article, like others, also featured the drug's revenues, indicating that Prozac would "pull in" a half a billion dollars in 1990 and was soon to be a billion-dollar product.

Buried in this article was the cautionary tale, endorsed by the manufacturer itself, that all drugs have the potential for adverse reactions, and that none works for everyone who takes it, including Prozac. For example, Prozac was noted in rare cases to be associated with mania, violence, or suicidality. Perhaps this comment was the antecedent for all the articles, lawsuits, and television specials that were to follow.

Despite the glamorous cover, the article itself had balance, and the most important message was left to the end: "As Prozac's success stories mount, so does the sense that depression and other mental disorders are just that—treatable illness, not failings of character. The stigma is receding and the search for still better treatments is accelerating" (Cowley 1990, p. 41). For some reason, this essential message became lost as the cited example of possible rare adverse effects, and not the larger picture, became the story. Within months, the name *Prozac* and the word *suicide* were to become inextricably linked while the forces driving this association were to remain obscure.

By the summer of 1990, newspaper and television reporters were detailing again and again a case series originally reported in the *American Journal of Psychiatry* describing the new onset of obsessional suicidal ideation in six patients who had been on Prozac (Teicher et al. 1990). The first of a series of lawsuits against Eli Lilly and Company had been filed alleging that Prozac had caused a woman to commit acts of self-destruction and to make multiple attempts at suicide. The first suit sought $150 million in damages. Quoted in *The Wall Street Journal* (Waldholz 1990), Leonard Finz, attorney for the plaintiff, claimed "the drug wasn't properly tested [and that] warnings of its horrendous effects haven't been made to the public" (p. B1). Eschewing response in the media, Eli Lilly responded, stating that "information about the drug should be communicated by [patients'] doctors, not by the media" (p. B1). In addition to the usual focus on the drug's commercial success and comments on the lawsuit, the article noted that it was the report by Teicher and colleagues that had suggested the link between the antidepressant and the suicidal thoughts and behavior.

By the fall of 1990, multiple lawsuits had been filed alleging both the induction of suicidal ideation and behavior as well as a number of

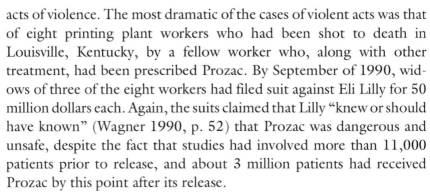

acts of violence. The most dramatic of the cases of violent acts was that of eight printing plant workers who had been shot to death in Louisville, Kentucky, by a fellow worker who, along with other treatment, had been prescribed Prozac. By September of 1990, widows of three of the eight workers had filed suit against Eli Lilly for 50 million dollars each. Again, the suits claimed that Lilly "knew or should have known" (Wagner 1990, p. 52) that Prozac was dangerous and unsafe, despite the fact that studies had involved more than 11,000 patients prior to release, and about 3 million patients had received Prozac by this point after its release.

The number of news articles, magazine stories, and television features are beyond counting. The Prozac backlash had clearly taken hold, as illustrated in the title of one article in *American Health* (Grady 1990) entitled "Wonder Drug/Killer Drug." The cover of the issue introduced the story: "The Prozac Scare: A Wonder Drug's Rise and Fall." Articles and reports detailed the same suits, the same plaintiff attorney, and the same *American Journal of Psychiatry* case report (Teicher et al. 1990). In *American Health,* Grady noted that "Prozac's strengths and weaknesses have now been blown far out of proportion. It must be judged against the terrible condition it was designed for—depression" (p. 65).

The attempt at balance, however, would not take hold. The "wonder drug" revisionism moved forward as, for example, the *Washington Post* news magazine *Health* asked on its cover, "Prozac: Is It Really the 'Wonder Drug' for Depression?" (Marcus 1990). Marcus noted "but into the life of a drug so successful, inevitably some rain must fall" (p. 12). Gradually, a kind of pseudo-balance would emerge in these articles as systematically assessed data from extensive clinical trials, FDA reviews, and postmarketing surveillance of patients numbering in the millions stood side by side with individual case reports and pictures of individuals who had suffered or perpetrated suicidal or violent acts. In the article, a New York woman is pictured pointing to a scar from a suicide attempt she had blamed on Prozac. Articles questioned whether Prozac should not be prescribed by nonpsychiatric physicians. The impact of this publicity was felt in the consulting room as new patients balked at the prescription of Prozac and even patients who were doing well on Prozac, either frightened by media or family members, elected to discontinue. The following letter, received at our unit, illustrates this.

> Dear Doctor,
>   I wish to discontinue my Prozac. I watched the Joan Rivers show yesterday and even though you had given me the paper explaining those negative things about Prozac, this program really gave me second thoughts.
>   I will just try harder to get myself together, to get to more Al-Anon meetings and hope for the best. I have limited medical coverage and I came to you with sincere hopes. Thank you for considering me, sorry for any inconvenience.

Even those who had had the "wonder drug" response began to feel the heat. Commenting on a neighbor who had extolled the virtues of her Prozac for having finally made her well, one woman declared "and she says she feels her depression is a thing of the past. Well if she wants to go ahead and commit suicide, I guess that's her problem."

An initial clue to some of the forces driving this attention was the fact that very few of the reports of tragic outcomes questioned the behavior of either the prescriber or the patients. If, indeed, some patients were getting worse with treatment, why was all the focus on the drug and not the treater? Denise Grady (1990) in the *American Health* magazine piece wrote, "Some experts wonder whether fluoxetine survivors are the victims of bad doctoring rather than a bad drug: people taking any psychiatric medication are supposed to be monitored closely, and those that get worse are supposed to be taken off the drug fast" (p. 62). For instance, a patient stayed on fluoxetine for a year and a half, yet she is suing Lilly, not her doctor. Unfortunately, by this point, some treatment responders were discontinuing treatments, and ironically and undoubtedly some of those had become suicidal. Further, some prescribers were likely changing therapy in favor of agents that would be less tolerable and therefore less effective or certainly more lethal if used in overdose.

The Data

By this time, six anecdotal cases—a highly controversial cluster of six complicated and atypical patients—were being referred to as a "major study" even by such sophisticated news reporters as Chris Wallace on the ABC news show *Nightline*. The original report was of six depressed patients who had become intensely preoccupied with suicide while on fluoxetine, and whose symptoms ultimately abated 60–106 days after treatment was withdrawn. The following was also true of some or all of these patients: 1) none had responded to prior treatments (e.g., one patient had failed to respond to more than 15 prior drug treatments); 2) all suffered well-known side effects of fluoxetine treatment, principally marked agitation or anxiety but also fatigue, which was responded to by dose escalation rather than reduction or counteractive treatment; 3) concurrent treatment included other drugs also known to cause agitation (e.g., neuroleptics and stimulants); 4) three patients had discontinued treatment with a monoamine oxidase inhibitor before Prozac; and 5) none had responded to fluoxetine. Additional complicating clinical features of these patients included temporal lobe epilepsy, paranoia, borderline personality, multiple personality disorder, and bipolar disorder. All of these patients had experienced some degree of suicidal ideation or behavior in the past prior to fluoxetine.

Teicher and colleagues (1990) were not the first to report a paradoxical worsening and emergence of intense suicidal ideation concomitant with antidepressant treatment. Damluji and Ferguson (1988) had previously described agitation and suicidal ideation, not present in their cases before treatment, which emerged with the use of the TCA desipramine. Of interest, two of these patients recovered when treatment was switched from a TCA to fluoxetine. Other paradoxical responses to TCAs had been reported, including paradoxical aggression (Rampling 1978). Indeed, events similar to those reported by Teicher and colleagues and Damluji and Ferguson have been seen with virtually all antidepressants. Known to this writer are similar individual reports with such diverse agents as amitriptyline, clomipramine, maprotiline, sertraline, bupropion, and others. What made the article by Teicher and colleagues most striking, however, was the clustering of six cases. That the agent had been prescribed, at that time, to almost 3 million patients would, however, make the observation of a cluster less remarkable. As noted by Frederick Goodwin (Burton 1991, p. A2), then Director of the Alcohol, Drug and Mental Health Administration, the number of persons on Prozac exceeded the population of Chicago, Illinois, where hundreds of people commit murder or suicide every year. Consider, furthermore, the rate of violent acts and suicide if the entire population of Chicago were made up of individuals meriting antidepressant pharmacotherapy. With the publicity associated with the initial case reports, a handful of other case reports followed, generally in groups of one or two cases featuring the emergence of suicidal ideation with treatment and its amelioration with treatment discontinuation. Given the denominator of patients on Prozac and the intense national interest in such cases, one could be struck either by the paucity of such reports or their similarity to the original observation.

Traditional postmarketing surveillance was becoming distorted and at risk of becoming useless to assess the relative risk of suicidal or violent acts of patients on Prozac compared with the risk for those on other treatments or no treatment at all. The relative risk of an event is calculated as a ratio, with the numerator derived from the number of individuals on drug A with a particular event divided by the number of persons on drug A during an interval, and the denominator the number of persons on drug B with the event divided by the number of persons on drug B in the interval. The reporting rate ratio, which would be an indication of the number of events reported in the population controlled for the number of prescriptions, would calculate events in the interval divided by prescriptions in the interval for drug A and events in the interval divided by the prescriptions in the interval for drug B. Unfortunately, the usefulness of these calculations disappears when publicity drives the reporting of events for only one of the drugs. When this happens it is necessary to turn to systematically ascertained data.

In the absence of systematically obtained data, even anecdotal reports begin to get dicey. In the frenzy of publicity, anecdote, and opinion, the value of additional open observations of individual cases diminishes dramatically. Three letters to the editor, in the year following the article by Teicher and colleagues (1990), illustrate this principle. One previous reporter of a case of suicidal ideation associated with fluoxetine wrote to report that follow-up observation of the same patient, 7 months after discontinuing fluoxetine and subsequent to two hospitalizations for depressive relapses while on other agents, revealed intermittent extreme suicidal ideation, leading the author to conclude "it is unlikely that fluoxetine has any relationship to the development of suicidal ideation" (Hoover 1991, p. 543). In another letter, Fetner and colleagues (1991) wrote:

> Teicher . . . and associates mention that Dr. Barbara Geller had discontinued an open study of fluoxetine in adolescents because of side-effects. This is a misstatement. We have never performed any protocol or any investigation on fluoxetine in adolescents. We have never presented this type of material at a meeting. (p. 1258)

The impact of publicity on expectation and reporting is dramatically illustrated by the communication of Dominguez and Goldstein (1992):

> A dramatic program aired on national television alerting consumers to the alleged dangers of fluoxetine. Our patient informed us that she had watched this program. It was then that she recognized and reported the serious effects the medication was having. . . . [S]he asserted that untoward effects from the drug emerged immediately after she began treatment. (p. 171)

The patient described aggression, homicidal thoughts, rage, aggressiveness toward family members, and an assault with a knife against her boyfriend. She stated, "This is not like me, I would never do this; I was a crazy woman." She noted also that she "wanted to jump off a cliff. . . . [T]here was a lot of hostility, it was constant, and all that I thought about: the hostility, the anger, and thoughts of suicide." As it turned out, these symptoms had emerged during 2 weeks of a single-blind, placebo lead-in to a double-blind, fluoxetine treatment study. It appears from this case that the media had triggered (at least the report of) suicidal and homicidal ideation in a psychiatric patient. Moreover, by chance, one of the original Teicher patients had been evaluated by this author in consultation both prior to the original case report and subsequent to it. A review of the detailed notes of the initial evaluation revealed no history given of emergence of intense and obsessive suicidal ideation and, on reevaluation, the patient was vague when directly queried and reported he was unable to distinguish this period of suicidal ideation from his chronic, baseline state. Although the patient's latter report is likely to be less reliable than the clinician's original observation, this observation underscores the risks in relying heavily on anecdotal data.

The indictment of an SSRI as a "cause" of suicidal ideation certainly ran counter to expectations, since the study of biological factors in suicide indicating central serotonin hypofunction predicted a specific antisuicidal effect of drugs of this class (Bourgeois 1991). Further, as noted by Mann and Kapur (1991), suicidal behavior reflects a complex etiology including multiple and interacting "neurobiologic, psychiatric, cognitive, and psychosocial factors" (p. 1027). Reviewing the case reports associating fluoxetine treatment and suicidal symptoms, these authors wrote,

> The presence of comorbid disorders, previous suicidal tendencies, and a highly variable time interval between the development of suicidal ideation and initiation of fluoxetine treatment, as well as the resolution of suicidal ideation after the cessation of fluoxetine, make it difficult to draw any clear conclusions. (p. 1029)

Surprised to hear that this antisuicidal, antidepressant drug with an extremely favorable safety record in overdose was being linked to suicidal behavior, my colleague, Maurizio Fava, and I conducted a survey study of 27 psychiatrists working in our department to assess the rate of emergence of suicidal ideation in patients on a variety of different antidepressants during a 1-year period (Fava and Rosenbaum 1991). The data were gathered on more than 1,000 depressed outpatients treated with tricyclics, fluoxetine, other antidepressants, and tricyclics combined with fluoxetine. None of the patients surveyed in this sample reported intense suicidal thoughts similar to those described in the report by Teicher and colleagues (1990). No significant difference in the emergence of suicidal ideation was observed across the groups, although it was apparent that suicidal symptoms did emerge after treatment was begun with a number of different antidepressants, including fluoxetine. Of 294 patients who had been treated with fluoxetine, clinicians reported suicidal ideation following the initiation of treatment in 8 patients. A follow-up of those patients revealed that none had made a suicide attempt while on Prozac, and 5 patients had continued on Prozac with a positive outcome, 2 after the addition of lithium to ongoing treatment with Prozac. In 1 patient, Prozac had been discontinued and later restarted with improvement in depression. Most of these patients had comorbid personality disorders, mainly borderline. Overall, our conclusions from these data were that suicidal ideation may occur after antidepressant treatment is initiated, that it occurs with a variety of antidepressants, and that it abates with treatment response. Although reassuring, retrospective reports, like case reports, have their limitations. Other retrospective reports of large series of patients treated with fluoxetine (e.g., Ashleigh and Fesler 1992) similarly observed no evidence of the emergence of intense, obsessive, violent suicidal preoccupation as described by Teicher and colleagues. These retrospective case series suggested that emergence of obsessive suicidal ideation was rare.

Thousands of patients, however, had been studied in clinical trials of fluoxetine for depression and other indications, including comparisons with both placebo and antidepressants. This data base, ascertained long before the case reports emerged and consisting of assessments of well-diagnosed patients, systematically and prospectively assessed, was available to explore further the association between fluoxetine and suicidal ideation. As reported in the *British Journal of Psychiatry* (Beasley et al. 1991), data from 17 double-blind, clinical trials of patients with major depressive disorder were pooled to compare the emergence of suicidal acts and suicidal ideation in 1,765 patients on fluoxetine, 731 patients on tricyclic comparisons, and 569 patients given a placebo. As was evident in the case reports, substantial suicidal ideation did indeed occur in patients following the initiation of treatment with fluoxetine (1.1%); however, this rate was significantly less than in patients on tricyclics (3.59%) or taking a placebo (2.63%). The emergence of suicidal ideation was significantly less likely on fluoxetine compared with tricyclic or placebo. Although such data cannot disprove the occurrence of a rare idiosyncratic adverse effect in a given patient, treatments are selected based on the likelihood of benefit outweighing risk. These data, therefore, were reassuring. Other similar reports found no association between fluoxetine and suicidality either in obsessive-compulsive disorder (Beasley et al. 1992) or in patients with bulimia nervosa (Wheadon et al. 1992) and found no association between fluoxetine and violence or aggression (Heiligenstein et al. 1992). Reviewing a number of studies of antidepressant pharmacotherapy and the occurrence of suicidal behavior, Montgomery and colleagues (1992) concluded that "the studies of serotonergic antidepressants do not suggest that they are suicide-provoking agents; rather they appear to be neutral or protective" (p. 275). Thus, retrospective reviews and prospective clinical trials did not associate fluoxetine with increased risk of suicidal ideation or behavior.

Another source to examine the issue of suicide and antidepressant treatment is population-based, epidemiologic data. Drawing on data from the annual report of the American Association of Poison Control Centers national data collection system, the Drug Abuse Warning Network, and the National Prescription Audit, Kapur et al. (1992) concluded that the risk of a suicide attempt did not appear to be different among antidepressants but that TCAs were associated with a higher rate of death in the event of an overdose than the newer agents. Fluoxetine, as expected, was relatively safe with respect to risk of fatal toxicity. Further, the data indicated that compared with desipramine, amitriptyline, and imipramine, in addition to having the lowest relative risk of death in overdose, fluoxetine had the lowest risk of being associated with a suicide attempt. The authors suggested that selective serotonergic drugs may be more effective in suppressing suicidal acts than noradrenergic antidepressants and stated that

> case reports of intensification or even emergence de novo of suicidal ideation and behavior in patients being treated with an antidepressant have been reported with almost all classes of antidepressant medications. Further systemic [sic] investigation is necessary to determine whether selective serotonergic drugs have an advantage in terms of suppression of suicidal acts. (p. 3443)

Despite data-based reports such as these, the Prozac controversy continued to percolate; one picture appeared to be worth more than 1,000 pieces of data.

The Prozac Defense

With claims in the millions of dollars, it was not surprising that an indictment of Prozac was featured in the August 1990 edition of *Trial*, a publication for trial attorneys. Inviting fellow attorneys to be in touch for "networking information" on Prozac, the authors (Lewis 1990) stated, "Unfortunately, this so-called wonder drug has a darker side"

(p. 62) and proceeded to review the report by Teicher and colleagues (1990), noting that "Prozac's product literature does not warn that the drug may induce suicidal thoughts" (p. 62). One attorney in particular, Leonard Finz of New York, is quoted as saying that his office had become "almost a national registry, the clearinghouse for Prozac" (Span 1991, p. C1). As reported in the *Washington Post* (Span 1991), his firm is reported to have filed "about 30 of the then estimated 75 civil cases against Eli Lilly and has hundreds more under retainer" (p. C1). Given the numbers of patients on Prozac, the likelihood of some being involved in dangerous or other antisocial behaviors was high, and attorneys began to defend criminal cases with the so-called Prozac defense claiming that clients would not be legally responsible for their acts if they had become violent when using Prozac. One attorney is quoted as saying, "As a defense lawyer, I don't have to prove that Prozac caused the murder. I just have to raise a reasonable doubt that my client acted voluntarily and that without the drug, the violence would not have occurred" (Marcus 1991, p. B1). Although, at the time of this writing, no criminal case has been successfully defended using the Prozac defense, this additional line of attack added to the negative publicity about Prozac and continued the pressure on patients and prescribers that eventually began to be seen in a leveling off of the drug's remarkable growth curve. In response to the Prozac defense, and beginning to stand up more aggressively for its product, Eli Lilly and Company took the position that it would offer to pay expert witness fees and provide expert consultation to prosecutors involved in cases attempting to employ the Prozac defense. Indeed, at the time of emergence of the Prozac defense, Eli Lilly, psychiatrists, and the general public began to become aware that there was an additional player involved in the attack on Prozac, a player familiar to American psychiatry, and one whose presence, according to some speculation, may have been important in fueling the whole Prozac controversy.

Eli Lilly Responds

In a "Dear Doctor" letter, in 1990, the Dista Product Company Division of Eli Lilly (personal communication, August 31, 1991) responded to the article by Teicher et al. (1990). Noting that their agent had, at that point, been prescribed to more than 2 million patients, they pointed out that clinical trial data and information did not support the hypothesis of a causal relationship between Prozac and suicidality. They cautioned all clinicians to remain vigilant about the possibility of the emergence of suicidality with any antidepressant therapy. Enclosed with this letter was a summary of some of the clinical trial data reviewed above. A subsequent brochure entitled "3 Years, 3 Million Patients" (Dista Products Company 1991) again addressed the issue, noting that more than 11,000 depressed patients in 18 countries had been studied in premarketing trials including more than 6,000 treated with Prozac. The brochure reviewed the postmarketing surveillance procedures of the company, referred to the "news media coverage" and the "highly sensationalized discussions" about Prozac, and mentioned that

> much of this negative coverage has appeared in the lay press and has been encouraged by the Church of Scientology, a California-based group with a long record of opposition to the practice of psychiatry and the use of psychotropic drugs. A group called the Citizens Commission on Human Rights, the arm of the Scientologists, has repeatedly attacked Prozac and distorted the facts about psychiatry. (p. 5)

The company noted that the "one-sided media coverage" was partly in response to their corporate decision not to participate in articles, newscasts, and talk shows.

The mention of the Church of Scientology, however, signaled that the company could not leave it to the researchers, the data, organized psychiatry, and certainly not to the media to inject balance into the discussion or to offset "pseudo-balance" where a case of a patient who responded to Prozac would be reported along with one who became violent during treatment, as if there were a 50/50 chance of either outcome. In June 1991, Lilly issued a letter of indemnification to physicians promising that "Eli Lilly and Company will defend, indemnify and hold you harmless against claims, liabilities or expenses, arising from personal injury alleged to have been caused by Prozac" (Eli Lilly and Company, personal communication, June 12, 1991). Assuming that prescribers had treated appropriately, Lilly was prepared to indemnify physicians for any liability associated with prescribing Prozac.

It had become apparent that despite clinical knowledge about safety and efficacy, and the known risk-benefit ratio of antidepressant pharmacotherapy, prescribers were increasingly daunted by the threat of medical and legal consequences that might occur despite appropriate diagnosis and treatment. Physicians knew that some patients on any treatment could become suicidal; some would attempt suicide or engage in criminal behaviors. This possibility, in light of the sensationalized accounts of lawsuits, threatened clinicians. How could physicians feel otherwise when shows like *Geraldo* and *Donahue* hyped the image of a "killer Prozac." For example, on February 21, 1991, the *Donahue* show was entitled "Prozac—Medication That Makes You Kill." On that show, a representative of the Citizens Commission on Human Rights (CCHR) accompanied "Prozac survivors" and Attorney Finz in their indictment of Prozac.

Advertisements were appearing in newspapers purporting to be public service information for patients beginning on Prozac; responders to these notices received warnings about the drug's dangers. Support groups of "Prozac survivors" were organized in various areas of the country. A series of large, full-page, attack ads against Eli Lilly and its drugs was purchased in *USA Today*. Lilly responded with another "Dear Doctor" letter advising prescribers, as documented in articles in *Time* (Behar 1991) and *The Wall Street Journal* (Burton 1991), that the Church of Scientology and the CCHR were "the primary sources of the unfounded attacks on Prozac" (Dista Products Company, personal communication, June 17, 1991). Noting that by this time 4 million patients in the United States had been prescribed Prozac and that the FDA along with 50 other regulatory agencies worldwide had found Prozac to be safe and effective, Lilly voiced extreme concern that many patients were daunted from treatment and "left vulnerable by fear and doubt" (Dista Products Company, personal communication, June 17, 1991). Indeed, Lilly reportedly ordered 250,000 special reprints of the *Time* article "The Thriving Cult of Greed and Power" (Behar 1991) to distribute to physicians. Lilly had broken from the corporate tradition of not engaging with the general news media about its products.

By mid-1991, most of the major media were beginning to attempt balance in the ongoing reporting of the Prozac story. In *Newsweek*, Cowley (1991) noted that "when researchers have gone looking for the 'Teicher syndrome' they haven't found it" (p. 67), but "if the Teicher syndrome is real, it is exceedingly rare—too rare to show up in studies designed to detect it, and too rare in the view of most psychiatrists to warrant big changes in prescribing practices" (p. 67). Despite the balanced reporting by the writer, the article was accompanied by photographs of shooting victims and the same forearm scar of the same woman featured in earlier stories.

Emboldened, psychiatrists and organized psychiatry began to fight back. A handful of cases out of millions treated had created a great adverse impact on physicians' ability to deliver treatment to depressed patients. This course of events made sense when viewed as more than a media feeding frenzy on a celebrity, billion-dollar drug, but rather as part of an organized assault on psychiatry in general. The American Psychiatric Association's *Psychiatric News* (Karel 1991) reported that "Scientology's ongoing war on psychiatry, now focused on the anti-depressant drug Prozac, was the topic of discussion" (p. 18) at the annual meeting. At that meeting, Frederick Goodwin had identified the CCHR as a Scientology group at war with psychiatry, identifying "their big target" as Prozac. The controversy was reframed as an assault on psychiatry aimed at its most visible, and successful, treatment, and with this the psychiatric field generated more vigorous responses. Even Teicher was quoted as stating "the Scientologists have made 'a real distortion of what we wrote'" (Karel 1991, p. 18). He also stated that most of his patients reacted positively to Prozac. Karel indicated that as early as July 12, 1990, the CCHR, whose executive director is reported to have compared modern psychiatry to Nazi eugenics, issued nationwide press releases (many published by newspapers without verification) noting that Prozac can cause intense, violent, suicidal thoughts and could cause patients to commit murder. Generalizing from the Teicher report, the CCHR had claimed that more than 100,000 people without any previous record of violence could "explode at any moment."

John L. Schwartz, M.D., the publisher of *Psychiatric Times,* also identified that the attack on Prozac was driven by Scientology and represented an attack on psychiatry in general. Indeed, the headline of the June 1991 *Psychiatric Times* was "Prozac Frees Ex-Scientology Leader From Depression." This issue summarized "Scientology's war on psychiatry," identifying organized psychiatry as the Church of Scientology's biggest financial competitor. Stating that the CCHR refers to itself as "psych busters," the article (Schwartz 1991, p. 28) noted that the CCHR had encouraged people to submit adverse drug reaction claims to the FDA and to bring lawsuits against Eli Lilly and psychiatrists. It also referred to efforts by the group to hurt the drug company's stock price, to foment national "Prozac Survivor Support Groups," and ultimately to lobby government officials to have Prozac removed from the market. Whether groups related to Scientology were specifically responsible for the Prozac story to date or simply fanned and fueled a weak flame to create a bonfire is a matter of controversy. Clearly, other individuals and entities, particularly in the media, exploited the controversy. Nonetheless, despite the general reassurances about the drug to prescribers, in the minds of many potential patients, the damage was done. Indeed, while the CCHR applied to the FDA requesting it withdraw marketing approval for Prozac, *The Wall Street Journal* ("L. Ron Nader" 1991) viewed these lobbying efforts as reflecting the combined energies of the Church of Scientology, Sidney Wolfe of Ralph Nader's Health Research Group, and trial lawyers, involved together in an effort to attack Prozac. *The Wall Street Journal* opined that the "anti-Prozac campaign" would have run down eventually if it had not been fueled by the self-interest of the Health Research Group and its association with contingency fee lawyers.

The result of the Scientology petition against Prozac was reported in an FDA article (Food and Drug Administration 1991); the agency had denied the request to withdraw marketing approval for Prozac. The FDA specifically stated that "the data and information available at this time do not indicate that Prozac causes suicidality or violent behavior" (p. 1). According to the article, the only evidence for the group's claim was "four incomplete anecdotal reports" (p. 2). This stood in contrast to the analysis of controlled clinical studies involving thousands of depressed patients. The National Mental Health Association, a patient advocacy group, and the American Psychiatric Association applauded the decision, the latter noting that the FDA had "chosen science over sensationalism" (English 1991, p. 1). It is worth noting that the American Psychiatric Association response came more than a year after that organization had published the original anecdotes in its journal. With respect to patient care and certainly with respect to the trajectory of growth of the market for the drug Prozac, the damage had been done. The American Psychiatric Association (English 1991) indicated that distraught patients had been calling physicians' offices and had been taking themselves off the medication, often without telling their doctors. Over time, the volume of sales of Prozac was to continue to grow, but never again at the rate that it had been experiencing prior to the unprecedented publicity. Mention of Prozac in the media would almost always be linked to the word "suicide" or to a recounting of the Prozac-suicide story.

The appropriate clinical response to the initial case reports was an obvious one: circumspection about the meaning of small numbers of anecdotes in the context of millions of psychiatric patients treated, recognition that idiosyncratic and rare events may occur with any treatment, and a reasoned approach to treatment preparation as summarized by Gelenberg (1991):

> A clinician might as part of routine instructions before prescribing, alert patients to a range of possible psychological effects—negative as well as positive—that sometime follow prescription of an antidepressant. The early weeks of treatment with any antidepressant can be crucial to a successful outcome, and a close working therapeutic dyad is a critical factor. (p. 16)

Since several of the case reports of emergence of suicidal ideation following the initiation of antidepressant treatment with fluoxetine have featured treatment-emergent akathisia or agitation (a side effect not limited to fluoxetine), clinicians should also inform patients about to begin an antidepressant about the possibility of treatment-emergent anxiety, agitation, or restlessness (particularly in patients with preexisting anxiety or panic disorder) and prepare the patients to alert their physician if these symptoms emerge. Patients should also know that there are potential strategies to minimize these effects, ranging from counteractive treatments to lowering of dose or changing treatment.

With respect to the issue of rage or violence while taking a drug, recent data indicate that a substantial number of patients with major

depression experience "anger attacks," spells of anger emerging dramatically and intensively from a background of depression-associated
irritability. More than 40% of untreated outpatients with depression
have reported anger attacks in the months prior to treatment (Fava et
al. 1993). The occurrence of these anger attacks is dramatically
reduced by treatment with 20 mg/day of fluoxetine. These data
indicate, however, that a minority of patients, despite treatment with
fluoxetine, continue to have anger attacks (Fava et al., in press). These
reports again remind us of the necessity to ground our conclusions on
cause and effect of treatments and symptoms on systematically ascertained data while remaining circumspect, vigilant, and careful in the
care of our patients.

Conclusion

Is the Prozac story over? To the extent that patients with depression
will commit angry acts and suicidal acts and also will continue to be
treated with Prozac, the story will remain alive, and the concerns about
medical and legal implications will persist. With the advent of younger
SSRIs, apparently comparably effective to Prozac, one ongoing impact
of the controversy will be to benefit drugs newer to the market. In the
absence of the Prozac story, several years of use and millions of
prescriptions would normally be a reassuring anchor for the older drug
of a class in the marketplace. The data for the newer agents are similarly
reassuring to those of Prozac, indicating no increase in emergent
suicidal ideation in clinical trials compared with placebo or TCAs. The
potential impact of newer SSRIs on Prozac, in light of the "suicide
story," is suggested by the cynical approach of a sales representative
for one of the newer agents who is reported by a colleague to have
described his drug on its introduction to the marketplace as "Prozac
without the lawsuit."

   At this point, we can only speculate as to the number of patients
who have refused treatment, abandoned treatment, or never presented
for treatment as a consequence of the Prozac story. How many of those
patients died of suicide, had marriages or work relationships disrupted,
or had children harmed by persisting parental dysphoria, irritability,

and impairment? What could have made a difference earlier on? Perhaps organized psychiatry, before it perceived the attack on Prozac as an attack on psychiatry, could have been more proactive. Organizations devoted to the scientific study of psychopharmacology, such as the American College of Neuropsychopharmacology, could have mounted a media response rather than a session at its annual meeting. At this point, a new organization, the American Society of Clinical Psychopharmacology, is emerging as a forum for enhancing clinical practice, research, and education in clinical psychopharmacology. A group such as this might in the future mobilize the field and expert opinion to respond. Perhaps, on the other hand, no organized response could have been sufficient.

In the media, science and clinical experience will never stand up to a dramatic case report. Is the Prozac story over? At best, like an infectious illness, it is in a carrier state, liable to reemerge at any time. Indeed, the headline of the *Wellington Evening Post* in New Zealand on January 8, 1993, was "Patients Told to Ignore 'Killer Drug' Claims," and the headline of the January 9, 1993, *Otago Daily Times* (Dunedin, New Zealand) was "Psychiatrists Oppose Scientology Drug Claim." On January 22, 1993, clinical researchers who had been involved in studies of fluoxetine were notified by a Lilly official that colleagues had been contacted by persons "identifying themselves as working with or for the Citizens Commission on Human Rights, an affiliate of the Church of Scientology who allege that Lilly and investigators engaged in fraud, negligence or other improper activity with respect to the testing of fluoxetine" (Eli Lilly and Company, personal communication, January 22, 1993). Thus, we must continue to identify the adversarial parties and their motives, to defend ourselves with data, and to protect our patients from untoward effects of treatment and the risks of nontreatment.

In June 1993, a book by Peter Kramer entitled *Listening to Prozac* was released featuring vivid examples of individuals who dramatically changed, clearly for the better, in a way unanticipated by their treating psychiatrist. These transformations, apparently of long-standing character problems, were associated with treatment with Prozac. Although the book is not a panegyric, including as it does details of the Prozac story and expectable adverse events and risks, we should expect these

remarkable, extremely positive, but atypical case studies to begin
another round of hype and backlash.

References

American Psychiatric Association: Diagnostic and Statistical Manual of Men-
    tal Disorders, 3rd Edition, Revised. Washington, DC, American Psychi-
    atric Association, 1987
Ashleigh EA, Fesler FA: Fluoxetine and suicidal preoccupation. Am J Psychi-
    atry 149:12, 1992
Beasley CM, Dornseif BE, Bosomworth JC, et al: Fluoxetine and suicide: a
    meta-analysis of controlled trials of treatment for depression. BMJ
    303:685–692, 1991
Beasley CM, Potvin JH, Masica DN, et al: Fluoxetine: no association with
    suicidality in obsessive compulsive disorder. J Affective Disord 24:1–10,
    1992
Behar R: The thriving cult of greed and power. Time, May 6, 1991, p 50
Bourgeois M: Serotonin, impulsivity and suicide. Human Psychopharmacol-
    ogy 6 (suppl):31–36, 1991
Bourne HR, Bunney WE Jr, Colburn RW, et al: Noradrenaline, 5-hydroxy-
    tryptamine and 5-hydroxyindoleacetic acid in hind-brains of suicidal
    patients. Lancet 2:805–808, 1968
Burton TM: Anti-depression drug of Eli Lilly loses sales after attacked by sect:
    Scientologists claim Prozac induces murder or suicide, though evidence
    is scant, campaign dismays doctor. Wall Street Journal, April 19, 1991a,
    p A1–A2
Cowley G: The promise of Prozac. Newsweek, March 26, 1990, pp 38–41
Cowley G: A Prozac backlash. Newsweek, April 1, 1991, pp 64–67
Damluji NF, Ferguson JM: Paradoxical worsening of depressive symptom-
    atology caused by antidepressant. J Clin Psychopharmacol 8:347–349,
    1988
Dista Products Company: 3 Years, 3 Million Patients (brochure). Indianap-
    olis, IN, Dista Products Company (a division of Eli Lilly and Co.), 1991
Dominguez RA, Goldstein BJ: Suicidal and homicidal ideations emerging
    during a placebo period. J Clin Psychiatry 53:171, 1992
English J: News release of the American Psychiatric Association on FDA
    denial of petition to ban Prozac. Washington, DC, American Psychiatric
    Association, August 1, 1991

Fava M, Rosenbaum JF: Suicidality and fluoxetine: is there a relationship? J Clin Psychiatry 52:108–111, 1991

Fava M, Rosenbaum JF, McCarthy M, et al: Anger attacks in unipolar depression; part I: clinical correlates and response to drug treatment. Am J Psychiatry 150:1158–1163, 1993

Fetner HH, Watts HE, Geller B: Fluoxetine and preoccupation with suicide. Am J Psychiatry 148:1258, 1991

Food and Drug Administration: FDA denies Scientology petition against Prozac (talk paper). Rockville, MD, Food and Drug Administration, August 1, 1991

Gelenberg AJ: Fluoxetine and thoughts of suicide. Biological Therapies in Psychiatry Newsletter 14:13, 16, 1991

Grady D: The Prozac scare: a wonder drug's rise and fall. American Health, October 1990, pp 60–65

Heiligenstein JH, Coccaro EF, Potvin JH, et al: Fluoxetine not associated with increased violence or aggression in controlled clinical trials. Annals of Clinical Psychiatry 4:285–295, 1992

Hoover CE: Suicidal ideation not associated with fluoxetine. Am J Psychiatry 148:543, 1991

Kapur S, Mieczkowski T, Mann JJ: Antidepressant medications and the relative risk of suicide attempt and suicide. JAMA 268:3441–3445, 1992

Karel R: Members react to campaign discrediting Prozac, psychiatry. Psychiatric News, June 7, 1991, p 18

Kramer PD: Listening to Prozac. New York, Viking, 1993

L. Ron Nader (editorial). The Wall Street Journal, June 25, 1991

Lewis J: Prozac: Dark Side of a Wonder Drug: The Exchange Report Trial, August 1990, pp 62–65

Mann JJ, Kapur S: The emergence of suicidal ideation and behavior during antidepressant pharmacotherapy. Arch Gen Psychiatry 48:1027–1033, 1991

Marcus AD: Murder trials introduce Prozac defense. The Wall Street Journal, February 7, 1991, p B1

Marcus E: Prozac: is it really the "Wonder Drug" for depression? Health: A Weekly Journal of Medicine 6:12–14, 1990

Montgomery SA, Montgomery DB, Green M, et al: Pharmacotherapy and the prevention of suicidal behavior. J Clin Psychopharmacol 12:27S–31S, 1992

Pollack MH, Rosenbaum JF: Management of antidepressant-induced side-effects: a practical guide for clinician. J Clin Psychiatry 48:3–8, 1987

Rampling D: Aggression: a paradoxical response to tricyclic antidepressants. Am J Psychiatry 135:117–118, 1978

Schumer F: Bye-bye blues: a new wonder drug for depression. New York, December 18, 1989, pp 47–53

Schwartz J: Prozac frees ex-Scientology leader from depression. Psychiatric Times 8:1, 24–28 1991

Snyder SH, Coyle JT: Regional differences in [3H]-norepinephrine and [3H]-dopamine uptake into rat brain homogenates. J Pharmacol Exp Ther 165:78–86, 1969

Span P: Leading the charge against Prozac. Washington Post, August 14, 1991, pp C1–C3

Teicher MH, Glod CA, Cole JO: Emergence of intense suicidal preoccupation during fluoxetine treatment. Am J Psychiatry 147:207–210, 1990

Waldholz M: Prozac said to spur idea of suicide. Wall Street Journal, July 18, 1990, p B1

Wagner R: Lawsuits claim drug caused suicidal ideation, homicide. Psychiatric Times, September 1990, p 52

Wheadon DE, Rampey AH, Thompson VL, et al: Lack of association between fluoxetine and suicidality in bulimia nervosa. J Clin Psychiatry 53:235–241, 1992

Wong DT, Horng JS, Bymaster FP, et al: A selective inhibitor of serotonin uptake: Lilly 10140 3-(p-trifluoromethylphenoxy)-N-methyl-3-phenyl-propylamine. Life Sci 15:471–479, 1974

CHAPTER TWO

Regulation of Electroconvulsive Therapy: The California Experience

Glen N. Peterson, M.D.

> What have our legislators gained by culling out a hundred thousand particular cases, and by applying to these a hundred thousand laws?
>
> Michel De Montaigne, *Essays of Michel de Montaigne* [1]

Electroconvulsive therapy (ECT) has had the historical distinction of being one of the earliest targets of antipsychiatric campaigns in the United States (Ayd 1975; Isaac and Armat 1990). ECT was introduced in Rome in 1938 as a more predictable replacement for convulsive therapy induced with pentylenetetrazole injection. The ill-conceived, large-scale use of ECT and early explorations of use in varied conditions damaged its early image (Abrams 1988). Acceptance of ECT was inhibited broadly from its inception by fears and prejudices of both the public and physicians and exacerbated by the early practice of treatment without anesthesia (Durham 1989; Endler and Persad 1988) and by the uneven availability of facilities and trained professionals. In recent decades, formal regulations in a number of states have limited the conditions under which ECT can be provided, distinguishing it from most general medical or surgical procedures (Mills et al. 1984). Regulations controlling ECT are so stringent that many of the most direly ill patients now have little or no chance of

---

[1] Cotton 1947, p. 416.

receiving this treatment (Bates and Smeltzer 1982; Clark et al. 1985; Mills and Avery 1978; Peterson 1984; Tenenbaum 1983). This unfortunate regulatory atmosphere has evolved despite overwhelming evidence of the safety and efficacy of ECT (American Psychiatric Association 1990; Consensus Conference 1985; Fink 1979).

The widespread suppressive regulation of ECT in the United States deprives far more patients of this specific treatment than even discriminatory insurance and other financial barriers, which have long stood between psychiatric patients and effective treatments (M. Freeman 1992).

The sense of helplessness that patients and their families experience in the face of an unrelenting mental illness meriting ECT is compounded by governmental policies that inhibit treatment. This unique besieging of a treatment with remarkable medical credentials fosters an ongoing toll of extended suffering and even death (California Department of Mental Health 1981; Roy-Byrne and Gerner 1981). This process demands closer examination in the interest of helping patients for whom ECT is relevant as well as to inform efforts to enlighten public policy.

The special regulation of ECT raises a number of public policy questions regarding the health interests of the community and the sensitive interactions of privacy, self-determination, competency, and the potential resort to involuntary treatment. Major tensions and controversies stimulated by the phenomenon of involuntary treatment have contributed to the overregulation of ECT (Heneberry 1982; Winslade et al. 1984; Winslade 1988). However, although the phenomenon of involuntary treatment represents a tiny portion of the total spectrum of psychiatric office and hospital services, it leads to sensationalization and polarization of many public debates about mental health policies. As one result of such conceptual illusions, the preponderance of patients, who freely select their professionals and treatments, become the unsolicited beneficiaries of unsought regulatory "protection." Such a shield of legal "rights" protections has developed in the United States for actual or prospective involuntary patients to the extent that treatment is often eliminated altogether, vastly delayed, or rendered meaninglessly transient (Gutheil and Appelbaum 1982; Isaac and Armat 1990). In this chapter, I explore the backstage interplay of designs and accidents that produce ECT policy, the process actually differing only modestly from the coarse fray of everyday "politics." The destructive impact of the regulatory suppression of this remarkable treatment will be clarified from the perspective of psychiatrists and individual patients and their families with an emphasis on the regulation of ECT in California.

The Anti-ECT Movement

Attitude surveys from the United States and Europe reveal that a substantial majority of ECT recipients, as well as psychiatrists, experience the treatment as positive (C. P. L. Freeman and Cheshire 1986; Weiner 1987). Of the 10%–20% (my estimate) of ECT patients who find the experience significantly distasteful, most still usually persevere with a treatment course in quest of relief from their painful mental disorder. Even those few who curtail their treatment course, or resolve not to accept future ECT should they relapse, are rarely inspired to dismiss their psychiatrists or to embark on a campaign against ECT. Whether their ECT experience has been on balance favorable or not, patients rarely campaign to impose their personal perspective on the community. Although more than 30,000 people receive ECT in the United States annually (Thompson 1986), my observations are that virtually the same handful of anti-ECT "ex-patients" appear at relevant functions year after year, with evidence of very few new "recruits." Oblivious to such crucial perspectives and responding to sensationalism and intense antipsychiatric lobbying, some public officials, perhaps intending well, mistake the vehemence of a tiny contingent of critics as proof of widespread evils. Their receptiveness to extremist arguments is easily exploited by the handful of maverick physicians who attempt to lend an aura of legitimate expert authority to antipsychiatric campaigns (Abrams 1988; Huber 1991; Isaac and Armat 1990; Isaac and Brakel 1992).

The courts have been a major spawning ground for radical changes in the regulation of psychiatric treatment. The promiscuous resort to litigation in the United States for all sorts of issues has encouraged the use of "hired-gun" experts, who are subject to few if any constraints on the misrepresentation of science, in profound contrast with the climate within professional conferences and the process of refereed publication (Huber 1991). Displaying contempt for consensually established wisdom and knowledge, the same predictable handful of physicians, skilled at polemics, routinely attack ECT in court or other public settings across the United States or Canada. As Isaac and Armat (1990) documented, most of them have had identifiable connections with Scientology's Citizens Commission on Human Rights (CCHR). They appear eager to join or promote court battles, whether for the sake of financial claims or social engineering (Isaac and Armat 1990).

As is illustrated later, many antipsychiatric activists or agents, especially in "public service" agencies and public office, exert their influence from paid positions of advantaged access to legislatures, regulatory agencies, and the courts. From these positions of regulatory advantage, the proponents of special regulations for ECT imply that the treatment would be wildly unconstrained in the absence of special laws. To the contrary, few endeavors in the United States face anything comparable to the plethora of regulations, community pressures, and professional guidelines that shape and discipline contemporary medical practice. Indeed, physicians are held to exacting levels of responsibility for their conduct, whereas public officials, whose actions can have more massive impact, are virtually immune from personal repercussions or sanctions, no matter the magnitude of harm done.

Sources of Regulation

The regulation of ECT derives from independent or interlocking actions of legislatures, courts, and executive agencies. The promulgation and application of such regulations involve a broad array of officials: legislators; legislative aides; judges and their clerks; local, regional, and national health agencies; district attorneys; public defenders; patients' rights advocates; and medical license boards. Public officials are often no more than supervisory authors of their official actions, which are usually given substance by hired staff, a less visible but highly influential tier of government. Pressure groups or persistent individuals can interact at virtually any of these levels and venues, shaping public policy at all points from conception to interpretation and execution.

Legislation

At least 37 states directly or by implication regulate ECT; California has provided a paradigm for stringent and intentionally repressive ECT legislation (Clark 1985). A general restructuring of the California State code for mental health care included some guidelines for ECT consent measures in the late 1960s. Assemblyman John Vasconcellos, father of California's existing ECT law, was strongly persuaded by anti-psychiatric activism in the mid-1970s when he composed two consecutive anti-ECT statutes. Honoring his convictions, a correspondence column in *Madness Network News* was entitled "Dear John . . . ." He reportedly met with Scientology-affiliated activists (CCHR). He embraced Szasz's (1961) dim views of psychiatry and purportedly had special animosity about ECT because of the experience of a relative. The bills succeeded easily in the legislature, reflecting commonplace anti-ECT prejudices. Medical and psychiatric society efforts moderated the author's original proposals slightly (Rudin 1978). The constraints that the California statute imposes are illustrated in the case examples below.

Berkeley, California.   In 1982 the voters of Berkeley passed a measure banning entirely the practice of ECT within the city limits. The American Psychiatric Association assisted the local and district components of the American Psychiatric Association in handling public relations during the preelection phase and the successful court challenge to the regulation. Psychiatric hospitals and the local and area levels of the American Medical Association joined the enterprise in a public show of support for ECT rarely seen before or since. Reflecting the scant respect for fact or dignity typical of most anti-ECT strategies, campaign handbills defamed by name the two psychiatrists who were performing ECT in the city, and the official election informational pamphlet maliciously and falsely purported that a young patient of one of the doctors had died because of ECT. (The patient died a number of months after her ECT while in physical restraints at a state hospital.)

Ultimately the ban was overturned by the courts.

Echoing anti-ECT proceedings in San Francisco, California, the Berkeley City Council passed an anti-ECT resolution in 1992. Other than for an abortive attempt by State Assemblyman Ferguson to promote the resolution's intent via legislation, no further visible consequences have ensued.

San Francisco, California. San Francisco had had only one ECT facility and two practitioners during a nearly 15-year drought of services and training traceable to California's prejudicial laws and local protests and publicity. In 1990, recognizing the enduring merits of ECT, several community hospitals and the University of California at San Francisco Medical Center revived ECT services. City Supervisor Angela Alioto proposed banning ECT from San Francisco in hearings in 1990–1991 in response to a coalition of groups antagonistic to the renewed local presence of ECT. Publicly funded groups such as Patients' Rights Advocacy Services (PRAS), the local contractor for the city-county patients' rights advocacy, and Protection and Advocacy, Inc., respectively coordinated the coalition or watched the process with an approving eye. Scientology's CCHR was part of the coalition, and its local leader attended board of supervisor hearings, even sitting at a prominent vantage point to the side of the supervisors on one occasion.

Melodramatic criticism of ECT is easily elicited in the San Francisco Bay Area since several inveterate ex-patient and physician activists live there. Another perennial gainsayer, Peter Breggin, M.D., was also brought in from Maryland for appearances and testimony, denouncing all ECT-practitioners as exploitive "electrolobotomists."

Alioto's office made a token request for information from the Northern California Psychiatric Society, which crafted an intensive informational and public relations response under the leadership of President Kathleen Unger, M.D., and Executive Director Joyce Jarvis. The San Francisco Medical Society and eventually the American Psychiatric Association, the latter by correspondence, also made valuable contributions. Several former ECT patients, troubled by the potential obstruction of an important treatment, volunteered for press or television contact, and a committee of psychiatrists was formed from several community hospitals, the University of California Medical Center, and the local United States Army base. The results included informational packets and videotapes for supervisors and press, public interviews and testimony, and the attendance of the ultimately un-swerving Alioto at ECT sessions for two consenting patients. (She registered the perplexing complaint that she met only patients receiv-ing maintenance treatment, at ease and articulate, rather than pro-foundly distressed or catatonic ones!)

The supervisors ultimately dropped a proposal to ban ECT, proba-bly on learning belatedly that the state constitution would vitiate such a move, as had happened in Berkeley. They voted to eliminate public spending for local patients who received ECT and encouraged the legislature to pass a statute allowing local governments to regulate the treatment. The fiscal restrictions were likely to be of limited actual impact. According to the local Department of Mental Health, only one of the few public facility patients referred for ECT in recent years was uninsured. At that, the city government never bothered to reim-burse the hospital or physician for services rendered.

Courts

The themes of court decisions about psychiatric treatments mirror the range of views, informed and otherwise, found in the general public. In some cases, physicians have been seen as the appropriate agents for treatment decisions, whereas in others, psychiatric treatments have been regarded as uniquely invasive or dangerous and a priori oppres-sive of patients' liberties (Mills 1985; Mills and Avery 1978; Whitcomb 1988). Since most patients who receive ECT do so by their own consent, courts become involved in special situations when standing laws are challenged, in issuing new public policy in the context of case rulings, or when legislatively mandated review of individual patients' ECT treatment is conducted. The "low visibility" setting of mental health hearings and the typical imbalance of legal advocacy that is often biased against treatment allow more latitude for the expression of a skeptical judge's personal opinion. In California jurisdictions, several types of misadventure can befall patients. Some judges have insisted that, although they will hear cases, no one under their review will ever receive ECT. At least one institutionalized patient in a northern California state hospital has been refused ECT on repeated hearings, despite the provision of unopposed expert testimony by multiple consultants and the assigned public defender's acceptance of ECT. At least one judge in California "dismissed" an ECT hearing in entirety after being irritated that a file was misplaced, refusing to allow rescheduling. In another instance, a judge assigned an ECT hearing, set only after substantial delay from a medical perspective, suggested canceling the hearing because of a personal distaste for ECT. A less flagrantly hostile judge skeptically inquired not only about clinical issues, but about the fee charged for ECT during review of a case.

The California statute poses the treating psychiatrist as the patient's adversary unless proven otherwise. This spirit, rather than the letter of the California law, is usually promoted in proxy consent hearings. Judges usually assume the authority to review the treatment's merits and declare whether or not ECT will be permitted, rather than ruling, as the law provides, simply on the patient's competency and, if appropriate, appointing a party to make the proxy consent decision.

Wyatt v. Stickney, Alabama, 1973. Suit was brought to intervene with a state hospital program where patients were uniformly suffering substandard habilitation, nutrition, and professional attention. ECT was given without anesthesia. In his zeal to set straight these wrongs, the judge incorporated demanding terms for ECT in his decision. Even voluntary, competent patients could not receive ECT without the involvement of three psychiatrists, one neurologist, and two attorneys. Ultimately, these rulings eliminated ECT from Alabama state hospitals entirely (American Psychiatric Association 1978).

Aden v. Younger, California, 1976. This suit brought by a psychiatrist challenged the 1974 anti-ECT statute authored by Vasconcellos, as an appeal of a lower-level suit filed by an ECT patient, *Doe v. Younger.* This law required that three consultants unanimously agree that ECT "is critically needed and that all other modalities have been exhausted." The California Court of Appeals found several portions of the statute unconstitutional on grounds of vagueness, of inadequacy of due process, and of invasion of privacy, especially for voluntary patients (Rudin 1978). The next statute, entitled "The Right to Refuse ECT," took effect in 1977 and included some moderations of the former provisions, but also the provision of court hearings for patients designated as involuntary or incompetent. Mechanisms and repercussions of this law are discussed in more detail later.

Doe v. O'Conner, California, filed 1987. This constitutional challenge to California's existing ECT laws received the support of the California Medical Association–California Psychiatric Association Joint Task Force on Electroconvulsive Therapy (California Medical Association–California Psychiatric Association 1990) but languished due to lack of funding for litigation.

In re Schuoler, Washington, 1986. Although this case occurred in Washington, it echoed the themes raised in California. This suit was brought by a publicly appointed attorney, supported by the state public defender association, "on behalf of" Ms. Schuoler, a public hospital patient, protesting the compression of a guardianship and ECT decision into one court hearing and the failure to delay the hearing when the attorney requested more preparation time. The ulterior goal appears to have been the abolition of ECT for public patients in the state. Such patients were routinely referred from county to state hospitals, with no ECT facilities, after 2 weeks. Since slowed and replicative legal proceedings would consume this brief interval, Schuoler and other public patients would then have had no access to ECT. Thus, through "due process" the patient would have been separated from scarce ECT resources and become the "beneficiary" of ineffective institutional confinement.

Fortunately, an industrious local district attorney carried the suit's defense, aided by an amicus curiae brief filed by the International Psychiatric Association for the Advancement of Electrotherapy, now known as the Association for Convulsive Therapy.

This case provides a vivid illustration of the myopia of many antitreatment activists, who indict psychiatry as being insensitive to patients' welfare and "rights," reserving to themselves the prerogative of wielding decisive powers over patients' lives regardless of whether the patients have requested their action or are even aware of it.

Ironically, Schuoler voluntarily (again) received ECT from the same physician and hospital for another relapse before "her" case was resolved.

Food and Drug Administration (FDA)

Antipsychiatric lobbying with the FDA succeeded in 1979 in tentatively gaining a potentially prohibitive "Class III" designation for ECT devices. Such a status would probably eliminate the development and manufacture of such devices in the United States, since Class III implies that extensive premarketing animal and clinical trials would be required to disprove the presumption of "unreasonable risk of illness or injury."

In 1982 the American Psychiatric Association petitioned to redesignate ECT devices as Class II. The FDA was receptive, supported by a review of extensive ECT literature and correspondence from many psychiatrists. Further sorties from ECT opponents have delayed final resolution of the debate, as has the articulation by the FDA of "performance standards" for devices. The standards will, in a manner parallel to the labeling of "approved" indications for new drugs, designate the disorders for which ECT is held to be indicated. Practitioners and manufacturers have been concerned that the presently proposed exclusion of disorders such as nonmelancholic depressions or schizophrenias will either serve to inhibit clinical practice unduly or to heighten the risk of frivolous liability suits for "off-label" but medically legitimate ECT uses (T. G. Goodwin, unpublished communication, October 22, 1990; Isaac and Armat 1990).

Other Administrative
Policy and Regulation

The administrative components of executive and judicial branches of government at all levels enact public policy via formal regulations and internal policies and by the impact of routine, daily decisions. For instance, given a medical request for ECT for an incompetent patient, a public guardian-conservator can decide when and whether to pursue the issue. In the same instance, the public defender and district attorney can each elect a time frame of action, the orientation of expert consultants used (if any), and which type of sentiment to promote regarding ECT.

County Mental Health Administration

Local and state health agencies can sustain or discourage the provision of ECT in public facilities. In the clinical care setting, the administration of a public hospital or of its psychiatric service likewise determines the mode of services provided. Two contiguous county psychiatric services in the Bay Area in California offer contrasting approaches to ECT. In Contra Costa County, the psychiatric staff and administration have regularly used ECT referral as a valuable clinical option, especially for treatment-unresponsive patients in their well-organized geriatric program. (They also cede that political pressures within their county government discourage the development of their own ECT facilities.) On the other hand, the director of psychiatry of Alameda County Mental Health Services has asserted that his program would resort to ECT referral only if a patient were imminently at risk of death. Cases in the county system have been allowed to deteriorate tragically, with resolute avoidance of ECT.

> *Case 1.* A psychotic, anorexic woman in mid-pregnancy had a history of recurring neuroleptic malignant syndrome on drug rechallenge. Her care included tube feeding and reliance on leather restraints for agitation. Her staff psychiatrist initiated contact with an ECT expert in the community, but was forced by the director to refrain from referral, to avoid "controversy."

> *Case 2.* This case also illustrates the functional severance of family ties and support that is promoted by the "rights" orientation of contemporary mental health regulation. An 18-year-old experienced a catatonic illness after a slow prelude of seclusiveness and an eruption of delusional excitement. He had a family history of major affective and psychotic disorders. He lingered in a county facility for months, mute and ungroomed for substantial time periods, until his mother protested his poor hygiene and unkemptness. Neuroleptic motor side effects were evident. The mother attempted to arrange a consultation by an eminent area psychopharmacologist. However, a local interpretation of "rights" allowed the patient to refuse—with a psychotically clouded utterance—disclosure of his treatment records, even though he was under the legal sway of a conservatorship for virtually all personal and treatment dispositions. I was

advised of the case and suggested consideration of ECT to a treating psychiatrist, who rejected this, suggesting that he thought further psychotherapy might be helpful. Ultimately a "social worker" told the family that no treatment would help, and placement in a boarding home ensued. The illness, and blockade of family inquiries, has endured for 6 years at the time of this writing.

The political sensitivity of ECT appears to ensure that it will not be provided by Bay Area county mental health programs in the visible future.

State Mental Health Administration

Under the sway of the Department of Mental Health, California's state hospitals have performed remarkably little ECT in recent decades, particularly in view of the large numbers of patients with severe, treatment-resistant disorders (Kramer 1990). A chain of review and approval for ECT extends beyond the statutory requirements, through ultimate review by a single psychiatrist in the central Department of Mental Health offices in Sacramento.

Case 1 ("Catch 22"). A state hospital patient considered capable of making his own consent decision, a rarity in the system, had an unusual delay before receiving treatment. The facility, and the Department of Mental Health, accustomed to the occasional involuntary or incompetent ECT candidate, had no procedure established to "process" the freely consenting patient, and so delayed ECT while devising such policy.

Case 2. A psychiatrist from Metropolitan State Hospital in southern California reported that about 20% of the facility's patients had disorders with affective features. No ECT had been provided at the hospital for 20 years, and referrals to ECT resources were rare.

Impact of ECT Regulations in California

Casual observers, including many psychiatrists who do not perform ECT, will be inclined to see a regulation promoting "informed consent" for ECT as innocuous, since the theme would appear to parallel our ethical codes and other prevailing laws. The champions of special ECT laws attempt to cast opponents of restrictive laws as opponents of the informed consent process. However, if the assorted arguments of the anti-ECT movement are put into some sort of order, it follows that this movement encourages refusal of ECT rather than an informed, reflective interaction with a physician.

Dissuasion and Intimidation

Naturally, the specific contents of an ECT law must be reviewed to discern the true impact on patient care. One significant way in which this statute regulates behavior is by threatening economic penalties and loss of professional license to anyone violating its provisions. The physician's good intentions do not suffice. The inhibiting power of the complex law (uninitiated attorneys require several readings to sort out technical requirements) is strengthened by the reality that unintended oversights could bring the same penalties as intentionally flouting the law.

Physicians and hospitals will respond according to the degrees of burden and perceived threat involved in contending with a statute. Observations of the California law in action since 1977 reveal that both medical and official interpretations of a statute may take broad dimensions, arising not just from the letter of the law, but as much from its spirit of antagonism to ECT, and the burdens it creates (California Medical Association–California Psychiatric Association 1990). As Montaigne observed, "There is as much liberty and latitude in the interpretation of laws as in their form" (Cotton 1947, p. 416). In this discussion, I address both the technical elements of California's anti-ECT law and its human impact.

Assault on the Doctor-Patient Alliance

Isaac and Brakel (1992) analyzed that mental health "rights" campaigns, which could address legitimate concerns, have been substantially crafted into a herd of Trojan horses for antipsychiatric, antitreatment zealots. This view is supported by the origins of California's ECT law and its title—not "informed consent guidelines" but "the right to refuse convulsive therapy." This statute clearly assumes that the ECT practitioner is not trustworthy, and the practitioner literally is treated as the patient's adversary when the court or "patients' rights advocate" is involved. In some court documents the hearing is actually on record as *"Dr. Doe v. Patient Roe."*

Biased Consent Form

The mandatory consent form is written by the Department of Mental Health with its contents prescribed by statute. It insinuates that a substantial lack of medical consensus exists about ECT and dwells vastly more on side-effect and risk issues than on potential benefits of treatment. Some of the alleged risks, such as ostensible damage to the brain or lungs, are included in obvious service of anti-ECT forces, without heed to scientific veracity. No attention is given to the risks of inadequately treated severe depression. This consent form invades the privacy of the doctor-patient relationship and hamstrings the potential for hospital medical staffs, eminent authorities, or professional societies to use evolving medical knowledge to shape consent discussions. The sketchy consent forms used for vastly more risky surgical procedures stand in ironic contrast to the ECT document, an attempt to corrupt the consent process into a dissuasive message.

Presumption of Incompetence

The voluntary patient, if considering ECT rather than other treatments, remarkably loses the legal presumption of competency and instead must undergo a mandated competency examination by an additional consultant. Patients under conservatorship, even if quite lucid and voluntarily admitted, as well as involuntary patients, require that a designated attorney, usually a public defender, concur with the treating psychiatrist's opinion of competency. If the patient is considered competent, the ponderous court hearing mechanism is obviated. However, most attorneys, insisting on "due process," seek the shelter of a full court hearing rather than allowing the patient to render his or her own choice.

Court Hearing and the Question of Access

Involuntary or incompetent patients will usually need a court hearing to resolve the consent mechanism. Paradoxically, despite setting this requirement, the state provides no mechanism by which the patient can have ready access to the courts. An attorney is required as the patient's counsel, usually a public defender. Since the California ECT law, like most "rights" regulations, implicitly impugns the family's role, an attorney retained by family in this situation would often be challenged as having an unacceptable conflict of interest. The defender is prepared to represent the patient in a hearing, but *not* to file for the hearing. In most jurisdictions, a patient who is in the charge of a public conservator will have the petition for hearing filed by the district attorney. Other patients will have no access to a hearing unless their family can retain an attorney, or they are, uncommonly, in a position to organize such for themselves. The lack of adequate funds will limit many, and finding counsel will be difficult at best since most private attorneys are unfamiliar with and intimidated by the issues. Families who otherwise have adequate resources may find the emotional burden of helping coordinate extended legal arrangements overwhelming.

> *Case 1.* A psychiatrist attempted to arrange a transfer for ECT for a psychotically depressed elderly woman who was seen in consultation in a general hospital medical ward. The receiving hospital had a policy of not accepting such transfers until the legal consent procedures were completed, since Medicare coverage would not redress the cost of a long period of pretreatment delay. The psychiatrist was sent several pages of instructions for pursuing an ECT hearing. This was not achieved, since there was no family or comparable party to sustain the effort.

> *Case 2.* A convalescent home resident in her 70s with deteriorating depression was wasting and feeble, raising concern for her survival on the part of her physicians and family. Her grandson, an attorney, overwhelmed by the outline of the arrangements necessary for an ECT hearing that had been sent to him, did not take the necessary initiative. (She recovered after a very slow response to medications.)

No Appeal

The statute contains no provision for review or appeal mechanisms should treatment be denied by the court.

No Emergency or Urgent Treatment Mechanism

The statute contains no provision for expeditious treatment for critically ill patients such as those with progressive physical debility, exhaustive psychosis, or neuroleptic malignant syndrome (Bach-y-Riata and DeRameri 1992). It is ironic that the very same patient to whose psychiatric treatment weeks of delay, reams of paper, and hours of officials' and physicians' energy have been devoted may require and receive emergency surgery or cardiac care without obstacle! Most such treatments would involve vastly more risk of morbidity or mortality than any psychiatric treatment. Yet the patient is not so "sheltered" from nonpsychiatric remedies (Applebaum and Roth 1984).

> *Case.* A cachectic, elderly, psychotically depressed woman had lingered for weeks in the referral hospital until her consent hearing was finally scheduled. During her eventual course of ECT she developed an incidental acute septic cholecystitis, requiring surgery. This was accomplished with no more formality than notifying her conservator.

Subjugation of the Family's Role

The confinement of proxy consent to legal mechanisms highlights the loss of the former consent roles of the family, physician, hospital administrator, and supportive consultants. Not only does the legalistic route entail substantial or insurmountable obstacles to appropriate ECT, but such legal requirements imply that the courts and other public agents are held by policymakers to be more respectful of the personal welfare of the patient than family members or physicians.

Invasion of Privacy

All ECT that occurs must be reported to county and state officials, with enumeration and demographics, including patients' hospital record numbers. Hence the private records of ECT patients are conspicuously flagged for governmental intrusion. Consent and clinical records are indeed reviewed during official inspections.

Elimination of ECT Resources

Is it an exaggeration to propose that a law that merely "regulates" and does not prohibit ECT actually does terminate a portion of services? Before proceeding with the factual demonstration that this is true, let me offer the historical quote: "The power to tax involves the power to destroy" (Marshall 1801/1978, p. 681). Substitute *regulation* for *tax* in the sense that governmentally imposed protocols extract energy, patience, and morale.

Promptly after the present California ECT statute took effect, a number of psychiatrists ceased offering ECT. Even more remarkably, a number of hospitals did likewise. In subsequent years, the areas of California with no ECT facilities at all increased (Kramer 1985). Especially in northern California, major psychiatric residency training centers, whether private, community, or university based, were conspicuously devoid of ECT. A generation of psychiatrists graduated here (and in many parts of the country) lacks meaningful experience with ECT. Further illustrating the intimidating impact of the law, even the psychiatric staffs and administrators of hospitals *exempt* from the law, "federal compounds," were strongly swayed by it. At least one Bay Area Veterans Administration hospital ceased ECT abruptly, and one military hospital considered doing so. A local veteran's facility has continued to refer ECT cases to a Los Angeles Veterans Administration hospital.

Disqualification by the Personnel Requirements

The subtle chilling effect of California's law is hardly the only obstacle to ongoing ECT in the smaller communities of the state. By statutory requirements, ECT requires one, or, with incompetent patients, two, pretreatment consultants and a posttreatment review "committee." Making the questionable assumption that all local psychiatrists were indeed willing to be involved with ECT, and allowing for at least one extra psychiatrist to allow vacation cross-coverage for ECT provision, a community or isolated hospital staff would require at minimum the participation of *four* psychiatrists for any provision of ECT. This is in the case of treatment of the voluntary, competent patients, where consent mechanisms themselves are not considered especially daunting by those who now give ECT. It appears that legislators, and urban psychiatrists, view medical matters in the context of cities, replete with professionals, and give limited regard to the plight of practitioners and patients in outlying settings.

Paperwork Burden

The California statute requires quarterly enumeration of ECT cases and of complications, with reporting to local and state mental health authorities. The necessary paperwork is not insignificant in volume and time required, and its inadvertent or intentional omission presumably risks the same severe sanctions as would the violation of other parts of the law.

Image of Inaccessibility and Impropriety

When the popular sleeping medication triazolam (Halcion) underwent another round of adverse publicity in 1992, a colleague of mine declared that he would no longer dispense it, although he had observed no special problems with it over years of prescribing it. The advocacy of ECT involves facing a far more disconcerting challenge than mere provocative news reportage. The "official government stamp of disapproval" leads many psychiatrists to consider or recommend ECT only reluctantly. Undoubtedly this same politically engendered self-consciousness has led some ECT practitioners to be unduly restrained in accepting referrals or in technical decisions that alter treatment efficacy (Hay et al. 1992). For instance, the outcome of ECT might be compromised by holding the lengths of treatment series to a cosmetically modest number rather than suiting individual patients' requirements.

Upper Hand for Antipsychiatrists:
Intimidation and Harassment

Censorial acts of government leave a profound impression. Although the ban on ECT in Berkeley lasted only a few months in 1982, local residents and nonpsychiatric physicians still commonly believe that the ban persists in the 1990s.

Local public officials who are hostile to ECT obviously gain encouragement from an anti-ECT state statute. The 1991 and 1992 anti-ECT resolutions in San Francisco and Berkeley served notice that the local governments, backed by the respective "patients' rights advocates," are poised to take ECT to task. Some hospitals in both communities have restricted their services in hopes of not drawing fire. One hospital specifically avoids extraregulatory agency interactions by not treating those incompetent for consent purposes. Another has overruled optional use of a sine-wave ECT stimulus device (for occasional patients not responding to conventional "brief-pulse" treatment despite enhancement techniques), for fear of drawing renewed official criticism and publicity.

> *Case 1.* I received a written accusation from a local patients' rights advocate official alleging that I had been covertly practicing office ECT without appropriate documentation and reporting to public agencies. The groundless charge was dropped, but the process depicts a discouraging, antagonistic atmosphere.

> *Other cases.* In a neighboring Bay Area county, the presence of at least one militant ECT opponent on the "advocates" staff colors the tone of all applications for court review of proxy consent. The request for a hearing usually is not made until several medication regimens are applied (even in the face of convincing failure or intolerance of such in the past) and/or the patient, often elderly, has gravitated toward serious medical deterioration. "Classical" syndromes are required, glossing over the large number of patients with variations of illness. I can attest to the psychiatrist's natural reluctance to enter into the court process after repeated experience with obstructive tactics, indifference, or hostility from various officials.

Pricing ECT Out of Reach

Under severe economic constraints due to Medicare and private insurance practices, hospitals are barely tolerating admissions long enough to encompass an ECT series of modest length. If patients' conditions involve impaired consent capacity, virtually no hospitals can viably invite such admissions, which would be vastly extended by court hearing requirements.

> *Case.* A woman in her 60s had a long history of atypical psychosis of the schizophrenic spectrum with a history of violence and severe self-burning. In a recent admission of several weeks she required restraints, tube feedings, and intensive nursing care. She had a pattern of limited benefit from neuroleptics and other classes of drugs, appearing to have some benefit from lithium with anticonvulsants. Seizures and a neuroleptic malignant syndrome had complicated an earlier trial of clozapine.
>
> Following a rapid relapse, her family sought ECT because of her history of benefit. The only East Bay hospital providing ECT was unable to readmit her

since her prior stay had not only outdistanced Medicare reimbursement substantially, but had exhausted the departmental budget for private-duty attendants for the fiscal period.

Officials: Authority Without Responsibility

If a judge, public conservator, district attorney, patients' rights advocate, public defender, or public mental health director were to cause harm or death by obstructing treatment in defiance of medical indications, no personal blame or retribution would derive. In stark contrast to the vulnerability of hospitals and physicians, public officials are generally given immunity by law from personal liability for their actions. The mind-set of officials is commonly colored by this psychological cushioning. An appearance of complying with regulations and procedures suffices, from this morally blunted stance.

> *Case.* Upon my request for state intervention for endangered patients, one deputy attorney general of California reassured me that I need not "worry" should a patient die due to regulatory treatment obstacles—as long as I followed statutory procedures!

Overwhelming Emotional and Logistical Obstacles

The family will frequently be so overwrought with concern over their loved one, including largely self-imposed reservations and guilty feelings about the prospect of involuntary treatment, that they will fail to marshal the necessary legal resources for an ECT hearing. Unless they have the supporting teamwork of a hospital staff and motivated family or public conservator, psychiatrists have no realistic way to seek ECT for deserving, incompetent patients. (Some public officials have suggested to me that it is the *psychiatrist's* place to hire an attorney for statutory proceedings. The physician who could hypothetically divert the energy and time required for this enterprise would also have to be independently wealthy, of course.)

> *Case 1.* A consulting psychiatrist referred an elderly psychotically depressed woman for ECT after evaluating her on an acute medical ward of a general hospital. Since she lacked family or other personal advocates, no one was at hand to carry the momentum for ECT hearing arrangements.

Case 2. The parents of a young woman with a refractory psychosis had an uneasy relationship with local officials because of battling the local public mental health system to procure acute and long-term hospital services for their daughter. Despairing over their daughter's scanty treatment benefit and prominent dyskinesias, they overcame their original aversion to ECT via consultations and perusal of literature. Since they feared that they would not succeed in pursuing ECT in East Bay courts, they admitted their daughter to a prestigious East Coast hospital for ECT. This required depletion of the father's retirement pension funds, whereas Medicaid would have financed treatment in California.

Case 3. An 82-year-old with a psychotic depression and past history of preferentially benefiting from ECT was admitted to an acute medical ward for hydration and support after several days of delusional refusal of sustenance. She had refused all medications starting several months before. Her internist and family were apprised of the weighty delays and legal hurdles that must precede ECT and that a psychiatric hospital could not accept her for an "administrative" stay. A gastrostomy feeding tube was promptly inserted, anticipating that, with or without pursuit of ECT, she would be in a convalescent home for the immediate future. She was more amenable to nursing care with neuroleptics and stimulants given via her feeding tube. At the time of this writing, a week after medical admission, her family was hesitating at retaining counsel for potential ECT proceedings, and she had developed a bacterial pneumonitis.

Even with some of the necessary resources in place, the imposing measures required by statute undercut the process more often than not. Only approximately 2% of patients receiving ECT in California have been treated with the statutory designation of involuntary status. (Some so designated on technical grounds are actually voluntarily admitted. Few "involuntary" recipients actually object to ECT, and even fewer express regret or resentment after gaining benefit from treatment.)

Hearing Delays

Anticipating the possibility that some treatment might be a matter of urgency, the statute indicates that a hearing shall be held within *3 days* of petition. I am aware of *no* hearings that have occurred within this time frame and very few that have come within a week of the mark. Seriously ill patients who require a court hearing must first have the uncommon prerequisite conjunction of a conducive hospital, psychiatrist, and legal agent. (It should be understood that contemporary clinical attitudes in most settings, as well as regulatory influences, will ensure that most patients will have remained unimproved, or will have deteriorated, for weeks, or even years, before ECT is advocated.)

Mechanisms of Delay

The conservator will demand that a formal explanatory letter, and probably the two consultants' reports, be in hand before a request is made to the district attorney to file for a hearing. Paperwork supersedes medical treatment needs.

The district attorney will naturally relegate an ECT case among a number of tasks demanding attention. If personal reservations about ECT apply, or special aspects of a case heighten the perceived level of "controversy," the petition will likely be filed with additional delay.

The public defender will require time to evaluate the patient and circumstances, and delayed scheduling of a hearing will result. The occasional defender who is adamantly opposed to all ECT will use delay as a tool in itself and may include the arrangement of an anti-ECT "expert" as grounds for more preparation time.

The court calendar, for mental health hearings as with other branches of the courts, is usually overflowing, hence leading to further delays.

Because of legal motions, a hearing can be continued without resolution of the treatment consent question.

As a consequence, the "3 days" timing of an ECT hearing is in practice several weeks, or even months. I have on occasion made special appeals to all officials involved, including the presiding judge of the superior court. The best outcomes have been in the range of 1–2 weeks' delay.

Callous Disregard for the Patients' Comfort and Safety

Other applicable statutes in California require that legal hearings be held in a setting that meets the patients' health and safety needs. In practice, most counties routinely require that patients be brought to a courthouse or other appointed facility, regardless of their tormented state, or severe agitation, or recent suicidal actions.

Debating the Relevance of ECT

The statute encourages a challenge to the merits of ECT. In its actual wording, the statute directs the court only to determine the patient's capacity for informed consent. Deviating from the instructions of the statute, however, the court hearing usually involves a debate over the choice of ECT, rather than a review of the patient's capacity for consent, and appointment of a proxy party when appropriate. Judges typically rule that ECT shall or shall not be performed.

Judicial Pharmacology

At least one Bay Area judge, without medical consultation to support his ruling, instructed the patient's psychiatrist to launch yet another medication program before asking that ECT be again considered.

The Judge as ECT Expert

I have learned of hearings in which judges approved ECT, but specified the electrode placement technique to be used, or the number of treatments to be provided.

ECT Is Forbidden

A judge in the Berkeley jurisdiction flatly declared that no patient under review by his court would have ECT. Another advised me on the day of the hearing that she took exception to ECT and wished to disqualify herself—which would have led to substantial further delay in treatment for the seriously disturbed patient. The staff of a state hospital has had the experience of a judge blocking ECT for a patient over a series of hearings, several months apart. Ironically, all other parties involved, including the patient and public defender, were supportive of ECT.

Illustrative Cases

Last Rites

Due to the combination of clinical and regulatory factors that typically delay choice of and approval of ECT in severe illness, I have encoun-

tered a number of cases wherein substantial physical detriment has
accompanied the mental duress suffered by patients. Transfer to general
medical or intensive care units has occurred due to intervening pneumo-
nia, cardiac crises, thromboembolism, inanition, and other illness.

> *Case 1.* A woman in her 60s, residing in a long-term care facility because of a
> psychotic bipolar disorder, had a history of neuroleptic malignant syndrome.
> After having ECT in a state hospital nearly 40 years before, she exhorted her
> family to spare her that treatment again. Even with renewed use of antipsychotic
> agents and adjunctive drugs, she dwindled with exhaustion and pneumonia while
> the family labored over the ECT issue. She had literally received the last rites of
> the Roman Catholic Church by the time a court approved ECT. One treatment
> improved her clouded, psychotic state dramatically. ECT was stopped at that
> point given the balance of her vast improvement and her sentiments about
> ECT—although she did not describe any specific part of her single treatment as
> particularly unpleasant.

> *Case 2.* A woman in her early 20s was admitted to a "nontraditional" (anti-
> somatic treatment) unit of a county hospital where the staff prodded her to
> "accept responsibility" for recovery from catatonia. After medical stabilization
> of her pneumonia and empyema in a community hospital, she was transferred,
> ankylosed in a fetal position, to a community psychiatric unit. Once legal
> preliminaries had finally been completed, she responded impressively to a brief
> course of ECT with a good social remission and eventual recovery of her physical
> capacities.

Interruption of ECT

Courts in the Bay Area have shown intolerance for maintenance ECT
by indirect evasive tactics. Instead of prohibiting or failing to order
approval of ECT, some courts have simply cut the thread of access to
further court hearings for patients under public conservatorship. By a
technical interpretation, in these cases the patients' public conserva-
torships were curtailed, citing that since they lived in chronic care
facilities (via arrangements by their protectors), they failed to
demonstrate an inability to obtain food, clothing, and shelter. The end
of conservatorship meant the end of ready access to court hearings,
necessary every 30 days by statute even if the maintenance treatment
pace were one treatment in that interval.

> *Case.* A young adult daughter of a political refugee immigrant family, formerly
> an excellent student, had had excellent remissions of two adolescent psychotic

episodes with ECT in her homeland. Her condition had relapsed within the first year of arrival in the United States, and, probably reflecting the reduced opportunities of her indigent status, the family interpreted professionals as representing that ECT was "not available" in Virginia, and later in the public mental health system in California. After 5 years of deterioration into a profoundly regressed, periodically explosive state, she was referred for ECT by a county mental health clinic.

Despite aggressive concurrent use of varied medications, she relapsed rapidly from her much-improved status obtained with acute ECT. The court began to interrogate the treating psychiatrist as sequential 30-day hearings were required to extend her continuation and maintenance treatment. The judge and public defender implied that an "end point" should be defined. The judge questioned the economic gain to the physicians (under Medicaid!), and at one point suspended hearings for several extra weeks. He was covertly seeking an independent psychiatric consultation to review both the ECT and *medications,* since a preliminary review of the latter with a county mental health official apparently cast doubt on those treatments also. That is, drugs such as carbamazepine (Tegretol) and divalproex (Depakote) were not then considered "standard" by the county program, which has a rigid formulary and procedure policy.

The consultant endorsed the quality of the patient's care. This was kept under wraps and never entered into the court record or related discussions of the patient's care. Further venting his displeasure with the case, the judge took exception, "on the record," to the psychiatrist's correspondence protesting delays in the patient's treatment. The patient's ECT was stopped after she could no longer obtain access to the courts, when the court canceled her public conservatorship.

Fatalities

Mortality figures related to deprivation of access to ECT will remain largely a matter of speculation. I have heard of deaths of patients who deteriorated in community psychiatric hospitals and died after transfer, and clinicians at the University of California, Los Angeles, described such an outcome (Roy-Byrne and Gerner 1981). As mentioned previously, some jurisdictions scrutinize ECT with a stern eye, imposing brinkmanship with the patient's health and even life.

Case. An elderly custodial patient in an excellent geriatric psychiatric facility experienced a deterioration in her immobilizing psychotic depression. She experienced profound anorexia and wasting and was transferred to a standard convalescent home for nasogastric tube feedings. A court hearing was finally scheduled after weeks of delay. The patient died 8 days before the date set for her hearing. (The reader will recall that the statute includes a 3-day time requirement from "petition" to hearing.)

Emergency Cases

Substantial delay and inaction is inherent in the California ECT law. In the face of pressure to respond rapidly in emergency situations, public officials frequently manifest a dense barrier of psychological denial, rationalization, intellectualization, and displacement, which allows them to invoke "due process" and "liberties" even at the cost of patients' bodily safety and integrity.

Psychiatrists and other medical and mental health professionals, meanwhile, will enhance standards of care by considering ECT as a measure that some severely disturbed patients merit on an emergency basis. Delays created by hesitant clinicians may precede those caused directly by public regulation.

Case 1. A formerly dynamic 18-year-old woman had lingered in a withdrawn state with her family after poor pharmacotherapeutic resolution of an explosive psychotic episode at age 15. Another delusional outburst preceded several weeks of deterioration with alternating catatonic inhibition and excitement. Several classes of neuroleptics, plus benzodiazepines, were minimally effective, and leather restraints and tube feeding were required because of food refusal, severe agitation, and repeated efforts at self-harm, such as self-strangulation. ECT was sought on an urgent basis due to the primary illness plus drug complications including recurrent hypotension, and concerns about airway safety with pro-longed tube feeding. The first cordons of officials insisted in having all paperwork in hand before contemplating any further steps. Only with extensive "lobbying" of the several departments of officials, including the presiding superior court judge of the involved county, was a special hearing "expedited" after 1 week, at continued jeopardy to the patient. (After the first, bilateral, treatment, the patient emerged dramatically from her profound disturbance into a more subdued level of psychosis. In place of her previous screams and groans, she awakened from ECT to greet her family pleasantly and ask for some doughnuts. The remarkable effectiveness of ECT renders it a priority consideration with catatonic syndromes.)

Case 2. A former nurse in her 40s who had a history of serious suicide attempts was admitted in an agitated state of psychotic depression. Involuntary ECT proceedings were sought when she failed to derive early benefit from substantial doses of sedative and neuroleptic agents with her antidepressant. She was absorbed with suicidal impulses, even grasping for items like pencils with intent of suicide. She was briefly in an intensive care unit after surgical repair of a neck laceration self-inflicted with a broken piece of concealed dinnerware. A probate court judge appeared to support a prompt ECT hearing, but "continued" the initial hearing to a later date to accommodate the "defense" counsel's prepara-tion. He blithely assured the dismayed attending psychiatrist that he was confident that the hospital staff would ensure the patient's safety in the interim. (Neither the nursing staff nor "patient's rights" regulations would sanction virtually continuous physical restraints or locked seclusion, despite the more certain safety margins of such options. Fortunately the patient was successfully attended and ultimately had a good remission with ECT.)

Younger Patients

In California, no ECT may be given to patients under age 12, and those age 12–16 must have three child psychiatric consultants concurring that the treatment is required as a lifesaving resort. (The relief of a persisting psychosis or depression is not an adequate foundation for proposing ECT in this age group.) Even without the life-and-death criterion, the need for three concurring child psychiatry specialists effectively eliminates the option of ECT. Most areas of the state have *no* such specialists. Even larger communities are unlikely to have many child psychiatrists who are both prepared to consider ECT as an option and willing to enter into the atmosphere of controversy posed by regulations. (As this chapter was being prepared, a bill passed in the Texas legislature that prohibits the use of ECT for anyone under the age of 16.)

Conclusion

It is easy to lose sight of the regulatory suppression of ECT. In his extensive contemplations, Montaigne suggested that we can become accustomed to even extreme social phenomena in a fashion analogous to the dulling of vivid sensory perceptions, such as tolerance to the scent of a perfume, or to sleeping in the vicinity of a clamorous bell tower (Cotton 1947). The clinical pattern of underuse of ECT in many areas naturally escapes the awareness of most office-based psychiatrists, because of preselection of patients by severity of disorder. The issue of suppressed and inadequate use of ECT also passes with limited notice on the part of many ECT practitioners. Psychological coping mechanisms, including desensitization, account for part of this shaping of perception. Also, events that take place are more easily registered than non-events. We are more aware of providing ECT for those who arrive at treatment, than of the less visible, hypothetical issue of the nontreatment of patients whose care is obstructed by regulations or other factors. By comparison, our profession takes justifiable pleasure in providing beneficial medication and psychotherapy for many with depression. Only when we are reminded by epidemiological researchers do we realize that the predominant portion of the depressed in our populace receive little or no such treatment.

Although we see the picket signs accusing practitioners of ECT or psychopharmacology of barbarism at meetings such as the annual American Psychiatric Association scientific meeting, we tend reflexively to mistrust characterizations of antipsychiatric regulations as arising from concerted, organized attacks on the profession. Such assertions sound too much like tabloid hyperbole, or troubled imagination. Psychiatrists, like most citizens of kindly manner, are disposed to attribute their own moral standards, such as intellectual honesty and altruism, to others, even in the political arena. Most of us who neither grapple with health care legislation or litigation nor follow antipsychiatric organizations closely are at risk of being ill-informed about the origins of restrictive regulation of treatments. Selected parties, however, have been aware of Scientology's anti-ECT intentions. The medical liability insurance industry in the 1970s did know of Scientology's encouragement of suits, and boosted premiums in the face of this (Anonymous 1978). (Later actuarial reviews have not supported the need for added premiums for ECT coverage [Slawson 1985].)

Political attacks on psychiatric treatment resemble campaigns of ethnic or religious denigration and do not aspire to civil, open debate (Isaac and Isaac 1983). Publication and public discussion of these social dynamics have been discouraged by the chilling effect of accounts of professionals or former group members who have experienced damage suits, personal harassment, and vilification after criticizing such antipsychiatric organizations as Scientology.

A government maintains safety and order by passing and enforcing rules, including health regulation. The United States has been undergoing, as have many Eastern and Western bloc industrial nations, an upsurgence of increasingly detailed lawmaking at all levels (Baldassarini and Cohen 1986). Ultimately, tensions arise over the relative deprivation of human freedoms that arises when government appoints to itself greater powers. Governments that intentionally inflict harm or death in other than legitimate police or national defense functions typically elicit internal or external challenge. But moral judgment and sanctions are not marshalled as easily when a destructive government policy causes injuries by unpublicized offenses of omission—such as prevention of ECT—rather than by active brutality, and when the victims are a small, inconspicuous, dispersed group. Patients deprived of adequate treatment, and their families, are likely not even to be cognizant of their missed opportunity, much less present a unified voice.

Public officials (and physicians) are prey to the same mechanisms of intuitive misjudgment as is the general public. Indictment, such as hostile ECT propaganda, leaves a more vivid and lingering impression than praise. We are familiar with the phenomenon of individuals or businesses publicly charged with a grave offense, struggling with the accusations and retaining a tainted image even if later exonerated. Likewise, maligning Ritalin (methylphenidate), Halcion (triazolam), Prozac (fluoxetine), or ECT fosters an image of blameworthiness.

Unlike professionals, lawmakers and courts obviously lack discerning knowledge of most areas for which they create policy. They are, as a result, more vulnerable to the dynamics of prejudice and can easily misread "experts" (Huber 1991). Unless officials observe reasonable criteria for assessing credentials, such as university or professional society status, they can confuse legitimate and fringe viewpoints, and authentic versus specious professional expertise. Thus, maverick physicians enjoy a measure of success in supporting antipsychiatric campaigns with fallacies such as the claim that ECT has not been properly researched, that (ostensible) "data" verify that it causes harm, or that ultimately the entire concept of mental illness is simply an exploitive fabrication.

The language of human "rights," made poignant by historical images of dismal psychiatric institutional settings, lends a facade of moral rectitude to campaigns to restrict biological psychiatric treatments. Once such public policy is enacted, the intimidating power of law demands compliance and looms large in shaping behavior and attitudes. This perceptual process lends even badly crafted law to be regarded as rational and morally sound. Physicians and the broader community are then placed in a dilemma wherein humane, ethical standards conflict with law.

The concept of informed consent is broadly and rightly valued as a major principle in providing medical care. The distinction between the fruitful promotion of informed consent and its perversion into a semantic tool for the obstructive regulation of psychiatric treatment, as with California's ECT law, eludes most lawmakers and many physicians. Most of the groups promoting antipsychiatric regulation may propose to be defending the free, informed interaction of patients and psychiatrists, but are additionally, openly aiming for regulations that impede or prevent treatment (Isaac and Brakel 1992).

For the complex case of consent for the incompetent patient, the avenue of court or less formal legalistic hearings has gained ascendancy in state or court-fostered regulations. Many psychiatrists find this model for proxy consent conceptually appealing, although they typically would also prefer not to attend court hearings personally. In this chapter, I have illustrated the varied ways in which aggressive regulation of ECT consent can delay or prevent treatment. The clinical cases illustrate the prevailing insensitivity of this legalistic consent approach to the patient's struggle with illness, or even the patient's survival. The option for timely proxy consent for treatment to be given by family, or additional medical consultants in urgent situations, has unfortunately fallen into disfavor for psychiatric treatments, even though these consent mechanisms appear to be on balance more humane than formal legal proceedings by all measures other than abstract legal arguments (Freedman 1987; Hoffman 1985; Levine et al. 1991). A major inconsistency of regulations is illuminated when the same patient who has endured delays and deterioration of health pending, or absent, ECT can promptly receive more risky cardiac or surgical care based on the medical judgment of need and informal consent alternatives (Mills and Avery 1978).

Ideally the legislatures and courts should offer ready redress for correcting misguided public policy. Of course, the expense of litigation alone impedes most recourse to the courts. Montaigne also recognized that laws aimed at details of human conduct are never insightful and flexible enough to fit adequately the complexities of life. Laws also become entrenched and are rarely reversed by subsequent legislation (Cotton 1947). Posing hypothetical efforts to moderate laws that restrict ECT or antipsychotic medication, one can imagine the dim likelihood of any legislator adopting a "pro-drug" or pro-ECT position in the current atmosphere.

An achievable goal in countering anti-ECT political campaigns is the blocking or moderation of proposed new or more extreme regulations by vigorous defensive, "reactive" efforts. This has been accomplished in several states, and in part at the local and state level in California. The American Psychiatric Association, the American Medical Association, and their respective state and local organizations have been foremost in these efforts. In the past decade the revival of ECT research, training, and publications; the convening of major scientific meetings on the subject; and informational efforts with the press have by degrees enhanced the public standing of ECT. Public discussions of ECT and the politics of the antipsychiatry movement by courageous former patients have added invaluably to this encouraging trend, as has endorsement of access to the treatment by such resourceful lay groups as the National Alliance for the Mentally Ill (1992). The uncertain prospects for correction of destructive ECT regulations rest especially on the continued efforts of psychiatric societies, teaching centers, and individual clinicians to clarify the proper role of ECT in medicine and to offer responsible guidance to public policymakers. Improved odds of success will also require confrontation of the deceptive propaganda efforts of zealous antipsychiatric groups and their allies.

References

Abrams R: Electroconvulsive Therapy. Oxford, Oxford Press, 1988

Aden v Younger, 57 Cal App 3d 622 (1976)

American Psychiatric Association: Electroconvulsive Therapy (Task Force Report No 14). Washington, DC, American Psychiatric Association, 1978

American Psychiatric Association: The Practice of Electroconvulsive Therapy; Recommendations for Treatment, Training and Privileging (Task Force Report). Washington, DC, American Psychiatric Association, 1990

Anonymous: Underwriter for Spero-Whitelaw Professional Liability Insurance, 1978

Appelbaum PS, Roth LH: Involuntary treatment in medicine and psychiatry. Am J Psychiatry 141:202–205, 1984

Ayd G: The contemporary attack on electroconvulsive therapy: a warning. International Drug Therapy Newsletter 10:2–4, 1975

Bach-y-Rita G, DeRameri A: Medicolegal complications of postpartum catatonia. West J Med 156:417–419, 1992

Baldassarini RJ, Cohen BK: Regulation of psychiatric practice. Am J Psychiatry 143:750–751, 1986

Bates WJ, Smeltzer DJ: Electroconvulsive treatment of psychotic self-injurious behavior in a patient with severe mental retardation. Am J Psychiatry 139:1355–1356, 1982

California Department of Mental Health: Response to the Citizens Advisory Council Report on Electroconvulsive Therapy. Sacramento, CA, December 17, 1981

California Medical Association-California Psychiatric Association: Joint Task Force on Electroconvulsive Therapy Report. San Francisco, CA, 1990

Clark CJ (chairman): Report of the Electro-Convulsive Therapy Review Committee. Ontario, Canada, Ministry of Health, 1985

Clarke D: Declaration of Dennis Clarke in support of motion to intervene. Re: Doe v O'Conner, October 8, 1987

Consensus Conference: Electroconvulsive therapy. JAMA 254:2103–2108, 1985

Cotton C (trans): Essays of Michel de Montaigne. Garden City, NY, Doubleday, 1947

Doe v O'Conner, C646194, County of Los Angeles, 1987

Doe v Younger, No 361769 (San Diego County Super Ct, filed Dec 30, 1974)

Durham J: Sources of public prejudice against electroconvulsive therapy. Aust N Z J Psychiatry 23:453–460, 1989

Endler NS, Persad E: Electroconvulsive Therapy: the Myths and the Realities. Toronto, Canada, Hans Huber, 1988

Fink M: Convulsive Therapy: Theory and Practice. New York, Raven, 1979

Freedman B: Why single out electro-convulsive therapy? Ethical arguments and analysis. Health Law in Canada 8:35–38, 58, 1987

Freeman CPL, Cheshire KE: Attitude studies on electroconvulsive therapy. Convulsive Therapy 2:31–42, 1986

Freeman M: Behavioral health management for self-insured employers. Journal of Health Care Benefits. May–June, 1992

Gutheil TG, Appelbaum PS: Clinical Handbook of Psychiatry and the Law. New York, McGraw-Hill, 1982

Hay D, Herzl S, Mills M, et al: The stigma of electroconvulsive therapy: a workshop, in Stigma and Mental Illness. Edited by Fink P, Tasman A. Washington, DC, American Psychiatric Press, 1992, pp 189–201

Heneberry JK: The right of the psychiatric patient to refuse treatment. Legal Medicine, 1982, pp 137–159

Hoffman BF: The impact of new ethics and laws on electroconvulsive therapy. Can Med Assoc J 32:1366–1368, 1985

Huber PW: Galileo's Revenge: Junk Science in the Courtroom. New York, Basic Books, 1991

In re Schuoler, Supreme Court, State of Washington, No 5133–1, August 7, 1986

Isaac RJ, Armat VC: Madness in the Streets. New York, Free Press, 1990

Isaac RJ, Brakel SJ: Subverting good intentions: a brief history of mental health law "reform." Cornell Journal of Law and Public Policy 2:1, 1992

Isaac RJ, Isaac E: The Coercive Utopians. Washington, DC, Regnery Gateway, 1983

Kramer BA: Use of ECT in California, 1977–1983. Am J Psychiatry 142:1190–1192, 1985

Kramer BA: ECT use in the public sector: California. Psychiatr Q 61:97–103, 1990

Levine SB, Blank K, Schwartz HI: Informed consent in the electroconvulsive treatment of geriatric patients. Bull Am Acad Psychiatry Law 19:395–403, 1991

Marshall J (Chief Justice, U.S. Supreme Court): McCulloch vs Maryland, 3–6, 1801, in Dictionary of Quotations. Edited by Evans B. New York, Avenel Books, 1978, p 681

Mills MJ: Legal issues in psychiatric treatment. Psychiatr Med 2:245–261, 1985

Mills MJ, Avery DH: The legal regulation of electroconvulsive therapy, in Mood Disorders: The World's Major Public Health Problem. Edited by Ayd FJ. Presented at the Tenth Annual Taylor Manor Hospital Psychiatric Symposium. Baltimore, MD, Frank J Ayd Communications, 1978

Mills MJ, Pearsall DT, Yesavage JA, et al: Electroconvulsive therapy in Massachusetts. Am J Psychiatry 141:534–538, 1984

National Alliance for the Mentally Ill: Board of Directors Resolution of June 7, 1992

Peterson GN: Competency and consent in psychiatric treatment: medical ethics in conflict with legal trends. American Journal of Forensic Psychiatry 5:33–42, 1984

Roy-Byrne P, Gerner RH: Legal restrictions on the use of ECT in California. J Clin Psychiatry 42:300–303, 1981

Rudin E: Psychiatric treatment: general implications and lessons from recent court decisions in California. West J Med 128:459–466, 1978

Slawson P: Psychiatric malpractice: the electroconvulsive therapy experience. Convulsive Therapy 1:195–203, 1985

Szasz TS: The Myth of Mental Illness. New York, Harper & Row, 1961

Tenenbaum J: ECT regulation reconsidered. Mental Disorders Law Review 7:148–157, 211, 1983

Thompson JW: Utilization of ECT in US psychiatric facilities, 1975 to 1980. Psychopharmacol Bull 22:463–465, 1986

Vasconcellos J: Dear John . . . (letter). Madness Network News, April 1975

Weiner R: Patient's attitudes toward ECT. Psychiatry October 1987

Whitcomb D: The regulation of electroconvulsive therapy in California: the impact of recent constitutional interpretations. Golden Gate University Law Review 18:469–494, 1988

Winslade WJ: Electroconvulsive therapy: legal regulations, ethical concerns, in American Psychiatric Press Review of Psychiatry, Vol 7. Edited by Frances AJ, Hales RE. Washington, DC, American Psychiatric Press, 1988, pp 513–525

Winslade WJ, Liston EH, Ross JW, et al: Medical, judicial and statutory regulation of ECT in the United States. Am J Psychiatry 141:1349–1355, 1984

Wyatt v Stickney, 325 F Supp 781 (MD Ala 1971); 334 F Supp 1341 (MD Ala 1971); enforced by 334 F Supp 373, 344 F Supp 387, appeal docketed sub nom Wyatt v Adernott, No 72-2634, 5th Cir, filed Aug 1, 1973 (in supra American Psychiatric Association, 1978)

CHAPTER THREE

Regulation of Psychostimulants: How Much Is Too Much?

Robert T. Angarola, J.D.
Alan G. Minsk, J.D.

Psychostimulant use, both for licit and illicit purposes, is part of American medicine and culture. Studies show that stimulants, such as amphetamine, methamphetamine, and methylphenidate, provide positive medical results in the treatment of narcolepsy, attention-deficit hyperactivity disorder, in some depressions (particularly in the elderly), and to a lesser extent in obesity. Most recently, they are being used as adjuvant drugs in reversing opioid-induced sedation in the treatment of cancer pain. However, their diversion and abuse have resulted in federal and state governments strictly regulating the availability and use of these substances. Negative publicity and lawsuits filed by special interest groups have exerted an additional regulatory-like effect. These efforts have reduced the abuse of these drugs. However, they have also led to inappropriate restriction of their medical use to the detriment of patient care.

In this chapter we describe the medical use of psychostimulant medications; analyze how the federal and state governments monitor and restrict their production, distribution, prescription, and use; review the medical and regulatory controversies surrounding these drugs; and evaluate the effects of federal and state regulation on their availability for legitimate purposes. The primary focus is on amphetamine, methamphetamine, and methylphenidate, the three most widely available psychostimulants.

History

Amphetamine was first synthesized in 1887 and used medically in 1927 (Encyclopedia Americana 1992). A. Ogata, a Japanese pharmacologist, developed methamphetamine in 1919 as an amphetamine derivative. Amphetamine was first marketed in the United States in 1931 as Benzedrine, a nonprescription inhaler designed for nasal decongestion. As physicians recognized that amphetamine could stimulate the central nervous system, they used it in the treatment of some forms of depression and narcolepsy, the neurological condition of uncontrollably falling asleep (Burton 1991). Drug manufacturers began marketing amphetamine and other prescription stimulants in the late 1950s and early 1960s (Holden 1976).

Soon after amphetamine appeared on the market, reports of abuse began to surface. Abusers took apart the spray bottles of Benzedrine to get to the paper inside that contained the amphetamine. They then consumed the drug by chewing or blending it into a beverage to get high (Burton 1991). Amphetamine became available in pill form in the 1950s, which facilitated abuse (Holden 1976).

By 1962, an estimated eight billion amphetamine tablets per year were being legally produced, ostensibly to treat conditions such as obesity. However, it was evident that there was widespread nonmedical consumption of these drugs: "Much of the amphetamine abuse of the 1950s and 1960s occurred as a result of prescription abuse by individual patients obtaining drugs from their private physician, many of whom knowingly were writing prescriptions for profit" (Burton 1991, p. 48). In the 1960s, an injectable form of methamphetamine, commonly known as "speed," emerged as a popular stimulant. Illicit sale and use of amphetamine continued through the 1960s. One commentator estimated a 50% diversion rate of legitimate amphetamine production to the black market (King and Ellinwood 1992).

By the mid-1960s, Congress recognized that the existing controls over depressants (e.g., barbiturates) and stimulants were inadequate to prevent diversion and abuse. Therefore, it enacted the Drug Abuse Control Amendments of 1965, amending the Federal Food, Drug, and Cosmetic Act (1965). These amendments imposed new requirements on producers and wholesalers to register depressant and stimulant drugs with the Food and Drug Administration (FDA) and maintain records of all stocks of each drug for 3 years.

In 1970, Congress enacted the Controlled Substances Act (1970). This act placed drugs in control schedules according to their abuse potential, from Schedule I, drugs such as heroin and LSD with high abuse potential and no established medical use, to Schedule V, legally marketed drugs with low abuse liability such as nonprescription codeine elixirs. Congress listed amphetamine, methamphetamine, and methylphenidate in Schedule III (21 U.S.C. § 812). Schedule III is defined as the following:

(A) The drug or other substance has a potential for abuse less than the drugs or other substances in Schedules I and II;
(B) The drug or other substance has a currently accepted medical use in treatment in the United States;
(C) Abuse of the drug or other substance may lead to moderate or low physical dependence or high psychological dependence. (21 U.S.C. § 812[b][3])

Schedule III controls require manufacturers and distributors to maintain records of production and movement of these drugs and to limit refills to five prescriptions in a 6-month period. In 1971, the Bureau of Narcotics and Dangerous Drugs, the predecessor agency of the Drug Enforcement Administration (DEA), rescheduled amphetamines and methylphenidate to Schedule II because of the continuing problems of overproduction, diversion, and nonmedical use. Drugs are placed in Schedule II if the following apply:

1) The drug or other substance has a high potential for abuse
2) The drug or other substance has a currently accepted medical use in treatment in the United States or a currently accepted medical use with severe restrictions
3) Abuse of the drug or other substances may lead to severe psychological or physical dependence. (21 U.S.C. § 812[b][2])

Schedule II controls allow DEA to place quotas (limits) on the production of the drugs covered and require the use of special order forms to transfer the drugs to the retail level. Prescription refills are prohibited. In nine states, Schedule II controls require the use of government-issued prescription forms, which significantly decrease the prescribing of the drugs covered (Angarola and Wray 1989).

The DEA administrator sets annual aggregate production quotas for all controlled substances in Schedules I and II (21 U.S.C. § 826, 28 C.F.R. 0.100). Quotas for amphetamine and methamphetamine have steadily declined from 1978 to 1992, although methylphenidate quotas have more than doubled since that time. Table 3–1 illustrates this trend.

This trend illustrates that the negative publicity concerning amphetamines affected the availability of these drugs for legitimate use. On the other hand, despite the controversy surrounding methylphenidate discussed later, quotas for that stimulant increased because it did not carry the same social stigma that amphetamine and methamphetamine shared. More important, parents and physicians found that methylphenidate was effective in the treatment of their hyperactive children and continued to use the stimulant for that condition.

Medical Uses of Psychostimulants

Obesity

The FDA has found the use of amphetamine and methamphetamine to be safe and effective for appetite suppression and for the treatment of obesity. The *Physicians' Desk Reference* (PDR) notes that "adult obese subjects instructed in dietary management and treated with 'anorectic' drugs, lose more weight on the average than those treated with placebo and diet, as determined in relatively short-term clinical

Table 3–1.   Quotas for amphetamine, methamphetamine, and methylphenidate (kg)

Year	Amphetamine	Methamphetamine	Methylphenidate
1978	3,562	448	1,837
1982	849	200	1,082
1992	626	23	3,708
1993	238	16	5,000

Source. Data from *Federal Register* (1977, 1981, 1992, 1993)

trials" (p. 1843). In addition, the PDR indicates that amphetamine and methamphetamine serve as a "short-term (a few weeks) adjunct in a regimen of weight reduction based on caloric restriction, for patients refractory to alternative therapy, e.g., repeated diets, group programs, and other drugs" (p. 1843).

The use of these drugs for this purpose has come into increasing disfavor in the medical community, primarily because of their high potential for abuse and questionable efficacy in long-term weight loss. The PDR recommends that the usefulness of amphetamine and methamphetamine "should be weighed against possible risks inherent in use of the drug" (p. 1843). However, Schedules III and IV anorectics, such as benzphetamine, fenfluramine, phendimetrazine, diethylpropion, and mazindol, are recommended in the management of "[e]xogenous obesity as a short-term (a few weeks) adjunct in a regimen of weight reduction based on caloric restriction" (p. 1843).

Attention-Deficit Hyperactivity Disorder (ADHD)

Methylphenidate hydrochloride is marketed in the United States, both as Ritalin and in generic form. Physicians prescribe it primarily in the treatment of children with ADHD (Gittleman-Klein 1987). Methylphenidate is an

> integral part of a total treatment program which typically includes other remedial measures (psychological, educational, social) for a stabilizing effect in children with a behavioral syndrome characterized by the following group of developmentally inappropriate symptoms: moderate-to-severe distractibility, short attention span, hyperactivity, emotional lability, and impulsivity. (Physicians' Desk Reference 1994, p. 835)

This stimulant is a short-acting compound with an onset of action within 30–60 minutes and a peak clinical effect usually seen between 1 and 3 hours after administration. Stimulants such as methylphenidate "diminish motor overactivity and impulsive behaviors seen in ADHD and allow the patient to sustain attention" (Biederman 1991, p. 535).

Ciba Pharmaceutical Company, a division of Ciba-Geigy Corporation, first marketed methylphenidate in 1956. It has been estimated that at least 800,000 children suffering from attention-deficit disorder, hyperactivity, and hyperkinesis benefit from methylphenidate therapy (Cowart 1988). ADHD affects approximately 3% of children (Wick 1993). As noted earlier, DEA production quotas for methylphenidate have increased significantly, reflecting growing medical acceptance of this form of therapy; since 1971, the number of prescriptions for methylphenidate has increased dramatically (Wick 1993).

Clinical studies show that methylphenidate use is "significantly better in improving classroom and behavioral manifestations of ADD [attention-deficit disorder] as compared to a placebo" (Garfinkel et al. 1983, p. 347). Treatment with methylphenidate was "effective in diminishing symptoms of aggression, impulsivity and attention deficits" (p. 347) and was found to be more effective in "ameliorating global disturbing classroom behavior" (p. 347). In addition, studies reveal that "methylphenidate can suppress physical aggression directed toward peers in the child's natural environment" (Gadow et al. 1990, p. 716). One study suggests that because methylphenidate is useful in reducing aggression, it might also be helpful in treating delinquent adolescents (Kaplan et al. 1990).

Short-term effects of this stimulant include less errors of omission and improvements on math and science performance tests. Children do more homework and receive better grades (Wick 1993). Methylphenidate has proven to be the most effective in the treatment of ADHD: "Methylphenidate has the longest and best track record of all the stimulants" (Wick 1993, p. 52).

Narcolepsy

Studies show that amphetamine, methamphetamine, and methylphenidate use helps individuals who suffer from narcolepsy, a neurological condition characterized by sudden and uncontrollable onset of sleep (Burton 1991). Mitler and colleagues (1992) indicated that "methamphetamine normalizes sleep tendency and performance in narcoleptic patients." Regestein and colleagues (1983) stated that "amphetamines are safe drugs in judicious chronic use [for narcolepsy]; many patients have used these agents continuously for decades. Further, we have not seen an amphetamine psychosis in any of our narcoleptic patients" (p. 170). Methylphenidate is also useful in the treatment of narcolepsy: "Methylphenidate has been recommended as the drug of choice . . . because of its prompt action and low incidence of side effects" (Soldatos et al. 1983, p. 4).

Other Indications

Some treatment of depression includes the use of amphetamine and methylphenidate; increases in dosage or abuse are rarely found (Nemeroff 1990). In addition, more physicians are using stimulants as adjuncts in cancer pain relief treatment (Max 1990). For example, dextroamphetamine is useful in the treatment of postoperative cancer pain (Foley 1993). Amphetamine has also been shown to improve pain control, activity, and appetite in cancer patients (Joshi et al. 1982). Studies (Bruera and Bertolino 1992; Forrest et al. 1977) indicate that amphetamine and methylphenidate "antagonize narcotic-induced sedation and cognitive impairment" (Bruera and Bertolino 1992, p. 3).

Psychostimulant Abuse and Trafficking

Abuse of Psychostimulants

Despite evidence that stimulants are medically beneficial in the treatment of obesity, narcolepsy, hyperactivity, and other conditions, several of these drugs have fallen into public and medical disfavor, in large part because of illicit manufacture, distribution, and nonmedical use. The responses of regulators and some physicians have resulted in decreasing the availability and use of these stimulants for legitimate medical purposes.

As amphetamine abuse increased in the 1960s and 1970s, the federal government tightened controls over production and distribution. Many of these stimulants reached the illicit market through diversion from legitimate channels, primarily from licensed physicians who prescribed and dispensed these drugs under the shield of medical usefulness (Burton 1991). The widespread abuse of these drugs 30 years ago still resonates today. For example, people fear that the use of stimulants in the treatment of hyperactivity will lead to abuse or misuse by the patient, even though studies have shown that this is rarely the case (Loney 1988).

Current stimulant abuse cannot be ignored:

> According to the 1990 National Household Survey on Drug Abuse (NHSDA), 1.4% of the general population 12 years of age or older [an estimated 8.5 million people] was currently using nonprescription psychoactive drugs (most commonly, controlled analgesics, followed by stimulants, tranquilizers, and sedatives). (Cooper et al. 1992, p. 1306)

The Drug Services Research Survey, a National Institute on Drug Abuse–sponsored national survey of drug treatment facilities, indicated that amphetamine is the fourth most frequently cited principal drug of abuse, taken by 5.9% of the patients, behind crack/cocaine, heroin, and marijuana/hashish (Cooper et al. 1992). In addition, amphetamine ranked third as the most widely abused class of illicit drugs among high school seniors in 1990 (National Institute on Drug Abuse 1991).

Despite figures showing that illegal manufacture of stimulants continues to rise, the trend of stimulant abuse among high school students and young adults shows a decline since 1982. Two reasons for this downward trend are media attention given to the dangers of drug abuse and the overall recognition that drug abuse is no longer fashionable. For example, the annual prevalence rate of stimulant use shows a decrease from 21% to 5% among college students. Other evidence indicates that high school students favor legal prohibition of amphetamine more than they did 10 years ago; peer disapproval of nonmedical amphetamine use stood at 84% in 1990, the highest level recorded in the study, which began in 1975 (National Institute on Drug Abuse 1991). Statistics collected by the National Institute on Drug Abuse through the Drug Abuse Warning Network (DAWN) show a slight decrease in amphetamine abuse from 1985 to 1990, with emergency room mentions of amphetamine reflecting 1.06% of the total episodes in 1985, compared with 0.91% of the total episodes mentioned in 1990. The data are collected from 770 hospital emergency rooms located primarily in 21 metropolitan areas and 87 medical examiners located in 27 metropolitan areas affiliated with the DAWN system (National Institute on Drug Abuse 1985).

However, DAWN figures reflect a sharp increase in methamphetamine abuse. Emergency room mentions rose from 0.76% of the total
episodes in 1985 to 1.41% of total episodes in 1990. The source of
methamphetamine abused is rarely legitimate prescriptions but rather
illegal manufacture (the DEA production quota for methamphetamine
was only 23 kg in 1992). On the other hand, although legal methylphenidate production more than tripled between 1982 and 1992
(from 1,082 to 3,708 kg in 1992), its abuse as tracked by the DAWN
system declined significantly. In 1985, emergency room mentions
involving methylphenidate equaled 0.36% of the total mentions in
1985 but dropped to 0.07% in 1990 (National Institute on Drug
Abuse 1990).

There were some concerns expressed that after amphetamines were
moved from Schedule III to Schedule II, the abuse of Schedule III
and IV stimulants would increase. This never happened. For example,
in 1985, there were only three Schedule III and IV anorectics (i.e.,
phentermine, diethylpropion, and phendimetrazine) listed in DAWN
emergency room mentions. There had been a 28% decrease in emergency room mentions for these drugs between 1981 and 1985,
resulting in a total of only 194 emergency room mentions out of
approximately 200,000 DAWN reports in 1985. The 1990 DAWN
figures do not list any emergency room mentions for the Schedule III
or IV anorectics (this includes all drugs listed by DAWN)[1] (National
Institute on Drug Abuse 1990).

Illicit Trafficking of Psychostimulants

Although psychostimulant abuse remains a major problem, the source
of these drugs has changed dramatically over the past two decades.
Diversion of amphetamine and methamphetamine from legitimate

---

[1] In 1990, the National Institute on Drug Abuse changed the format for reporting
DAWN emergency room mentions and reduced the number of drugs reported.
This may explain in part why these three drugs were not mentioned.

channels has sharply declined. Once a significant problem in the 1960s and 1970s (Puder et al. 1988), enforcement efforts have led to reduced diversion opportunities (General Accounting Office 1982). By the late 1970s, diversion of amphetamine from pharmacists and physicians made up only 20% of the illicit market of these stimulants, and diversion of methamphetamine only 5% (Drug Abuse Policy Office 1982). Similarly, DEA reports that

> data collected and analyzed by the DEA for more than a decade indicate that approximately 40% of all drug abuse and illicit drug traffic in the United States today involves controlled substances that have been legitimately manufactured and subsequently diverted through illicit channels into nonmedical use, that is, abuse. This figure represents a 30% decrease from 5 or 6 years ago, when 60% to 70% of illicit drugs were diverted from legitimate sources. (Haislip 1989, p. 205)

However, although diversion opportunities from legitimate channels are decreasing, the number of illegal production sources continue to increase. "It is important to emphasize that the source of most amphetamines currently abused is illicit production, not diverted prescribed stimulants" (Cooper et al. 1992, p. 1306).

Another indication that the source of drug abuse today comes from the illegal production of stimulants is the increase in the number of clandestine laboratories seized. For example, seizures of illegal methamphetamine laboratories rose 600% during the late 1980s (Irvine and Chin 1991). Since 1987, more than 80% of all clandestine laboratories seized by DEA involve the synthesis of methamphetamine (Irvine and Chin 1991). Some laboratories illegally manufacture drugs with a street value of more than $300,000 in 1 week (Burton 1991).

Continuing reports of the abuse and diversion of amphetamine and methamphetamine have affected physicians' willingness to prescribe these drugs for legitimate purposes. Likewise, many pharmacists are reluctant to dispense or even stock them (Joranson 1990). Tight production quotas at times have affected patient access to needed medications. For example, in 1988, the administrator of the Drug Enforcement Administration ordered his staff to recalculate the aggregate production and individual manufacturing quotas for methylphenidate to "provide . . . for the estimated medical, scientific, research, and industrial needs of the United States" (Federal Register 1988, p. 50592). The administrator had found that quota restrictions were unduly limiting medical supply.

Actual abuse of stimulants led to tighter regulation and lower medical use. It is likely that this, in turn, has left many patients without needed medication.

Regulation of Psychostimulants

One commentator noted the following:

> For a long time, there has been a tendency to confuse legal and illegal use of drugs like the narcotic analgesics. . . . [I]t is silly to impose draconian restrictions on legitimate use of analgesics by health professionals in a simple-minded attempt to cut down on diversion and illicit use. Such measures tend to have little effect on illegitimate use of drugs and add considerably to the burdens on legitimate health care providers. (Lasagna 1989, p. 238)

The same can be said about psychostimulants. Although diversion of stimulants from legitimate sources was a significant problem in the 1960s and 1970s, the illicit manufacture of these drugs is the primary source today. Federal and state regulation of legitimate manufacturers, distributors, prescribers, and dispensers fails to address illegal production. Although the government must continue to regulate the legitimate channels of manufacture and distribution to prevent diversion to the illicit market, responsible regulation must ensure that stimulants are available for legitimate use.

Federal Regulation of Psychostimulants

Congress enacted the Controlled Substances Act to restrict the production and distribution of drugs that are subject to abuse. The strict regulation of stimulants resulted from two somewhat unrelated facts. First, the potent stimulants such as methamphetamine provided a strong sense of euphoria, a "rush" that some people found intensely pleasurable. There was little disagreement that these drugs met the Controlled Substances Act criterion for having a "high potential for abuse." At the same time that this pharmacological fact was being recognized, the medical community and federal and state regulators were becoming increasingly skeptical over the efficacy of stimulants for weight loss. This combination of events led to the early rescheduling of amphetamine, methamphetamine, and methylphenidate to Schedule II at the federal and state levels and to calls for even stronger regulatory action.

Despite the passage of the Controlled Substances Act, some members of Congress considered removing amphetamines from the market altogether. For example, Senator Gaylord Nelson (D-WI), chairman of the Monopoly Subcommittee of the Senate Small Business Committee in the mid-1970s, wanted to prohibit the commercial sale of amphetamines (at that time 2.25 million Americans were taking prescribed amphetamines). At hearings held before this subcommittee, the director of the FDA's Bureau of Drugs contended that the Controlled Substances Act had failed to reduce amphetamine abuse and testified that "the only meaningful next step which can be taken is to remove the indication for obesity from the labeling for amphetamines or to remove them from the market" (Holden 1976, p. 1027).

Because of abuse problems, the FDA noted specific concerns relating to the use of amphetamine and dextroamphetamine (21 C.F.R. 310.504[e] 1992). The FDA has made clear that it does not find much support for the efficacy of amphetamines in the treatment of obesity in the long term. In July 1972, the Final Report to the Director of the Bureau of Drugs by the Consultants on Anorectic Drugs concluded that adult obese subjects lost more weight with anorectic drugs than placebos and diet in short-term trials (National Institutes of Health 1973). However, the report concluded with a medical finding that the drugs were not the sole reason for the weight loss and that the "total impact of 'drug-induced' weight loss over that of diet alone must be considered" (p. 502).

The report recommended that all anorectics reviewed, with the exception of fenfluramine, should be placed in Schedule II on the basis of the drugs' potential for abuse and that "amphetamines prepared for or in a form suitable for parenteral use not be approved for use in the treatment of obesity" (National Institutes of Health 1973, p. 501). The report also indicated that amphetamine and methamphetamine were widely abused and concluded that it was in the best interest of the public health "to limit the use of amphetamines as far as is compatible with adequate therapy" (p. 501). Nevertheless, FDA decided in the late 1970s not to remove the obesity indication.

Two important physicians' reference guides also question the use of amphetamine and methamphetamine for obesity treatment. The PDR's listing of amphetamine includes a warning box for the physician (Physician's Desk Reference 1994). The drug is noted to possess a "high potential for abuse" (p. 1843) and is to be used only for weight reduction when "alternative therapy has been ineffective" (p. 1843). Amphetamine prescriptions are to be given "sparingly" (p. 1843).

The American Medical Association's (1986) *Drug Evaluations,* 6th Edition, uses even stronger language to describe amphetamine, dextroamphetamine, and methamphetamine, and their abuse potential: "None are advocated for the treatment of obesity because the risk of dependence is great. The FDA Bureau of Drugs has concluded that the amphetamines have no advantage over other anorectic drugs that have less risk" (p. 929).

State Regulation of Psychostimulants

States have also taken an active role in limiting the illegal production and distribution of stimulants. Although states must comply with federal law and regulations, many have imposed stricter regulations to curb nonmedical use of stimulants, particularly amphetamine and methamphetamine. Wisconsin was the pioneer in the late 1970s, and other states followed its efforts to curb the diversion and abuse of these drugs.

Following the FDA's decision not to remove the obesity indication for stimulants and in response to diversion and abuse in the Medicaid program, in 1976 the Wisconsin State Department of Health and Social Services restricted reimbursement of Medicaid claims for amphetamine products, unless prior authorization had been granted. Following preliminary investigations of numerous physicians, the Medical Examining Board promulgated an administrative rule making it "unprofessional conduct" to prescribe or dispense amphetamine for other than limited clinical indications, such as in the treatment of narcolepsy, hyperkinesis, drug-induced brain dysfunction, and depression (Treffert and Joranson 1981). Obesity was not one of these indications. In addition, several physicians were disciplined. In 1989, responding to a request from the Wisconsin Cancer Pain Initiative, Wisconsin modified its regulation specifically to allow physicians to prescribe amphetamines to treat persistent opioid-induced sedation in patients with cancer who require opioid analgesics for the relief of pain. The Wisconsin program effectively stopped the diversion and abuse of amphetamines and eliminated the use of these drugs for the treatment of obesity (D. E. Joranson, personal correspondence, January 1993). Following the sharp decline in diversion and abuse of amphetamines, the prior authorization restriction was lifted (D. E. Joranson, personal correspondence, January 1993).

Other states followed Wisconsin's lead. For example, in Kansas, Schedule II amphetamines may not be used for long-term treatment of obesity. Despite evidence of their efficacy, they are also proscribed in the long-term treatment of narcolepsy and hyperkinesis (Richard and Lasagna 1988). In addition, prescriptions for Schedule III and IV anorectic drugs are restricted to short-term obesity treatment (Richard and Lasagna 1988). Louisiana imposed strict regulations on stimulants used for the treatment of obesity. For example, prescriptions beyond 3 months' duration or a refill without a demonstrated loss of weight is "per se evidence" of a violation of the Louisiana Medical Practice Act (Richard and Lasagna 1988).

Kansas, Louisiana, and Wisconsin are not alone in imposing stricter controls over Schedule II stimulants. Georgia, Michigan, Texas, and many other states have similarly tightened requirements for the prescription and distribution of stimulants for legitimate medical uses (Richard and Lasagna 1988). The impact of these regulations is to limit severely the availability of stimulants for legitimate purposes. Controls placed over the specific use of these drugs such as those imposed in Wisconsin and Kansas can impede physicians' and researchers' development and use of appropriate drug therapies.

Negative Publicity and Medical Use

In the United States and throughout the world, there are some drugs we like and some we do not like. Nobody questions the use of insulin to treat diabetes or digitalis to control a heart condition. However, the taking of drugs that affect the central nervous system is often under attack. For example, although the World Health Organization has designated benzodiazepines as "essential drugs," consumer groups and other medical "experts" often questioned the use of these drugs to control severe anxiety attacks and panic disorder ("High Anxiety" 1993). Likewise, the prescribing of drugs to treat obesity, narcolepsy, and hyperactivity is subject to intense scrutiny. It is possible this disfavor is related to the condition being treated. Although clinically significant anxiety is one of the most common forms of mental illness, some people think that a person should just toughen up and not use a drug as a crutch. Children who cannot focus on schoolwork or normal play activities because of ADHD are "just being kids" and should not receive medications that have been proven to allow them to function normally.

The American Academy of Child and Adolescent Psychiatry and other medical organizations have strongly supported the use of stimulants as appropriate in the treatment of hyperactivity. However, methylphenidate in particular has been in the center of controversy. Lawsuits, adverse television reports, and newspaper articles critical of stimulant treatment for ADHD are major reasons for parental rejection of methylphenidate use (Safer and Krager 1992). Critics complain that methylphenidate can cause dangerous side effects and that psychiatrists are too eager to label children with conditions that might not exist. It is ironic that "while claims of overutilization are frequently made, research suggests that significant underutilization occurs" (Cooper et al. 1992, p. 1308).

The controversy found its way to the daily talk shows, such as *Donahue* and *Oprah*. Parents and children, school administrators and teachers, and physicians and lawyers assembled on these shows to discuss how methylphenidate has either positively or negatively affected their lives. Law enforcement officials highlighted the dangers of drug abuse. The emphasis was invariably on the adverse consequences of using these drugs.

Some individuals object to methylphenidate and other psychostimulant use because of a fear of overuse or abuse; others share philosophical objections to using drugs that affect the brain. For example, the Scientologists formed a group called the Citizens Commission for Human Rights in 1969. This group spawned more than 20 lawsuits against physicians who prescribed and distributed methylphenidate (Safer and Krager 1992).

There are no reports of any plaintiff ever winning any of these cases. However, the controversy over methylphenidate led to a decline in its legitimate use. For example, in Baltimore County, Maryland, the medication rate for treatment of hyperactivity had doubled every 4–7 years from 1971 to 1987 (Safer and Krager 1992). By 1987, almost 4% of all public elementary schoolchildren were receiving stimulant medication. However, after a media blitz against methylphenidate in 1987 and a highly publicized lawsuit in Baltimore, the medication rate dropped 39% in 1989 and 1991 surveys. The biggest decline related to kindergarten and elementary schoolchildren who had never received the drug (Safer and Krager 1992). Parents were affected by the negative publicity and had not seen the positive results that methylphenidate had had on hyperactive children. On the other hand, this publicity had little effect on those parents of children who had benefited from methylphenidate administration (Safer and Krager 1992). They knew that the medication had helped their children cope with their condition and continued to use the drug.

In Maryland, sales dropped 23% in response to the lawsuits and negative publicity. From 1986 to 1990, methylphenidate pharmacy sales in the Baltimore metropolitan area declined 60%. The decrease in methylphenidate use most prominently affected children attending schools in the less affluent areas of the county. In particular, slightly more than one-third of the total decline in the student medication rate from 1989 to 1991 was attributed to a reduced use in hyperkinetic clinics, designed specifically for children suffering from this disorder. DEA also reported that the medication rate in the Baltimore area decreased more than the national average (Safer and Krager 1992).

This public controversy over the use of methylphenidate has contributed to increased media and governmental scrutiny of the drug's use. A small number of parents and physicians learn of the problems and side effects that a few patients who take methylphenidate have experienced and ask their legislators to pass measures to control the prescription and distribution of the drug. The media are all too willing to highlight the problems associated with any central nervous system drug while downplaying or ignoring the benefits to patients. Many parents of children who are hyperactive choose not to start stimulant use because they fear the potential problems associated with taking a Schedule II drug. However, the evidence suggests that those who have used these drugs continue to use them, despite the negative publicity (Safer and Krager 1992). The consequences of the underutilization of appropriate medication are telling. Of the children taken off methylphenidate during the period studied, 47% developed mild to moderate adjustment problems, and 36% developed major adjustment problems such as school failure or frequent suspensions or both (Safer and Krager 1992).

Regulation: How Much Is Too Much?

Amphetamine, methamphetamine, methylphenidate, and other psychostimulants have clear medical usefulness. However, in response to the illicit manufacture and distribution of these drugs and the negative publicity surrounding their abuse, both the federal and state governments have implemented programs that may overregulate their availability. Today, few physicians or pharmacists illegally divert stimulants for nonmedical use, overprescribe the drugs, or incompetently diagnose children as hyperactive. However, rather than find and punish the small number of wrongdoers, the government's attitude is often to restrict access to the drug and thereby penalize the innocent patient.

One of the effects of negative publicity and overregulation is to make stimulants less available for legitimate use. For example, 27% of those responding to a 1991 American Narcolepsy Association (1992) survey stated that their pharmacist had, at some point, "refused to fill all or part of" their prescription for narcolepsy medication, in large part for fear of censure (Cooper et al. 1992). In addition, adverse publicity deters those suffering severe anxiety disorders or ADHD from using needed drugs (Nemeroff 1990).

Patients rarely abuse stimulant medications or increase dosages. Restrictions over legitimate production and distribution have little impact on the availability of the stimulants for abuse purposes because illicit production is the major source of these drugs (Cooper et al. 1992). The evidence reflects a steady decline in stimulant abuse. Amphetamine, methamphetamine, and methylphenidate provide beneficial results for thousands of Americans in the treatment of narcolepsy, hyperkinesis, cancer pain, and, to a lesser extent, depression and obesity. Yet fear of dangerous side effects and hyperbolic media accounts have led to increased regulation and reduced availability. For example, in those states having multiple copy prescription programs, prescribing of the drugs covered, including stimulants, declined more than 50% (Angarola and Wray 1989).

Although federal and state efforts to restrict the legitimate diversion of stimulants were necessary in the 1960s and 1970s, the problem today relates to the illicit manufacture, sale, and use of these drugs. "The problem of diversion can and should be addressed without in any way compromising legitimate medical practice or patient care" (Joranson and Dahl 1989, p. 198). Greater focus should be placed on those few physicians and pharmacists who divert stimulants and other drugs for illegal use. When justified, law enforcement actions should be applied to practitioners who knowingly prescribe or dispense stimulants for nonmedical purpose. State health departments and professional medical organizations should educate physicians who overprescribe on the proper use of these drugs. State governments should follow Wisconsin's lead and remove unnecessary restrictions on their use. Indeed, Wisconsin might wish to consider further modifications to its amphetamine regulation if it is not needed to prevent drug diversion.

Legislators and regulators must walk a fine line between preventing drug abuse and diversion and ensuring needed availability of controlled substances. They must keep foremost in their minds the welfare of the vast majority of patients who appropriately use stimulants and other controlled substances for medical purposes. There is no justification for initiatives like government-issued prescription forms that have a demonstrated negative impact on patient care. Well-intentioned policymakers and self-serving special interest groups need to know when their actions result in too much regulation. Practitioners and patient groups have to be ready to convey this message rapidly, forcefully, and effectively.

References

American Medical Association: Drug Evaluations, 6th Edition. Chicago, IL, American Medical Association, 1986, p 929

American Narcolepsy Association: Eye opener: report on discrimination: ANA survey finds 50% face discrimination. San Francisco, CA, The American Narcolepsy Association, 1992, p 4

Angarola RT, Wray SD: Legal impediments to cancer pain treatment, in Advances in Pain Research and Therapy, Vol 2. Edited by Hill CS, Fields WS. New York, Raven, 1989, pp 213–231

Biederman J: Psychopharmacology, in Textbook on Child and Adolescent Psychiatry. Edited by Wiener JM. Washington, DC, American Psychiatric Press, 1991, pp 545–570

Bruera E, Bertolino M: Cancer pain: neuropsychologic findings and opiate analgesics. IASP Newsletter, July/August 1992, pp 2–3

Burton BT: Heavy metal and organic contaminants associated with illicit methamphetamine production, National Institute on Drug Abuse Res Monogr Ser No 115 (DHHS Publ No ADM-91-1836). Washington, DC, U.S. Government Printing Office, 1991, pp 47–49

21 C F R 310.504 (1992)

28 C F R 0.100 (1992)

Controlled Substances Act, Pub L No 91-513, USC § 812, 826, 84 Stat 1247 (1970)

Cooper JR, Czechowicz DJ, Petersen RC, et al: Prescription drug diversion control and medical practice. JAMA 268:1306–1310, 1992

Cowart VS: The Ritalin controversy: what's made this drug's opponents hyperactive. JAMA 259:2521–2523, 1988

Drug Abuse Policy Office, Office of Policy Development: Federal Strategy for Prevention of Drug Abuse and Drug Trafficking. Washington, DC, The White House, 1982, p 18

Encyclopedia Americana, Darbury, CT, Grolier, 1992

Federal Food, Drug, and Cosmetic Act, Pub L No 89-74, 79 Stat 226 (1965)

42 Federal Register 61,520 (1977)

46 Federal Register 56,956 (1981)

53 Federal Register 50,591 (1988)

57 Federal Register 47,120 (1992)

58 Federal Register 42,327 (1993)

Foley KM: Management of cancer pain, in Cancer: Principles and Practice of Oncology, 4th Edition, Vol 2. Edited by DeVita VT, Hellman S, Rosenberg SA. Philadelphia, PA, JB Lippincott, 1989, pp 2428–2436

Forrest W, Brown B, Brown C, et al: Dextroamphetamine with morphine for treatment of postoperative pain. N Engl J Med 296:712–715, 1977

Gadow KD, Nolan EE, Sverd J, et al: Methylphenidate in aggressive-hyperactive boys; I: effects on peer aggression in public school settings. J Am Acad Child Adolesc Psychiatry 29:710–718, 1990

Garfinkel BD, Wender PH, Sloman L, et al: Tricyclic antidepressant and methylphenidate treatment of attention deficit disorder in children. Journal of the American Academy of Child Psychiatry 22:343–348, 1983

General Accounting Office: Comptroller general's report to the Congress: comprehensive approach needed to help control prescription drug abuse (GAO/GGD-83-2). Washington, DC, General Accounting Office, 1982

Gittleman-Klein R: Pharmacology of childhood hyperactivity: an update, in The Third Generation of Progress. Edited by Meltzer HY. New York, Raven, 1987, pp 1215–1224

Haislip GR: Impact of drug abuse on legitimate drug use, in Advances in Pain Research and Therapy, Vol 2. Edited by Hill CS, Fields WS. New York, Raven, 1989, pp 205–211

High anxiety: Consumer Reports, January 1993, p 19

Holden C: Amphetamines: tighter controls on the horizon. Science 194: 1027–1028, 1976

Irvine GD, Chin L: The environmental impact and adverse health effects of the clandestine manufacture of methylphenidate, National Institute on Drug Abuse Res Monogr Ser No 115 (DHHS Publ No ADM-91-1836). Washington, DC, U.S. Government Printing Office, 1991, pp 33–34

Joranson DE: Federal and state regulation of opioids. Journal of Pain and Symptom Management 5:S12–S23, 1990

Joranson DE, Dahl JL: Achieving balance in drug policy: the Wisconsin model, in Advances in Pain Research and Therapy, Vol 2. Edited by Hills CS, Fields WS. New York, Raven, 1989, pp 197–204

Joshi J, De Jongh C, Schnepper N, et al: Amphetamine therapy for enhancing the comfort of terminally ill cancer patients (ASCO abstracts C-213). Philadelphia, PA, WB Saunders, 1982

Kaplan SL, Busner J, Kupietz S: Effects of methylphenidate on adolescents with aggressive conduct disorder and ADHD: a preliminary report. J Am Acad Child Adolesc Psychiatry 29:719–723, 1990

King RK, Ellinwood EH: Amphetamines and other stimulants, in Substance Abuse: A Comprehensive Textbook, 2nd Edition. Edited by Lowinson JH, Ruiz P, Millman RB, et al. Baltimore, MD, Williams & Wilkins, pp 247–270

LA REV STAT § 37:1261–37:1292

Lasagna L: Regulation from the perspective of a researcher and clinician, in Advances in Pain Research and Therapy, Vol 2. Edited by Hill CS, Fields WS. New York, Raven, 1989, pp 233–240

Loney J: Substance abuse in adolescents: diagnostic issues derived from studies of attention deficit disorder with hyperactivity, in Adolescent Drug Abuse: Analysis of Treatment Research. Edited by Rahdert ER, Grabowski J. Rockville, MD, National Institute on Drug Abuse, 1988, pp 19–26

Max MB: Improving outcomes of analgesic treatment: is education enough? Ann Intern Med 113:885–888, 1990

Mitler MM, Hajdukovic R, Erdman M: Methamphetamine normalizes sleepiness and performance in narcoleptics (abstract). Sleep Research 21:1–8, 1992

National Institute on Drug Abuse: Statistical series: annual data 1985: data from the Drug Abuse Warning Network (DAWN) (DHHS Publ No ADM-86-1469). Washington, DC, U.S. Government Printing Office, 1985

National Institute on Drug Abuse: Statistical series: annual emergency room data 1990: data from the Drug Abuse Warning Network (DAWN) (DHHS Publ No ADM-91-1839). Washington, DC, U.S. Government Printing Office, 1990

National Institute on Drug Abuse: Drug abuse among American high school seniors, college students and young adults, 1975–1990, Vol 1 (high school seniors) (DHHS Publ No ADM-91-1813). Rockville, MD, National Institute on Drug Abuse, 1991

National Institutes of Health: Obesity in perspective (DHEW Publ No NIH-75-708). Bethesda, MD, National Institutes of Health, 1973

Nemeroff CB: The rational use of narcotic analgesics, benzodiazepines and psychostimulants in medical practice. N C Med J 51:240–243, 1990

Physicians' Desk Reference, 46th Edition, Revised. Montvale, NJ, Medical Economics Co, 1992

Puder KS, Kagan DV, Morgan JP: Illicit methamphetamine: analysis, synthesis, and availability. Am J Drug Alcohol Abuse 14:463–473, 1988

Regestein QR, Reich P, Mufson MJ: Narcolepsy: an initial clinical approach. J Clin Psychiatry 44:166–172, 1983

Richard BW, Lasagna L: Anorectic drugs: drug policy making at the state level. J Clin Pharmacol 28:395–400, 1988

Safer DJ, Krager JM: Effect of a media blitz and a threatened lawsuit on stimulant treatment. JAMA 268:1004–1007, 1992

Soldatos CR, Kales A, Cadieux RJ: Treatment of Sleep Disorders 2: Narcolepsy, in Rational Drug Therapy. American Society for Pharmacology and Experimental Therapeutics 17:1–7, 1983

Treffert DA, Joranson D: Restricting amphetamines. JAMA 245:1336–1338, 1981

Wick JY: Use of psychoactive medications in children and adolescents. Am Pharm NS § 3:51–58, 1993

CHAPTER FOUR

Antipsychotic Medication: Regulation Through the Right to Refuse

Rodney Deaton, M.D., J.D.
Harold Bursztajn, M.D.

In his famous 1977 article, law professor Robert Plotkin launched the first salvo in an interprofessional war of words when he challenged fellow lawyers to protect psychiatric patients from the "therapeutic orgies" inflicted on them by their doctors. Within a few short years, after phrases such as the "right to treatment" and the "right to refuse treatment" had become commonplace in both professional literatures, Appelbaum and Gutheil (1979) fired back the next famous round of verbal ammunition, lamenting that the legal "cures" for these psychiatric "orgies" were causing patients in state hospitals simply to "rot with their rights on" (p. 306).

During these last 15 years the pitch of the rhetoric on both sides of the issue has waxed and waned between these two poles (Brakel and Davis 1992; Sauvayre 1991), yet one fact remains clear: the topic of involuntary treatment with antipsychotic medication continues to divide doctors from patients and their advocates, and scholars from clinicians. In many ways, despite all the ink spilled on this subject year after year, consensus on the subject remains, at best, tenuous.

In this chapter we focus on the controversies surrounding the regulation of antipsychotic medication, primarily regulations that have developed as the result of efforts of those within the "right to refuse treatment" movement in the United States. For the most part, both federal and state courts have driven the development of this area of psychiatric law, but legislatures and administrative bodies have also come to play an important role in the unfolding struggle.

We begin by outlining the major public policies that have driven the movement, primarily by explaining how the doctrines of different types of law—constitutional, common, legislative, and administrative—have framed the salient issues. We then outline the three major types of approaches legal decision makers have taken to resolve these issues.

Next, we look at the recent empirical data examining the impact of this "right to refuse treatment" on the clinical use of antipsychotic medication with involuntary patients to see what effects the law has had on the type of care these patients are receiving. We end by describing not only some potential pitfalls that clinicians need to recognize in this area of law and psychiatry, but also some potential benefits that they may reap if they learn to use these laws wisely and effectively.

Public Policies and Legal Theory

Federal Constitutional Issues

For many years the legal question in this area that puzzled lawyers and mental health professionals alike had been the most fundamental and encompassing one: to what extent does the United States Constitution grant involuntary psychiatric patients the legal right to refuse treatment with antipsychotic medication or other forms of psychiatric treatment?

Simply put, the Constitution governs the ways that the federal and state governments govern. Not only does it outline how the federal government is to be set up, but it also sets the legal parameters within which any state government is to govern justly.

Clearly the text of the Constitution says nothing directly about the subject of the involuntary medication of committed patients. The Bill of Rights and other Constitutional provisions instead spell out certain "enumerated" rights such as the freedom of speech, the free exercise of religion, the freedom from unreasonable searches and seizures, and the equal protection of the rights of all citizens under the law.

Nevertheless, for years the justices of the United States Supreme

Court have held that these enumerated rights are not the only rights guaranteed by the Constitution. In the modern bureaucratic state the government can interfere with our lives in a number of ways, some obvious, some not, some positive, some not. No matter what the interference, however, as citizens we have some rights—coined *unenumerated rights*—against unbridled government action.

Yet as to these unenumerated rights one question remains: how personal, how important or "fundamental" is the area of our lives into which the government is intruding? Most government actions concern areas of our lives that are indeed important (e.g., how we make our living) yet that do not touch areas of our lives that somehow define our "core" selves. The Court has labeled these more routine areas of our lives as "liberty interests."

On the other hand, the Court has deemed certain areas of our lives—especially our political selves and our sexual selves—as so important that we possess certain "fundamental rights" against government interference in those areas. The most well known of such rights are our "privacy rights," which include our right to marry, our right to use the contraceptive method of our choice, and the right of women to terminate a pregnancy in its early stages (Tribe 1988).

The difference between the two classes of unenumerated rights is not trivial, and it goes to the heart of the controversy over the involuntary use of neuroleptics. In either class the government can interfere with our exercise of our rights, but as to interference with fundamental rights (and most enumerated rights), the government must show that the interference is very narrowly fashioned so as to satisfy the most important government objectives. In contrast, interference with liberty interests need only be reasonable in light of important, yet not vital, government interests (Tribe 1988).

Basically both supporters and detractors of the right to refuse treatment recognized that the government should only have limited power to force citizens to accept medical treatments without their consent. They differed markedly, however, in defining the breadth of that power—and thus the complexity of the procedures necessary to protect that right. Moreover, for many years each side had quite plausible arguments from Constitutional precedent to support its own particular position.

Then in 1990 the Court decided the case of *Washington v. Harper*. In that case the Court recognized that a prisoner in jail had a liberty interest, and thus some right, to be free from unnecessary involuntary treatment with antipsychotic medication. Government officials could not simply medicate prisoners at whim, to silence them or to punish them, for example. Yet in clear contrast to the dissenters, the majority justices did not deem this right to be fundamental. Thus they did not require the state of Washington to hold formal judicial hearings to determine whether involuntary treatment was justified. The state's less formal administrative procedures for review of involuntary treatment sufficed.

The Court revisited this issue in *Riggins v. Nevada* (1992), a case involving the involuntary medication of prisoners to make them competent to stand trial. Although two dissenters claimed the Court was turning to a more strict standard of judicial scrutiny in these cases, the majority clearly stated that they were not retreating from the holding in *Harper*. The right to refuse involuntary treatment with antipsychotic medication is a more limited liberty interest, not a fundamental right.

Supporters of the more broad right of refusal do have some ground to argue that these cases should be interpreted in light of their criminal context: the interests of the government in the treatment of prisoners may not be the same as those in the treatment of civilly committed mental patients. Yet it appears that advocates of the broad right must look to some other legal source to support their policies of "medical self-determination."

Other legal sources for the broader right, however, are quite available. They are the remedies afforded by state laws (Blackburn 1990b).

State Law Issues

The state remedies are justified by one fundamental principle: in our federal system of government, in which the central government has limited but superior powers, the United States Constitution sets the minimal standards a state must meet to ensure that its laws are equitable. Nevertheless, each state has the power to set more stringent standards to evaluate laws within that state, just as long as those laws do not interfere with the routine business and social relations between citizens of different states.

For example, each state has its own constitution. Therefore, the high courts of each state could potentially determine that under their state constitution, the right to refuse treatment is indeed a fundamental right, and thus it is one requiring formal judicial proceedings to override it. Most famously, the high courts of Massachusetts (*Rogers v. Commissioner* 1983) and New York (*Rivers v. Katz* 1986) have taken this exact position in the definition of their state's right to refuse treatment.

Furthermore, each state has its own common law, the general body of law passed down from generation to generation, judicial in origin rather than legislative, that regulates the routine affairs of our private lives, such as the transfer of property or the just recompense for injury (tort law). Under the tort theory of battery, persons have always been able to refuse the unwanted physical contacts of others (Restatement 1965). State courts then extended this refusal right specifically to physical contact by medical professionals (*Mohr v. Williams* 1905), holding that doctors may treat at least their voluntary patients only with their patient's informed consent (*Schloendorff v. Society of New York Hospital* 1914). Several courts, including the *Rogers* and *Rivers* courts, have grounded their holdings in these state common law rights as well.

Finally, many state legislatures have granted civilly committed patients certain rights to refuse involuntary treatment with antipsychotics. Usually, there are certain administrative procedures that are then delineated to ensure proper reviews of treatment refusal (Blackburn 1990b).

In all these cases the underlying public policy is essentially the same: as far as possible, citizens should be allowed to determine for themselves what psychiatric treatment they will or will not receive. The differences are in the meaning of the "as far as possible," specifically in how broad the right is to be and thus how stringent the procedures must be for treaters to override that refusal right. In essence three major approaches to review of treatment refusals are being employed in the United States (Appelbaum 1988; Blackburn 1990b).

Legal Consequences

Medical Review

The most liberal review procedure might be termed the *medical review procedure* (Blackburn 1990b). Under this system, the treating medical professional, perhaps in consultation with the broader treatment team, reviews the patient's reasons for refusal of the antipsychotic. If the treater makes a reasonable medical judgment that treatment with the medication is necessary, the treater may go ahead with the treatment. The patient may or may not have recourse to administrative or judicial review of the decision, but these reviewers are only to determine whether a "professional judgment" for treatment was made. Absent malice or gross negligence, the reviewers are to respect the decision of the treater.

Clearly this is the system most preferred by psychiatrists and least preferred by mental health advocates. The professional judgment standard comes from a related Supreme Court case, *Youngberg v. Romeo* (1982), which reviewed standards for the use of physical restraints in institutions for the severely developmentally disabled. In that case the Court clearly meant for lower reviewing courts to review such treatment decisions with great deference to the medical decision maker. In using the *Youngberg* case as an analogy, the courts promulgating this standard have shown similar deference to treatment decisions involving the use of antipsychotics.

Surprisingly this standard may not be as uncommon as one might think. It is the standard that has been adopted by most federal courts that have ruled on this issue (*Charter v. United States* 1988; *D'Autremont v. Broadlawns Hospital* 1987). The *Harper* and *Riggins* cases do not appear to cast doubt on these holdings. That federal courts have adopted this liberal standard is important for psychiatrists in states that have not yet adopted their own standard of review, either through judicial decision or legislation. Arguably patients in these states may refuse only under the color of this more limited federal right, as the federal right would apply in the absence of any specific state right, and federal appeals courts tend to follow each other in deciding cases such as these.

Administrative Review

Perhaps most common of the three review methods is the administrative method. Under this scheme, either the treater or the patient has the right to request administrative review of the decision to treat with antipsychotics. Actual procedures vary widely from state to state: in some cases a panel of disinterested professionals reviews the treatment plan; in others the medical director of the facility reviews the decisions. In most cases some appeal to the state courts is available to the party adversely affected by the administrative decision, but the state court review is usually quite deferential to the administrative decision maker.

This type of administrative review was lent credence by the federal court review of the New Jersey procedures analyzed in one of the first major right to refuse cases, *Rennie v. Klein* (1978/1981). After a long series of reviews, one of which even briefly reached the Supreme Court, the federal courts eventually approved those procedures. Perhaps equally well known in the psychiatric and legal literature are the procedures set up by officials in the state of Ohio. These procedures have been discussed extensively and empirically tested as to their outcomes (Appelbaum and Schwartz 1992).

If one could say that any consensus has been reached between professionals about the "best" review procedures—and we again stress, such consensus would only be tenuous at best—it would be that the administrative review procedures are perhaps the best, at least in terms of the consequences of the procedure. Certainly not all legal decision makers, however, have been convinced of its superiority.

Judicial Approach

The third approach, the judicial approach, is by far the most procedurally exacting and without doubt the most controversial in psychiatric circles. Inspired by the landmark or infamous Massachusetts case of *Rogers v. Okin* (1979) (choice of adjective depending on your orientation), this approach requires judges to make independent assessments of the need for involuntary treatment of patients with antipsychotics, with the assessments being carried out in the context of formal judicial proceedings, with patients having full rights to counsel and cross-examination (*Rogers v. Okin* 1979).

The standard by which the reviewing judge is to assess the refusal is usually some version of the "substituted judgment" test (*Rogers v. Commissioner* 1983). Under this somewhat convoluted test, the judge is to receive evidence about the patient's current and past wishes and then, by some turn of reasoning or imagination, decide what the patient would want done if the patient were in fact competent to make the choice.

Such procedures are most supported by mental health advocates, as they are the procedures most like those employed in the criminal justice system. By the same token they are the procedures most maligned by psychiatric critics (Appelbaum and Gutheil 1979; Gutheil 1980). Given the extensive amount of psychiatric and legal time consumed by these procedures (Schouten and Gutheil 1990), they have been extensively studied by empirical researchers to determine their impact on clinical care, as is discussed later.

Other Review Procedures

Although the above three approaches are the most common ones in the right to refuse cases, one other procedure should be mentioned: pharmaceutical review. This review actually does not arise out of a treatment refusal. Nevertheless the impetus for the review does seem to arise from the general suspicion of antipsychotic medication that has been generated by the refusal cases.

Specifically, the Omnibus Budget Reconciliation Act of 1987 included add-on provisions governing the evaluation and treatment of individuals in nursing homes with mental illnesses. Since the nursing home industry is now a large, multistate industry, the United States Congress has the power under the Commerce Clause of the Constitution to regulate its activities. This law contains provisions for the routine review of the administration of antipsychotic medication, with such review possibly carried out by a pharmaceutical consultant.

It is unclear whether further nonrefusal review procedures will be set up in other contexts, but this specific situation within nursing homes does point to the far-reaching effects of the right to refuse treatment movement. Still another expansion of the impact of this movement can be seen in regulations in several jurisdictions requiring signed informed consent forms before antipsychotic medication can be administered to even voluntary patients. Such requirements stand in contradistinction to the absence of equivalent requirements for other classes of drugs equally (or more) prone to side effects and place antipsychotics in a class with experimental agents or surgical procedures that have traditionally required written consent forms.

Empirical Consequences

Ever since the *Rogers* and *Rennie* cases were first adjudicated, psychiatrists have persistently asked one crucial question: what will be the impact of the right to refuse treatment doctrine on patient care?

In the ensuing 15 years many researchers have examined the consequences of this doctrine empirically (Binder and McNiel 1991; Ciccone et al. 1990; Cournos et al. 1991; Farnsworth 1991; Godard et al. 1986; Levin et al. 1991; Sheline and Beattie 1992). Unfortunately, generalizations are difficult to draw from the studies: states vary widely in the procedures being evaluated, and research subjects vary widely on a number of parameters, including stage of commitment and length of refusal. Although written some time ago, the observations of Appelbaum and Hoge (1986) still seem accurately to reflect the general picture of the treatment refuser:

> Short-term refusal is frequent, but long-term refusal less common. Refusers are likely to be sicker than accepting patients, but it is unclear if most of them are legally incompetent. Over the short term, many refusers do poorly in the hospital, but if ultimately treated they do at least as well as other patients. Finally, patients' refusals are usually not upheld, with the vast majority of refusing patients being treated, at least initially, over the objections of the patient. (p. 290)

Hoge and his colleagues have done the most extensive work to date looking at treatment refusal in a prospective fashion, and their data provide good evidence of the clinical impact of treatment refusals (Hoge et al. 1990).

Their study reviewed the treatment of 1,434 committed patients who were admitted to four different acute state hospital wards in

Massachusetts over the course of 6 months. They reported an overall incidence of refusal of 7.2%; 61% of the refusals first occurred within 72 hours of the patient's admission.

Of this group, 50% of the patients eventually agreed to take the medication voluntarily, and 23% of the patients received no antipsychotic treatment because their treaters eventually concurred in the patients' refusals. The remaining 18% of patients were taken to court for review of their treatment refusal.

As noted above, Massachusetts follows a judicial review model, involving a special court proceeding to determine competency of the patient and treatment plan. All of the refusing patients (19 in total) who went to court were adjudicated incompetent and ordered to take antipsychotic medication.

When compared with a control group of nonrefusers, the refusers were usually more acutely ill, with higher initial Brief Psychiatric Rating Scale ratings for psychosis and agitation. They were more likely to be hospitalized for a longer period of time (apparently not solely because of the length of the refusal period) and were more likely to require some type of physical or chemical restraint. They had a higher rate of actual or threatened violence to self or others, and 50% of the patients were noted to have had a negative effect on the ward milieu and other patients.

Perhaps most notable are the data from the prehearing period. The average time between patient refusal and judicial hearing was 36.7 days. More amazing, however, are separate data published by the Massachusetts Department of Mental Health, outlined in the study by Hoge and colleagues (1990): over the course of an 18-month period, review of competency/treatment petitions to the mental health court consumed 10,500 hours of time for state attorneys, 3,000 hours of time for various paralegals, and 4,800 hours of time for mental health professionals.

Fortunately the patients in this study were almost all eventually treated, so none of them ended up "rotting" acutely. Without a doubt, however, treatment refusals led to significant treatment delay and had a considerable impact on resource utilization. The other studies cited basically come to the same conclusions as the study by Hoge and colleagues (1990). It is worth noting that at least one study (Schwartz et al. 1988), although based on a small sample, found that the majority of involuntarily medicated patients, once adequately treated, are approving of the decision to have overridden their treatment refusal and assert that, should they refuse again in similar circumstances, they would wish to be involuntarily medicated again.

None of these studies addresses the issue of what happens to patients who "fall through the cracks," those whose treatment is delayed by the refusal, leading to the less quantifiable, yet no less real costs of psychosis and destruction of the treatment milieu. Thus the clinical and ethical questions one is then left with in these cases are certainly more disturbing and complex than what one would otherwise hope.

Clinical and Ethical Consequences

Several important questions arise as a result of the theoretical and empirical information presented thus far. First, what is the role of "informed consent" in the whole right to refuse treatment process? One of us (H. B.), along with colleagues, has written extensively on the need for clinicians to view informed consent as a process, not as an event (Bursztajn et al. 1990; Gutheil et al. 1984).

To avoid costly legal proceedings, to what extent are psychiatrists seeking pro forma, written consent for treatment, using standardized forms without adding any discussion to the process? On the other hand, are there physicians who are in fact not treating patients who should be treated, primarily because they fear patients will not take medications if they are apprised of their effects? Some work has already been done in this area (Munetz and Roth 1985), demonstrating the positive effects of a therapeutic dialogue and challenging the notion that properly informing patients of the risk of tardive dyskinesia will lead to treatment refusal. Further work, however, is needed.

Second, has all this regulation just added to the stigmatization of severely mentally ill persons by labeling their medical treatment so negatively? In another study, marked differences were found between judges and physicians in their assessments of actual risk for tardive dyskinesia in patients on neuroleptics, with judges markedly overestimating the risk (Bursztajn et al. 1991). Have regulations brought on by such overestimates actually encouraged treatment refusal, thereby discouraging needed treatment?

How do these judges' perceptions, especially if they are appellate judges, affect their opinions—or even influence the tone of their opinions, sending out negative messages about antipsychotic drugs? Although a few articles in the legal literature attempt to cast a positive light on neuroleptics and their salutary effects on patient health (Brakel and Davis 1992), even a cursory review of law review articles on the subject would make one think that psychiatrists are more poison merchants than healers. Even clozapine has come under the pall of the treatment refusal shadow (Blackburn 1990a). How many psychiatrists are not adequately treating severely ill patients because they do not want to face the hassles of judicial scrutiny or perhaps even the threat of public censure?

Third, what will be the effects of related regulations on the use of antipsychotics, such as those promulgated by the Omnibus Budget Reconciliation Act? Rovner and colleagues (1992) studied prescription practices in Baltimore, Maryland, nursing homes over a 6-month period. They found that significant changes were made in the types of psychotropic medications prescribed in those homes, fortunately mostly for the better.

Nevertheless, one of us (R. D.) has anecdotally noted several cases in his practice in which family physicians providing medical coverage for a nursing home have reduced residents' antipsychotic medications on the advice of a pharmaceutical consultant, without conducting any independent mental status examination on the patient or seeking a psychiatric consultation. As a result, several residents with severe chronic mental illness acutely decompensated, requiring emergent hospitalization for stabilization. Further rigorous empirical study is necessary to determine whether such regulations will improve or hinder good patient care in these nursing homes—whether patients will receive needed treatment or just "fall through the cracks."

Finally, one interesting question never seems to be asked in these discussions: to what extent is all the discussion about the right to refuse treatment one way to avoid the more difficult public policy problem of inadequate treatment resources for mentally ill persons? If state hospitals and community mental health centers were adequately staffed with well-trained professionals, with good coordination of services between facilities, how often would these issues arise? Would there ever have been litigation in the first place? Appelbaum and Gutheil (1981) went so far as to suggest that constitutional arguments for the right to refuse treatment are no more than a smoke screen for the actual policy objectives of patient advocates and the courts, which is to improve the quality of psychiatric care. One would hope that the litigation has eliminated the worst abuses of psychiatric practice, but has it done so—and at what cost to the legitimate use of antipsychotic medication? Has the litigation had any effect on the legislators and administrators who earmark state funds for spending?

Still, although the right to refuse treatment doctrine has, indeed, negatively affected the appropriate use of antipsychotic medications, we do not want to appear solely negative in our concerns. Clinicians should also look at the positive aspects of the right to refuse treatment movement and utilize them fully in their practices.

For example, certainly one would hope that psychiatrists are now at least considering how open discussion with patients about medications may improve long-term compliance. Indeed, authors of major textbooks on law and psychiatry now stress the alliance-building aspects of the right to refuse treatment doctrine (Appelbaum and Gutheil 1991; Simon 1992).

Furthermore, Schmidt and Geller (1989) pointed out how even potentially cumbersome procedural systems such as the one in Massachusetts may be used as part of an overall treatment strategy for refractory patients. In a series of anecdotes drawn from cases from western Massachusetts, they suggested that with excellent coordination of services and information between all agencies involved in a patient's care, treaters can enhance compliance with wise judicial intervention, perhaps either by impressing on the patient the seriousness of the treatment endeavor or by broadening the range of options available to ensure compliance (e.g., judicial contempt of court orders, with state marshals bringing the patient in for depot neuroleptic treatment).

Finally, as Hoge and colleagues (1990) pointed out, patients may simply perceive the treatment system as fundamentally more fair and trustworthy when they are allowed actively to participate in their treatment decisions, even if those decisions are eventually overridden. Thus it is inappropriate simply to carp about the right to refuse treatment. Instead, psychiatrists should continue to work to improve the system to optimize care for their patients.

Conclusion

In the final analysis, however, once one has studied all the policy and empirical issues and has contemplated the actual and potential effects of the regulation of antipsychotic use by means of the right to refuse treatment doctrine, one fact remains clear: the tension between the right to refuse treatment and the relative absence of the right comes down to a choice based on values, not just doctrines and facts. We can measure the monetary value of services required to effect the right to refuse treatment, but what correspondingly is the monetary value of liberty or freedom from coercion? What is the value of freedom from unnecessary illness? Similarly we can speak eloquently of the human rights of persons to decide, think, and feel as they wish, but what of the thoughts, feelings, and even safety of those around the persons, their family, their friends, their fellow sufferers who are wanting voluntarily to take the choices offered them by their treaters?

The back and forth game of words goes on. One could probably identify the author of a particular piece of writing on this subject as a lawyer or a mental health professional simply by the vocabulary the author uses in the piece. One person's care is another's paternalism. One person's liberty is another's license. We can only suggest that the reader take the most difficult path of all: support patient autonomy and seek to treat patients appropriately.

The right to refuse treatment movement has indeed usefully enhanced clinicians' awareness of the value of promoting patient autonomy. At the same time it has led to various regulations and practices that have often discouraged the appropriate use of antipsychotic medication. Thus the difficult task of the mental health professional is finally the most complex one: to continue to promote patient autonomy while resisting regulatory encroachment on appropriate treatment.

References

Appelbaum PS: The right to refuse treatment with antipsychotic medications: retrospect and prospect. Am J Psychiatry 145:413–419, 1988

Appelbaum PS, Gutheil TG: Rotting with their rights on: constitutional theory and clinical reality in drug refusal by psychiatric patients. Bull Am Acad Psychiatry Law 7:306–315, 1979

Appelbaum PS, Gutheil TG: The right to refuse treatment: the real issue is quality of care. Bull Am Acad Psychiatry Law 9:199–202, 1981

Appelbaum PS, Gutheil TG: Clinical Handbook of Psychiatry and the Law. Baltimore, MD, Williams & Wilkins, 1991

Appelbaum PS, Hoge SK: The right to refuse treatment: what the research reveals. Behavioral Sciences and the Law 4:279–292, 1986

Appelbaum PS, Schwartz WF: Minimizing the social cost of choosing treatment for the involuntarily hospitalized mentally ill patient: a new approach to defining the patient's role. Connecticut Law Review 24:433–485, 1992

Binder RL, McNiel DE: Involuntary patients' right to refuse medication: impact of the Riese decision on a California inpatient unit. Bull Am Acad Psychiatry Law 19:351–357, 1991

Blackburn CE: New directions in mental health advocacy? Clozapine and the right of medical self-determination. Mental and Physical Disability Law Reporter 14:453–461, 1990a

Blackburn CE: The "therapeutic orgy" and the "right to rot" collide: the right to refuse antipsychotic drugs under state law. Houston Law Review 27:447–513, 1990b

Brakel SJ, Davis JM: Taking harms seriously: involuntary mental patients and the right to refuse treatment. Indiana Law Review 25:429–473, 1992

Bursztajn HJ, Feinbloom RI, Hamm RM, et al: Medical Choices, Medical Chances: How Patients, Families, and Physicians Can Cope With Uncertainty. New York, Routledge, Chapman & Hall, 1990

Bursztajn H, Chanowitz B, Kaplan E, et al: Medical and judicial perceptions of the risks associated with use of antipsychotic medication. Bull Am Acad Psychiatry Law 19:271–275, 1991

Charter v United States, 863 F2d 302 (4th Cir 1988)

Ciccone JR, Tokoli JF, Clements CD, et al: Right to refuse treatment: impact of Rivers v Katz. Bull Am Acad Psychiatry Law 18:203–215, 1990

Cournos F, McKinnon K, Stanley B: Outcome of involuntary medication in a state hospital system. Am J Psychiatry 148:489–494, 1991

D'Autremont v Broadlawns Hospital, 827 F2d 291 (8th Cir 1987)

Farnsworth MG: The impact of judicial review of patients' refusal to accept antipsychotic medications at the Minnesota Security Hospital. Bull Am Acad Psychiatry Law 19:33–42, 1991

Godard SL, Bloom JD, Williams MH, et al: The right to refuse treatment in Oregon: a two-year statewide experience. Behavioral Sciences and the Law 4:293–304, 1986

Gutheil TG: In search of true freedom: drug refusal, involuntary medication, and "rotting with your rights on" (editorial). Am J Psychiatry 137:327–328, 1980

Gutheil TG, Bursztajn HJ, Brodsky A: Malpractice prevention through the sharing of uncertainty: informed consent and the therapeutic alliance. N Engl J Med 311:49–51, 1984

Hoge SK, Appelbaum PS, Lawlor T, et al: A prospective multicenter study of patients' refusal of antipsychotic medication. Arch Gen Psychiatry 47:949–956, 1990

Levin S, Brekke JS, Thomas P: A controlled comparison of involuntarily hospitalized medication refusers and accepters. Bull Am Acad Psychiatry Law 19:161–171, 1991

Mohr v Williams, 104 NW 12 (Minn 1905)

Munetz MR, Roth LH: Informing patients about tardive dyskinesia. Arch Gen Psychiatry 42:866–871, 1985

OBRA: Omnibus Budget Reconciliation Act of 1987, Pub L No 101-508 (1987), codified as 42 USCA 1396r, 1396r(c)(1)(D) (suppl 1993)

Plotkin R: Limiting the therapeutic orgy: mental patients' right to refuse treatment. Northwestern University Law Review 72:461–525, 1977

Rennie v Klein, 462 FSupp 1131 (D NJ 1978), 653 F2d 836 (3d Cir 1981)

Restatement (Second) of Torts, 18 (1965)

Riggins v Nevada, 112 SCt 1810 (1992)

Rivers v Katz, 67 NY2d 485, 495 NE2d 337, 504 NYS2d 74 (1986)

Rogers v Commissioner of the Department of Mental Health, 390 Mass 489, 458 NE2d 308 (1983)

Rogers v Okin, 478 FSupp 1342 (D Mass 1979)

Rovner BW, Edelman BA, Cox MP, et al: The impact of antipsychotic drug regulations on psychotropic prescribing practices in nursing homes. Am J Psychiatry 149:1390–1392, 1992

Sauvayre P: The relationship between the court and the doctor on the issue of an inpatient's refusal of psychotropic medication. J Forensic Sci 36:219–225, 1991

Schloendorff v Society of New York Hospital, 211 NY 125, 105 NE 92 (1914)

Schmidt MJ, Geller JL: Involuntary administration of medication in the community: the judicial opportunity. Bull Am Acad Psychiatry Law 17:283–292, 1989

Schouten R, Gutheil TG: Aftermath of the Rogers decision: assessing the costs. Am J Psychiatry 147:1348–1352, 1990

Schwartz HI, Vingiano W, Bezerganian Perez C: Autonomy and the right to refuse treatment: patient's attitudes after involuntary medication. Hosp Community Psychiatry 39:1049–1054, 1988

Sheline Y, Beattie M: Effects of the right to refuse medication in an emergency psychiatric service. Hosp Community Psychiatry 43:640–642, 1992

Simon RI: Clinical Psychiatry and the Law, 2nd Edition. Washington, DC, American Psychiatric Press, 1992

Tribe LH: American Constitutional Law, 2nd Edition. Mineola, NY, Foundation Press, 1988

Washington v Harper, 494 US 210 (1990)

Youngberg v Romeo, 457 US 307 (1982)

CHAPTER FIVE

Medical Marijuana

Richard B. Karel

One of the most controversial and striking examples of governmental regulation of a medicine is the complete ban on use of marijuana for any purpose, medical or otherwise.[1]

The ban, in practical terms, means that marijuana is relegated to the federal Schedule I category under the federal Controlled Substances Act. A Schedule I drug is deemed to have no medical use and to have high abuse potential. Such a drug may not be prescribed to patients and may be obtained only by federally authorized researchers for investigational purposes.

The federal Controlled Substances Act was enacted by Congress in 1970. Up until that time, it was technically legal under federal law for physicians to pay a special tax and receive a license to prescribe marijuana, although the complicated regulations for actual use made this virtually impossible (Brecher 1972; Musto 1987; Randall 1988).

This scheduling of marijuana contrasts with the scheduling of drugs such as cocaine and morphine for medical use under Schedule II, despite their popularity as illicit recreational drugs and their greater toxicity.

THC (delta-9-tetrahydrocannabinol), marijuana's primary active ingredient, was approved by the Food and Drug Administration (FDA) in 1985 for use in combating nausea and vomiting associated with cancer chemotherapy and was placed in Schedule II (National

---

[1] The term *marijuana* will be primarily employed, but, for the purposes of this discussion, may be used interchangeably with the words *hemp, cannabis,* or *hashish.* The latter technically refers to the resin of the marijuana plant, which contains a high concentration of the primary active constituents.

Institute on Allergy and Infectious Diseases 1992). The drug, under the trade name Marinol, received expanded FDA approval in December 1992 as an appetite stimulant for patients with acquired immunodeficiency syndrome (AIDS) (Buterbaugh 1993).

In contrast with its stubborn resistance to rescheduling marijuana for any use, the Drug Enforcement Administration (DEA) has shown some tolerance toward physicians prescribing Marinol for non-FDA approved uses. In response to an inquiry, the deputy assistant secretary for public health policy at the United States Department of Health and Human Services wrote the following in November 1992 (prior to FDA approval of Marinol for AIDS wasting syndrome):

> The Drug Enforcement Administration's policy statement published in the *Federal Register* on May 13, 1986 states that the DEA *may* revoke registrations or criminally prosecute physicians who prescribe Marinol for medical indications outside the approved use associated with cancer treatment if such prescription is considered inconsistent with the public interest. My staff have had several discussions with DEA on this issue, however, and we have been assured that as a matter of policy, DEA *will not* revoke a registration or take criminal action against a physician who prescribes Marinol for medical indications other than nausea associated with cancer chemotherapy as long as the medication serves a direct, legitimate purpose in a patient's care. It should be noted that DEA has never taken adverse action against any physician for prescribing "off label" use of Marinol. Physicians who appropriately prescribe Marinol for medical purposes other than cancer chemotherapy should not be affected. (J. C. Chow, unpublished communication, 1992)

THC, however, has not proven suitable for all patients who might benefit from marijuana, hence the existence of Marinol has failed to put the issue to rest. This matter came to a head in March 1992 when the federal Department of Health and Human Services rescinded its compassionate exception program, which had provided marijuana for medical use to 13 Americans ("U.S. Rescinds Approval . . ." 1992).

Yet marijuana, like opium, has a medical history dating back thousands of years. A substantial body of knowledge about marijuana's medical applications has accumulated over the centuries, gained both through application in day-to-day medical practice and in clinical trials. There is a large body of anecdotal evidence and a number of substantial clinical trials, but a relative absence of double-blind trials. This paucity of double-blind studies is a function of several factors. These include the ethical concerns of physicians confronted with suffering patients in trials where the medications with which marijuana is being compared prove ineffective; the particular nature of smoking marijuana, which complicates establishing a double-blind and carefully measuring dosage; and the existence of hurdles created by marijuana's prohibited status. Grinspoon and Bakalar (1993) have discussed the implications of this research dilemma.

The legal status of marijuana has created major barriers to systematic study of therapeutic applications, providing a convenient rationale for opponents who circularly argue that more systematic research is needed before marijuana is rescheduled for medical use. Such opponents choose to ignore a substantial body of clinical and anecdotal data.

A particularly repressive era began in 1980 with the expansion of the war on drugs under the administration of Ronald Reagan and George Bush, heralding 12 years of harshly inflexible drug policy that culminated in the March 1992 Department of Health and Human Services decision ending the federal compassionate exception program. As of this writing, there is cause for guarded optimism, as the newly elected administration of Democrat Bill Clinton appears likely to approach drug policy and research more rationally. President Clinton's choice for Surgeon General, Jocelyn Elders, has said she favors legalizing medical use of marijuana to treat glaucoma, relieve nausea, and stimulate appetite ("Choice for Surgeon General . . ." 1992).

To understand why marijuana is prohibited today, even for medical use, it is necessary to take a brief look at the drug's tangled but fascinating regulatory history in the United States.

Regulatory History of Marijuana in the United States

The regulatory history of marijuana in the United States effectively begins with the passage of the Food and Drugs Act of 1906. Although this legislation did not restrict the sale of marijuana preparations, it required, for the first time, the listing of ingredients on all remedies sold. Within a few years of passage, the sale of remedies containing marijuana, opiates, and cocaine—all of which were freely available in over-the-counter patent medicines—dropped by an estimated one-third as health-conscious Americans opted for non–habit-forming remedies (Musto 1987). Much of the historical data reviewed here were assembled by David F. Musto (1987) for a chapter entitled "Marijuana and the Federal Bureau of Narcotics" in his book *The American Disease: Origins of Narcotics Control.*

Marijuana escaped the constraints of the Harrison Narcotic Act of 1914. Although the Harrison Narcotic Act is widely viewed as the beginning of United States antidrug legislation, the act was not, in fact, prohibitory, and marijuana was entirely exempt from its provisions, which applied to morphine, heroin, opium, and cocaine. The act required only that all those dealing in and dispensing narcotics be registered and keep records. Patent medicines containing opium, morphine, heroin, and cocaine were still readily available in pharmacies, in general stores, and by mail order. Only with later judicial interpretations did the act become prohibitory (Musto 1987: see discussion of *U.S. v. Jin Fuey Moy* 1916, *U.S. v. Doremus* 1919, and *Webb et al. v. U.S.* 1919). After 1906, the next major regulatory effort to control marijuana came with passage of the Marijuana Tax Act of 1937.

There is substantial evidence that early efforts to control marijuana, smokable opium, and cocaine were spurred by racial and ethnic prejudice (Musto 1987). At the first international drug control conference at the Hague in 1911, for example, American delegate Henry Finger, arguing for control of world traffic in marijuana, commented that Californians were frightened by "the large influx of Hindoos . . . demanding *cannabis indica*" and initiating "the whites into their habit" (qtd. in Musto 1987, p. 218).

From 1920 to 1934, domestic fear of marijuana rose, becoming particularly intense in areas with large concentrations of Mexican immigrants.

Mexican immigration, both legal and illegal, rose rapidly during the 1920s. With the economy booming, the immigrants were welcomed by employers in search of cheap labor for the factories and fields of the nation.

Xenophobia and racism were always present, however, and, as

medical historian Musto (1987) observed, "by the mid-twenties horrible crimes were attributed to marijuana and its Mexican purveyors" (p. 219). Law enforcement and medical officials in the New Orleans area, who believed it was a dangerous sexual stimulant that removed civilized inhibitions, began publishing articles linking marijuana to many of the region's crimes, further fueling fear of the drug. This triggered requests to add marijuana to the list of substances covered by the Harrison Narcotic Act.

The notion of marijuana as a dangerous drug prone to cause not only criminality but sexual excess was given legitimacy by some in the medical profession. Walter Bromberg, for example, told a 1934 meeting of the American Psychiatric Association that marijuana "releases inhibitions and restraints imposed by society and allows individuals to act out their drives openly, [and] acts as a sexual stimulant [particularly to] overt homosexuals" (qtd. in Musto 1987, p. 220).

Despite the mounting pressures for the federal government to act to control marijuana, some officials, including Harry Anslinger, commissioner of the Federal Bureau of Narcotics (FBN), believed any prohibitive federal regulation would intrude into the police powers of the states.[2] But Anslinger believed that such constitutional objections could be bypassed by enacting legislation based on mutual treaty obligations with other nations (Musto 1987, p. 358). Federal regulators had successfully employed this approach in other areas.

Among the concerns cited by Anslinger in a confidential memorandum to Assistant Secretary of the Treasury Stephen Gibbons in February 1936 was how to eliminate "certain phases of legitimate traffic" in marijuana to facilitate a broad prohibition on the drug. These included "a small medical need for marijuana," which Anslinger said the pharmaceutical industry had "agreed to eliminate" entirely.

---

[2]The FBN, created in July 1930, was part of the Treasury Department until 1968, at which time it became part of the Justice Department and was renamed the Bureau of Narcotics and Dangerous Drugs. This bureau remained in the Justice Department, but was somewhat revamped and renamed the DEA in 1973 (Musto 1987).

Only veterinarians would have a continuing medical need, and that could be satisfied by foreign imports, Anslinger told Gibbons. He added that "we are now working with the Department of Commerce in finding substitutes for the legitimate trade, and after that is accomplished, the path will be cleared for the treaties and for federal law" (qtd. in Musto 1987, p. 224).

The United States State Department agreed to give Anslinger the chance to present a measure that would establish international treaty obligations at the June 1936 Conference for the Suppression of the Illicit Traffic in Dangerous Drugs in Geneva, Switzerland. The 26 other nations involved, however, showed little interest in signing an international treaty to regulate marijuana.

At this juncture, it became clear that a domestic approach employing traditional federal powers would have to be employed. The general counsel for the United States Treasury then suggested that to avoid constitutional constraints against intruding into the police powers of the states, a federal transfer tax be enacted similar to one passed in 1934 to reduce the use of machine guns by gangsters. Under that law, the National Firearms Act, Congress decreed that machine guns could be transferred only on payment of a special transfer tax. The tax was later challenged but eventually upheld as constitutional by the Supreme Court in March 1937 (Musto 1987).

Anslinger, in 1936, still had doubts about the constitutionality of what became known as The Marijuana Tax Act, but was heartened by Congress' apparent ignorance on the matter and observed that "the only information they had was what we would give them in our hearings" (qtd. in Musto 1987, p. 225).

Although the Treasury Department dutifully collected scientific and medical information on marijuana, officials, concerned about presenting a united front and worried about the legislation's chances for passage, chose to ignore anything that minimized the hazards of marijuana. This made the marijuana hearings "a classic example of bureaucratic overkill" (Musto 1987, p. 225).

The hearings hence presented a one-sided view of marijuana's dangers and benefits, the historical record shows. The Division of Public Hygiene in the Public Health Service, precursor to today's National Institute of Mental Health, was not represented, although it made experts available for months before the hearings (Musto 1987), and the Treasury Department's testimony was accepted uncritically by Congress.

The Marijuana Tax Act passed easily, becoming effective on October 1, 1937. Musto (1987) concluded the following:

> Why the marijuana law was so eagerly desired by some and, when enacted, so effectively placating are fundamental questions. From the evidence examined, the FBN does not appear to have created the marijuana scare of the early 1930s. . . . When viewed from the narrow goal of placating fears about an "alien minority," the Act was serviceable for more than a quarter of a century. For the broader significance of the marijuana law and an understanding of the dynamics involved in prohibitive legislation, the Tax Act must be placed in its cultural and institutional context. (p. 229)

From Patriotic Pot to the Reagan Revolution

Although the passage of the Marijuana Tax Act was the single most significant development affecting the legal status of marijuana in the United States, the four decades following the act were witness to radically shifting attitudes on the role of marijuana in American society.

In the aftermath of the Marijuana Tax Act, medical use of marijuana became negligible, leading to the dropping of the drug from *The Pharmacopeia of the United States of America* (1936) after 1942 (Brecher 1972).

Ironically, that same year, the United States Department of Agriculture launched an ambitious campaign portraying war-related domestic hemp cultivation as a patriotic act. From 1942 to 1945, American farmers were encouraged to grow hemp as a remedy to the shortage of imported hemp for rope caused by World War II. The department even produced a film entitled "Hemp for Victory" (United States Department of Agriculture 1942), which has been reproduced for sale by marijuana legalization advocates (Herer 1992).

From 1940 to 1970, increasingly punitive legislation proliferated throughout the United States, arrests grew, and the press continued to publish sensational and misleading accounts of the consequences of marijuana use (Brecher 1972).

An analysis of state laws governing marijuana that appeared in the

Congressional Record in January 1970 (Analysis of State Laws Governing Marijuana) revealed how draconian the penalties had become. The
examples below were cited in a Consumers Union report on licit and
illicit drugs (Brecher 1972).

> Alabama: Possession of one marijuana cigarette required a minimum sentence
> of 5 years, with suspended sentences and probation prohibited. A second
> possession offense could bring up to 40 years.
>
> Georgia: First offense sale of marijuana to a minor was punishable by a
> minimum sentence of 10 years and a maximum of life imprisonment. A second
> offense was punishable by a minimum of 10 years and a maximum of death.
>
> Illinois: First offense sale required a minimum 10-year sentence and a maximum
> of life imprisonment. Second sale offense required a mandatory life sentence.

A major shift in cultural attitudes beginning in the 1960s led to an
increase in recreational marijuana use and, beginning in 1972, a
widespread revision of state laws governing marijuana possession
penalties. From 1972 to 1978, 11 states, encompassing one-third of
the United States population, decriminalized possession of small
amounts of marijuana, making the offense similar to a traffic ticket.
During that same period, another 33 states enacted measures providing for conditional discharge that would leave the marijuana offender
with no criminal record (K. B. Zeese, personal communication, April
23, 1993).

From 1978 through 1993, 35 states legalized prescription use of
marijuana, with legislation pending in several more states as of early
1993. The difficulty in providing a pharmacologically consistent supply, caused by the end of the federal compassionate exception program, however, made it impossible to secure medical marijuana. Some
state legislatures, however, passed measures allowing use of confis-
cated marijuana for medical purposes, setting up a potential confrontation between the state and federal governments (K. B. Zeese,
personal communication, April 23, 1993).

Although the legal pendulum continued to swing in a positive
direction for medical marijuana from 1978 to the present, laws affecting recreational marijuana use began to swing back the other way from
the 1980s through 1992, creating the paradox of increasing accep-

tance of marijuana as a medicine and increasingly harsh punishment of marijuana offenders, including those caught cultivating the plant for medicinal reasons.

The increased use of urinalysis for marijuana and other drugs; the application of federal and state forfeiture provisions permitting seizures of homes, automobiles, and boats for relatively minor marijuana offenses; and the passage of state laws mandating denial or revocation of driver's licenses and professional licenses for minor marijuana offenses—all resulted in a growing litany of horror stories related to citizens losing property, licenses, and freedoms for marijuana offenses.

Although some individuals have been successful in having property returned and charges dropped or reduced, the cost, financially and in terms of disrupted lives and damaged health, has been high.

In August 1992, for example, Valerie Corral, a 40-year-old woman from Santa Cruz, California, who had smoked marijuana for 18 years to control epileptic seizures, was arrested for growing five plants in a vegetable garden near her porch (Rogers 1993). Under California law, she faced up to 3 years in prison for her offense.

Corral had started using marijuana to control grand mal seizures she began having after a severe head injury in 1973. Prior to her marijuana use, she had become addicted to phenobarbital and diazepam in an effort to control her seizures. She found that by smoking marijuana when she felt a seizure approaching, she could lessen the severity of the seizure or prevent it.

The judge in the case decided to accept a medical necessity defense after Corral's physician, Dr. James Ishaq, wrote a letter stating he would prescribe marijuana for her were it legal. At this juncture, the Santa Cruz district attorney dismissed the charges, saying he was convinced that he could not get a jury to convict her. But the district attorney also said the case was unique and that he would continue to prosecute other marijuana offenders.

In November 1992, Santa Cruz County voters had approved a nonbinding referendum recommending that police and prosecutors use discretion in cases involving marijuana offenders known to be using the plant for medical purposes.

In February 1993, an organization based in Washington, DC, called the Emergency Coalition for Medical Cannabis was formed to promote medical legalization of marijuana. In an appeal, the coalition reported that a 56-year-old California woman, Shirley Dorsey, had committed suicide rather than testify against her 73-year-old friend, Byron Stamate. Stamate was facing serious legal charges after admitting to growing marijuana for use in treating a painful chronic spinal condition.

During hearings before the DEA from 1986 through 1988, numerous personal accounts of the positive medical use of marijuana were presented. The hearings, discussed later, ultimately led to a recommendation for the medical rescheduling of marijuana, which was ignored by the DEA (Randall 1988, 1989, 1990, 1991b).

Therapeutic Use of Marijuana in Antiquity

As noted, therapeutic use of marijuana is clearly established back into antiquity, and it has an unbroken history of use in India and the Far East, despite its changing legal status over the centuries.

There is strong evidence of medicinal use dating back to more than 1000 B.C. (Brecher 1972; Mikuriya 1973). Evidence of earlier use is imprecise, but is most often based on a reference to medicinal use of marijuana in a Chinese pharmacology treatise attributed to the Emperor Shen Nung and alleged to date from 2737 B.C. According to historian Edward M. Brecher, however, Shen Nung was a mythical figure, and the treatise was actually compiled much later than 2737 B.C. A Chinese text dating from 1200 to 500 B.C. documents medical use of marijuana (Brecher 1972; Walton 1938).

Marijuana, as the sacrament *soma,* is mentioned in India's Atharva Veda, one of the earliest portions of the Veda, the scriptural text embodying the basic truths of Hinduism, thought to date back to 1500 B.C. or earlier (De Bary 1958; Walton 1938). Another mention occurs in the Susruta, an Indian treatise dating from before the fourth century A.D. In Persia (Iran), the Zend-Avesta, the sacred text of Zoroastrianism, dating back several centuries B.C., makes reference to marijuana (Walton 1938).

An archaeological dig at Beit Shemesh in Israel provided the first convincing archaeological, as opposed to literary, evidence of medicinal use of marijuana in antiquity, according to anthropologist Joel Ziss of the Israel Antiquities Authority (*Intermountain Jewish News* 1992). The evidence dates to the fourth century A.D.

Professor Rafael Meshulam of Hebrew University's Pharmacy School examined residue found on the abdominal remains of a 14-year-old girl in her ninth month of pregnancy. He found a chemical constituent present only in marijuana in a small mound of burned grasses and fruit deposited on the girl's abdomen. "Presumably the hashish was burned so she could inhale it to ease the pain," said Meshulam. "They then placed the burnt material on her abdomen" (Intermountain Jewish News, p. 23).

Ironically, both contemporary supporters and opponents of legalizing the *recreational* use of marijuana have gone to great lengths, with limited success, to find evidence that marijuana was used as an intoxicant in antiquity. What is relatively clear, however, is that marijuana's medicinal properties were well known for thousands of years. In a paper on marijuana in ancient Greece and Rome, classics professor Theodore F. Brunner (1977) noted that

> the evidence available from Greek and Latin literary sources—while establishing the fact that certain properties inherent in cannabis were known and used for *medicinal* purposes—does not permit us to postulate use of the plant as an intoxicant in [ancient] Greece and Rome. (p. 225; italics added)

In the Greek literature, only Herodotus, thought to have lived from 485 B.C. to 425 B.C., makes clear reference to use of marijuana as an intoxicant. The reference, which refers to the Scythians, by now has become famous to drug historians. It describes the practice of inhaling the vapor from marijuana seed thrown onto red-hot stones inside of tents, after which "the Scythians, delighted, shout for joy" (Brunner 1977, p. 222).

Although this passage and others discussing only medicinal properties of marijuana refer to the seeds, there is reasonable speculation that this might have included the flowering tops that contain the seeds (Brunner 1977).

Dioscorides, a Greek surgeon in the Roman army from A.D. 54 to 68 credited with being the originator of the study of the *materia medica*, described use of crushed seed, placed in the ear, for treatment of earache (Brunner 1977; Stedman 1966).

Galen, a Greek physician who lived from A.D. 130 to 201 and practiced medicine in Rome, referred to use of the seed as an appetite stimulant and antiflatulent. Like Dioscorides, he described use as an analgesic for ear obstruction (Brunner 1977).

Pliny the Elder, who lived from A.D. 23 to 79, also described use of various parts of the marijuana plant to treat a variety of conditions, including gout and digestive upset. But, as Brunner (1977) noted, "While Pliny reports a rather wide variety of domestic and medical applications of cannabis, he appears to be totally unaware of its potential as an intoxicant. Subsequent writers on the subject show a similar unawareness" (p. 224).

East Meets West: Marijuana in Western Medicine

In the introduction to his book written more than 20 years ago, psychiatrist and medical historian Tod Mikuriya (1973) observed that "medicine in the Western World has forgotten almost all it once knew about therapeutic properties of marijuana" (p. xiii). That statement is only slightly less descriptive of the state of knowledge today.

Marijuana was mentioned in various publications in European medicine in the 17th and 18th centuries, notably in the *Edinburgh New Dispensary* of 1794, which described the oil as useful in treating coughs, venereal disease, and urinary incontinence (Grinspoon and Bakalar 1993). But it was not formally introduced into Western medicine until 1839, when a young physician, W. B. O'Shaughnessy, exposed to its medical virtues while serving with the British in India published a 40-page treatise dealing with therapeutic uses of marijuana, particularly as an antispasmodic (O'Shaughnessy 1842).

O'Shaughnessy was a disciplined scientist, known more for his studies on electrolyte therapy than his work with marijuana. He carefully tested the effects of cannabis preparations on animals before using them to treat humans (Mikuriya 1973). After satisfying himself that the drug was safe, he administered various extracts to humans, finding analgesic and sedative properties.

But, according to Mikuriya (1973), "his most spectacular success" (p. xv) was use of marijuana to quiet the wrenching muscle spasms of tetanus and rabies. O'Shaughnessy's observations on the antispasmodic properties of cannabis have been repeatedly confirmed by contemporary users, who continue to testify to its efficacy while being forced to act criminally to obtain the drug (Randall 1991b).

When O'Shaughnessy returned to England in 1842, he brought samples of cannabis to pharmacists. By 1854 it was listed in the *United States Pharmacopeia,* and by the 1860s it had become a popular remedy both in England and America (Grinspoon and Bakalar 1993). It remained in the *United States Pharmacopeia* until 1941, 4 years after passage of the Marijuana Tax Act (Mikuriya 1973).

From its introduction by O'Shaughnessy until about 1900, marijuana was viewed as an important therapeutic agent. During that era, more than 100 papers were published in the Western medical literature describing therapeutic applications of marijuana (Walton 1938).

O'Shaughnessy's success with the drug as an antispasmodic was replicated by others, as McMeens reported to the Ohio State Medical Society in 1860. He included case histories and opinions from a number of physicians who found it effective in alleviating spasmodic conditions, from painful uterine contractions to spasmodic cough and tetanus.

McMeens (1860/1973) quoted a Dr. Fronmueller of Fuerth on the use of marijuana as an opium substitute:

I have used hemp many hundred times to relieve local pains of an inflammatory as well as neuralgic nature, and judging from these experiments, I have to assign to the Indian hemp a place among the so called hypnotic medicines next to opium; its effects are less intense, and the secretions are not so much suppressed by it. Digestion is not disturbed; the appetite rather increased; sickness of the stomach seldom induced; congestion never. . . . It disturbs the expectoration far less than opium; the nervous system is also not so much affected. The whole effect of hemp being less violent, and producing a more natural sleep, without interfering with the actions of the internal organs, it is certainly often preferable to opium, although it is not equal to that drug in strength and reliability. (p. 134)

In a 1938 discussion of therapeutic applications of marijuana, Walton (1938/1973) observed that when it was first introduced, which was prior to the introduction of synthetic analgesics and hypnotics, cannabis offered major advantages over the opiates, which were the only drugs then in general use as sedative hypnotics and analgesics.

> The most attractive feature of the hemp narcotics was probably the fact that they did not exhibit certain of the notorious disadvantages of the opiates. The hemp narcotics do not constipate at all, they more often increase rather than decrease appetite, they do not particularly depress the respiratory center even in large doses . . . and most important, the liability of developing addiction is very much less than with opiates. (pp 160–161)

In an 1891 paper, Mattison (1891/1973) stressed the safety of marijuana and its efficacy as a hypnotic and analgesic, with emphasis on its use in migraine: "Its most important use is in that opprobrium of the healing art—migraine" (p. 152).
He cited testimonials from a number of other physicians as to the efficacy of marijuana in migraine and closed his paper with a final plea and admonition:

> I close this paper by again asking attention to the need of giving hemp in migraine. Were its use limited to this alone, its worth, direct and indirect, would be greater than most imagine. . . . Recollect that hemp eases pain without disturbing stomach and secretions so often as opium, and that competent men think it not only calmative, but curative. (pp. 156–157)

Mattison then quoted a colleague who wrote to tell him that "the young men rarely prescribe it" (p. 157), and said "to them I specially commend it. With a wish for speedy effect, it is so easy to use that modern mischief-maker, hypodermic morphia, that they are prone to forget remote results of incautious opiate giving" (p. 157). He concluded that "Indian hemp is not here lauded as a specific. It will, at times, fail. So do other drugs. But the many cases in which it acts well entitle it to a large and lasting confidence" (p. 157).

Some contemporary physicians familiar with the historical use of cannabis in migraine have found Marinol useful as a supplementary therapy for this condition (T. H. Mikuriya, personal communication, May 1993).

In his treatise on medical marijuana, psychiatrist Mikuriya (1973) reviewed and summarized the potential therapeutic uses of marijuana as found in the Western literature through the early 1970s. These included analgesic, hypnotic, appetite stimulant, antiepileptic, antispasmodic, migraine treatment, tranquilizer, antiasthmatic, childbirth analgesic, oxytocic, antitussive, topical anesthetic, withdrawal agent for opiate and alcohol addiction, antibiotic, intraocular hypotensive, and hypothermogenic (Anderson 1863; Berger 1971; Birch 1889; Boyd and Merritt 1965; Ciba Foundation Study Group 1964; Cunningham 1894; Davis and Ramsey 1949; Eli Lilly 1898; Hare 1887; Hare and Chrystie 1892; Hepler and Frank 1971; *Journal of the American Medical Association* 1930; Jones 1970; Mattison 1891; Mayor's Committee on Marijuana 1944; McMeens 1860; Nadkarni 1945; O'Shaughnessy 1842; Osler and McCrae 1916; Ratnam 1916; Reynolds 1890; Stevens 1903; Suckling 1881; Thompson and Proctor 1953; Waring 1874).

Recent Recognition of Marijuana's Therapeutic Potential

Although it is important to examine the more distant historical record in tracing the evolution of marijuana as a therapeutic agent, it is of more immediate relevance to examine recent clinical and anecdotal accounts. Some contemporary therapeutic applications of marijuana, although foreshadowed by those in the historical record, are a function of recent medical developments. These developments include the increase in the incidence of cancer attributable to increasing longevity; the advent of more effective, but highly toxic, cancer treatments; and the appearance of human immunodeficiency virus and its medical sequelae, particularly cachexia, or wasting syndrome (Miller et al. 1992; National Institute on Allergy and Infectious Diseases 1992).

The increasing incidence of cancer—the National Cancer Institute (Miller et al. 1992) estimated there would be 520,000 cancer deaths in the United States in 1992—combined with the proliferation of radiotherapy and chemotherapy, has brought with it the problem of medically induced nausea as a serious toxic side effect of cancer treatment. Persistent nausea may be life threatening, by causing systemic weakening through reduced caloric intake or by necessitating the discontinuation of therapy that would otherwise prolong life.

AIDS-related phenomena, including wasting syndrome and reactions to the therapeutic drug zidovudine (AZT), present problems that may, like the side effects of cancer treatment, be directly or indirectly life threatening. AIDS cachexia involves the loss of appetite during the progression of the illness. With AZT, some patients experience severe nausea.

Marijuana's properties as an antispasmodic and appetite stimulant, combined with its remarkably high margin of safety, have proven critical for increasing numbers of both cancer and AIDS patients afflicted by nausea and appetite loss. By calming gastrointestinal spasms, it permits cancer patients who respond poorly to standard antiemetics to continue therapy. By stimulating appetite, both the cancer patient and the AIDS patient are better able to maintain adequate nutritional intake.

Safety becomes particularly critical when patients are already being exposed to a variety of highly toxic agents, as in chemotherapy, or when they are suffering from compromised immunity, as in AIDS.

In a 1987 affidavit to the DEA during hearings on the rescheduling of marijuana, Weil (1987/1988) commented that "nearly all medicines have toxic, potentially lethal effects. But marijuana is not one of these drugs. There is no record in the extensive medical literature describing a cannabis induced fatality" (p. 432). Similarly, in an essay on the historical use of cannabis in Western medicine, Mikuriya (1969) compared the margin of safety for THC with that for barbiturates and

Doonesbury   BY GARRY TRUDEAU

alcohol, based on the difference between the generally effective oral dose and the minimum lethal dose. For secobarbital, the margin is about 3–50, that is, the minimum lethal dose is 3–50 times the effective dose. For alcohol, the margin is approximately 4–10 times the effective dose, and for THC the margin is about 40,000–1, based on the oral dose required to kill a mouse (Mikuriya 1969).

Concerns about the alleged immunosuppressive effects of marijuana have been raised to justify denying the drug to patients. But a major 18-month study of almost 5,000 homosexual men with AIDS found no correlation between marijuana use and immune status, and no effect of marijuana use on the speed at which the disease progressed (Kaslow et al. 1989). As Hollister (1992) observed in an article on marijuana and immunity

> [the evidence has been contradictory and is] more supportive of immunosuppression only when one considers *in vitro* studies. These have been seriously flawed by the very high concentrations of drug used to produce immunosuppression and by the lack of comparisons with other membrane-active drugs. The closer that experimental studies have been to actual clinical situations, the less compelling has been the evidence. (p. 7)

There is a fairly extensive literature involving recent controlled clinical trials with oral THC and related cannabinoids, and a somewhat more modest literature of recent controlled and uncontrolled clinical trials with whole marijuana. The clinical data are supplemented by a proliferation of well-documented anecdotal accounts. Taken together, the clinical and anecdotal data constitute an impressive body of contemporary evidence validating the therapeutic efficacy of marijuana as an antiemetic and, to a lesser but still significant extent, as an intraocular hypotensive and antispasmodic.

An extensive compilation of clinical and anecdotal accounts was assembled from DEA and other hearings on marijuana in medicine by Robert Randall of the Alliance for Cannabis Therapeutics in a four-volume series, *Marijuana, Medicine and the Law* (Randall 1988, 1989, 1990, 1991b) and in a book on use of marijuana in AIDS (Randall 1991a). Grinspoon and Bakalar made extensive use of anecdotal accounts in their 1993 book *Marijuana, the Forbidden Medicine*, including a moving personal account of the remarkable role marijuana played in enabling Grinspoon's terminally ill son Danny to tolerate treatment for acute lymphatic leukemia (Grinspoon and Bakalar 1993). Many of the other accounts of patients' struggles to ease their suffering through illegal use of marijuana are equally compelling.

The best account of the clinical studies on use of marijuana in controlling emesis and glaucoma is contained in a brief to the DEA by the Alliance for Cannabis Therapeutics. The brief can be found in the *Marijuana, Medicine and the Law* series (Randall 1989).

The Alliance for Cannabis Therapeutics cited both published and unpublished studies, including two academic clinical trials and six trials conducted under the aegis of six different state governments, some involving more than 100 people treated with smoked marijuana as part of the investigational protocol.

In one trial of THC versus placebo, about one-fifth of the 50 participants dropped out after telling the researchers that smoked marijuana obtained on the street was more effective than oral THC. The researchers had only oral THC available (Sallan et al. 1975). The researchers noted that the use of illicit marijuana, although impossible to quantify, was a significant variable that could not be ignored in interpreting the results. The suggestion that the mass defection to marijuana over THC was clinically significant has been dismissed by opponents of therapeutic legalization (Randall 1990).

A double-blind, controlled trial of placebo, oral THC, and smoked marijuana was conducted by Chang and colleagues (1979) over a 6-month period. They found a 93% reduction in nausea and vomiting in chemotherapy patients who combined THC and smoked marijuana. The authors identified problems with adequate absorption of oral THC as resulting in less than adequate blood plasma THC levels in more than 60% of patients exposed to oral THC only. This compared with a 71% level of blood plasma adequacy in patients who inhaled marijuana. Oral THC, unlike inhaled marijuana, proved highly inconsistent, and Chang and colleagues reported that later trials showed no statistical significance between oral THC and placebo.

The six controlled, state-sponsored studies most frequently cited by medical experts testifying in support of rescheduling marijuana occurred in New Mexico, Michigan, New York, Georgia, California, and Tennessee (Randall 1989, 1990). All involved comparisons of smoked marijuana with other antiemetics in cancer patients.

In New Mexico, oral THC was found effective in 60% of the cases and smoked marijuana in 90% (Randall 1990, p. 148). In a Michigan program comparing thiethylperazine (Torecan) with marijuana, patients were permitted to switch after initial trial; 50% chose marijuana, 13% switched *to* marijuana from Torecan, and only 5% switched *from* marijuana to Torecan (Randall 1990, p. 285). Marijuana effectively reduced nausea in almost 80% of the patients. In a smaller Tennessee study involving 27 patients, marijuana proved effective for more than 90% and oral THC for only 67% (Randall 1989, p. 55). The New York program found marijuana effective in 83%, with researchers noting that it was effective in about 50% more patients than prochlorperazine (Compazine) (Randall 1989, p. 50). In Georgia, about 70% of both marijuana smokers and oral THC users reported success (Randall 1989, p. 41). In the California study, which had by far the most narrow qualifying requirements, 59% of the physicians rated marijuana moderately or very effective (Randall 1989, 1990).

In the cancer treatment literature, one substantial pilot study found smoked marijuana effective in 78% of a group of 56 patients who had *failed* to respond to standard antiemetics while undergoing cancer chemotherapy (Vinciguerra et al. 1988). More than a third (34%) rated it "highly effective," and 44% found it "moderately effective." The positive respondents included 29% of patients who had failed to respond to oral THC, leading the authors to observe the following: "Failure to respond to oral THC does not preclude benefit from inhaled marijuana. . . . This is not unexpected, since only 5%–10% of orally administered THC is absorbed, whereas inhaled marijuana has a five-to-tenfold greater bioavailability." Some patients vomit up oral THC, either after chemotherapy, or prior to chemotherapy, from conditioned anticipatory vomiting.

The combination of formal research findings supporting use of smoked marijuana as an antiemetic and the growing body of anecdotal evidence has led a growing number of oncologists to recommend it, despite the drug's forbidden status, according to a national survey (Doblin and Kleiman 1991). The survey, conducted through Harvard University, found that 44% of the respondents admitted recommending the use of marijuana for controlling emesis in cancer chemotherapy patients, despite the drug's illegality. Almost half said they would prescribe marijuana in smoked form to some of their patients were it legal, and a majority (54%) thought smokable marijuana should be legally available by prescription.

The antispasmodic properties of smoked cannabis have been successfully applied to treatment of tremors in patients with multiple sclerosis and to treatment of muscle spasm in para- and quadriplegic patients (Grinspoon and Bakalar 1993; Institute of Medicine 1982; Petro 1980; Randall 1991b).

In addition to numerous recent anecdotal accounts and historical clinical data, effective use in multiple sclerosis was verified under clinical conditions in a 30-year-old man (Meinck et al. 1989). In this case study, conducted at the Department of Clinical Neurophysiology at the University of Gottingen in Germany in October 1985, marked improvements in motor handicaps were quantitatively assessed by means of clinical ratings, electromyographic investigation of leg flexor reflexes, and electromagnetic recording of hand action tremor after the subject smoked a marijuana cigarette. In addition, the man, who complained that multiple sclerosis had made him impotent, told the researchers that marijuana allowed him to have a satisfactory sex life. The authors stated the following:

> At the time of our experiments he was bound to a wheelchair because of severe limb and gait ataxia and spastic tetraparesis. . . . He complained of impotence, with erections lasting less than 5 minutes and lacking ejaculation. He tried a marijuana cigarette about 1984 and noted an instantaneous improvement of his motor and sexual functions lasting for several days. Since then, he regularly took some marijuana biscuits each week, which enabled him to climb stairs, to walk on even ground, and to have erections for more than 30 minutes, allowing him a quite satisfactory sexual life.

Use to control muscle spasm among paralyzed Americans is so commonplace that one neurologist testified before the DEA that "you cannot walk down a neurology ward in a Veterans Administration hospital without smelling marijuana" (Randall and O'Leary 1989, p. 7).

The ability of inhaled marijuana to lower intraocular pressure has led to occasional use as an antiglaucoma agent, although one of the original backers of this application later retrenched and testified against rescheduling marijuana for any medical use, in keeping with the official position of the American Academy of Ophthalmology (Hepler 1978/1988, 1987/1988). A reading of the research and clinical case studies, however, confirms that inhaled marijuana has a significant effect on intraocular pressure and, at least in one longitudinal case study, has been proven effective in stopping damage to the optic nerve over an extended period of time when conventional antiglaucoma agents failed (Grinspoon and Bakalar 1993; Institute of Medicine 1982; Merritt 1987/1988; Randall 1987/1988). That nearly 10,000 people are blinded yearly by glaucoma strongly suggests that the addition of marijuana to the therapeutic arsenal has the potential to save the sight of some glaucoma patients not helped by other therapies (National Eye Institute 1978 in Randall and O'Leary 1993, p. 7).

The National Eye Institute expressed opposition to use of marijuana in glaucoma in a policy statement provided to the author of this chapter in 1992. The statement was provided by a spokesperson for the United States Public Health Service as background for the government's decision to withdraw further provision of marijuana under the compassionate exception program. The National Eye Institute ignored research, such as that cited by the National Academy of Sciences in their 1982 Institute of Medicine report, showing marijuana could lower intraocular pressure enough to prevent optic nerve damage from glaucoma.

> Smoking marijuana produces undesirable side effects for glaucoma patients, such as elevated blood pressure, dry eye, and euphoria in the majority of patients studied. Glaucoma patients who regularly and chronically smoke marijuana would also be at risk for respiratory system damage. . . . There is considerable variability in the composition and quality of marijuana from supply to supply. In addition, smoking is a less than optimal drug delivery system. Without a standardized product and method of assuring the bioavailability of its active ingredients, marijuana is problematic as a therapy for glaucoma. (National Eye Institute 1992, pp. 2–3)

The concern expressed by the National Eye Institute regarding the side-effect profile of marijuana must be balanced against the toxic nature of standard antiglaucoma agents, including acetazolamide (Diamox) and timolol. According to testimony by ophthalmologist John Merritt, acetazolamide can destroy a patient's kidneys, and timolol has been held responsible for 32 *deaths* when used as indicated for glaucoma over an 8-year period (Merritt 1987/1988). Although marijuana is not an initial drug of choice in glaucoma therapy, its use may allow a treating physician to reduce or eliminate the use of more toxic conventional therapies.

There is also evidence confirming historical use of cannabis as an anticonvulsant and antiasthmatic, a migraine treatment, and, at least for some people, an anxiolytic and antidepressant. In some, however, marijuana may be anxiogenic or dysphoria-inducing, exacerbating underlying pathology (Grinspoon and Bakalar 1993; Institute of Medicine 1982; T. H. Mikuriya, personal communication, 1993; Tashkin et al. 1974).

Although marijuana compared favorably with isoprenaline as a bronchodilator in one clinical study, its use as an antiasthmatic is intrinsically limited by the irritant effects of inhaled smoke (Tashkin et al. 1974). Marijuana smoke contains more tars and carbon monoxide than tobacco smoke, and the tars are likely to be retained because of the way in which marijuana is usually inhaled (Tashkin et al. 1980; Wu et al. 1988). These effects may be mitigated by the use of water pipes or other types of filtering mechanisms (Grinspoon and Bakalar 1993).

There is a substantial animal literature on use of cannabis as an anticonvulsant, as well as one substantial double-blind, human trial of use of a cannabis derivative, but not whole cannabis, in human epilepsy (Cunha et al. 1980; Institute of Medicine 1982). There are also anecdotal accounts (Grinspoon and Bakalar 1993). In the human study (Cunha et al. 1980), 15 patients with temporal lobe epilepsy were randomly divided, with 8 receiving the cannabis derivative and 7 receiving placebo in a double-blind procedure lasting up to 4.5 months. Of the 8 receiving the active drug, 4 were almost seizure free during the trial and 3 showed partial improvement. Those on placebo showed no change in seizure frequency.

The major arguments against legalizing medical use of marijuana were summarized by Dan Spyker of the United States Public Health Service in a March 1992 statement explaining the Public Health Service decision to end its compassionate exception program that had provided marijuana legally to 13 patients:

Clinically, marijuana has many drawbacks as a medicine. Marijuana is not a pure drug and may be contaminated with pathogens such as mold and fungi. Smoked marijuana delivers irritants that could be highly noxious to patients with chronic illness or immunosuppression. In addition, after reviewing the available data, scientists at the National Institutes of Health have concluded that existing evidence does not support recommending smoked marijuana as the treatment of choice for any medical condition. Further, there are effective and safer alternatives available for all illnesses for which marijuana is being requested. (United States Public Health Service 1992)

The DEA Hearings: Recommendation and Rejection

In response to an earlier court order, the DEA held hearings to hear arguments for and against the medical rescheduling of marijuana from 1986 through 1988. The critical testimony was distilled into Randall's *Marijuana, Medicine and the Law* series of books (Randall 1988, 1989, 1990, 1991a, 1991b).

The outcome of the hearings was widely publicized when DEA Administrative Law Judge Francis Young ruled that marijuana did have an accepted medical use under provisions of the Controlled Substances Act of 1970, and recommended that the DEA reschedule marijuana from Schedule I to Schedule II (United States Department of Justice 1988). In making the ruling, which was ultimately rejected by DEA, Young chided the agency, stating

the evidence in this record clearly shows that marijuana has been accepted as capable of relieving the distress of great numbers of very ill people, and doing so with safety under medical supervision. It would be unreasonable, arbitrary, and capricious for DEA to continue to stand between those sufferers and the benefits of this substance in light of the evidence in this record.

The Administrative Law Judge recommends that the Administrator conclude that the marijuana plant considered as a whole has a currently accepted medical use in treatment in the United States, that there is no lack of accepted safety for use of it under medical supervision and that it may lawfully be transferred from Schedule I to Schedule II. The judge recommends that the Administrator transfer marijuana from Schedule I to Schedule II. (p. 68)

The DEA waited 4 years before categorically rejecting Judge Young's recommendation. Administrator Robert Bonner blasted Young's ruling, commenting, "Lay testimonials, impressions of physicians, isolated case studies, random clinical experience, reports so lacking in details they cannot be scientifically evaluated and all other forms of anecdotal proof are entirely irrelevant" (Treaster 1992, p. B11). The agency made its announcement 1 week after the Department of Health and Human Services terminated its compassionate marijuana provision program (Treaster 1992).

On December 31, 1991, Massachusetts became the 35th state to recognize marijuana's medical value, as Governor William Weld signed new legislation. The law protects medical use and allows doctors to prescribe marijuana after they receive approval from state and federal health officials. But the cancellation of the federal compassionate exception program, which had provided the only legal source of marijuana for medical use, has, for the time being, effectively nullified the various state actions to legalize medicinal marijuana use (Drug Policy Foundation 1992).

Conclusion: Bad Policy, Bad Medicine

The appropriate medical use of marijuana has the potential to help hundreds of thousands of suffering Americans with conditions including chemotherapeutically induced nausea, pathological muscle spasm, AIDS cachexia, and glaucoma, and perhaps others. Unlike the broad proposals to legalize marijuana or other drugs for nonmedical use, marijuana's legalization for medical use has broad bipartisan support and broad support among the public (see also Randall and O'Leary 1993).

Where it is possible to substitute marijuana for other medications, there may be a significant enhancement of therapeutic safety as well as efficacy. Where marijuana is being used to offset side effects of intrinsically toxic therapies, as in cancer, marijuana's benign nature is even more critical.

Federal policy on medical marijuana is both bad policy and bad medicine, and should be categorically rejected as a cruel, irrational, and intolerable intrusion into the appropriate prescribing of a psychoactive substance.

References

Allentuck S: LaGuardia report: medical aspects (1944), in Marijuana: Medical Papers: 1839–1972. Edited by Mikuriya TH. Oakland, CA, Medi-Comp Press, 1973, pp 179–211

Analysis of state laws governing marijuana. Congressional Record, January 20, 1970, pp S240–S245

Anderson GS: Remarks on the remedial virtues of cannabis indica, or Indian hemp. Boston Medical and Surgical Journal 67:427–430, 1863

Berger AD: Marijuana. Medical World News, July 16, 1971, pp 37–43

Birch EA: The use of Indian hemp in the treatment of chronic chloral and chronic opium poisoning. Lancet 1:625, 1889

Boyd ES, Merritt DA: Effects of a tetrahydrocannabinol derivative on some motor systems in the cat. Arch Internat de Pharmacodynamie et de Therapie 153:1–12, 1965

Brecher EM: Licit and Illicit Drugs: The Consumers Union Report on Narcotics, Stimulants, Depressants, Inhalants, Hallucinogens and Marijuana—Including Caffeine, Nicotine and Alcohol. Boston, MA, Little, Brown, 1972

Brunner TF: Marijuana in ancient Greece and Rome? The literary evidence. Journal of Psychedelic Drugs 9:221–225, 1977

Buterbaugh L: FDA drug approvals spurt at year's end. Medical Tribune, January 28, 1993, p 10

Chang AE, Shling RC, Stillman NE, et al: Delta-nine-tetrahydrocannabinol as an antiemetic in cancer patients receiving high-dose methotrexate: a prospective randomized evaluation. Ann Intern Med 91:819–824, 1979

Choice for Surgeon General favors medicinal marijuana use. Washington Post, December 20, 1992, p A16

Ciba Foundation Study Group: Hashish: its chemistry and pharmacology. Ciba Foundation Study Group, 1964, pp 45, 49

Controlled Substances Act, 21, USC § 801 (1970)

Cunha JM, Carlini EA, Pereira AE, et al: Chronic administration of cannabidiol to healthy volunteers and epileptic patients. Pharmacology 21:175–185, 1980

Cunningham DD: Report by Brigade-Surgeon Lt Col DD Cunningham, FRS, CIE, on the nature of the effects accompanying the continued treatment of animals with hemp drugs and with datura, in Report of the Indian Hemp Drugs Commission, 1893–1894, Vol 3. Simla, India, Government Central Printing Office, 1894, pp 192–196

Davis JP, Ramsey HH: Antiepileptic action of marijuana-active substances. Federal Proceedings 8:284–285, 1949

De Bary WT: Sources of Indian Tradition, Vol 1. New York, Columbia University Press, 1958

Doblin RE, Kleiman MA: Marijuana as antiemetic medicine: a survey of oncologists' experiences and attitudes. J Clin Oncol 9:1314–1319, 1991

Drug Policy Foundation: Massachusetts becomes thirty-fifth state to recognize medical marijuana. Drug Policy Action 3:3, 1992

Eli Lilly: Lilly's Handbook of Pharmacy and Therapeutics. Indianapolis, IN, Eli Lilly & Co, 1898

Food and Drugs Act of 1906, 34 Stat 768 (1906)

Grinspoon L, Bakalar JB: Marijuana, the Forbidden Medicine. New Haven, CT, Yale University Press, 1993

Hare HA: Clinical and physiological notes on the action of cannabis indica. Therapeutic Gazette 11:225–228, 1887

Hare HA, Chrystie W: A System of Practical Therapeutics, Vol 3. Philadelphia, PA, Lee Brothers, 1892

Harrison Narcotic Act of 1914, Pub L No 223, 63rd Congress (1914)

Hepler RS: Affidavit of Robert S Hepler, MD (1978), in Marijuana, Medicine and the Law: Direct Testimony of Witnesses on Marijuana's Medical Use in the Treatment of Life- and Sense-Threatening Diseases Including Cancer, Glaucoma, Multiple Sclerosis, Para- and Quadriplegia, Chronic Pain, and Skin Disorders in Hearings Before the US Drug Enforcement Administration. Edited by Randall RC. Washington, DC, Galen Press, 1988a, pp 51–57

Hepler RS: Direct testimony of Robert S Hepler, MD, and information statement of the American Academy of Ophthalmology (1987), in Marijuana, Medicine and the Law: Direct Testimony of Witnesses on Marijuana's Medical Use in the Treatment of Life- and Sense-Threatening Diseases Including Cancer, Glaucoma, Multiple Sclerosis, Para- and Quadriplegia, Chronic Pain, and Skin Disorders in Hearings Before the US Drug Enforcement Administration. Edited by Randall RC. Washington, DC, Galen Press, 1988b, pp 355–359

Hepler RS, Frank IR: Marijuana smoking and intraocular pressure. JAMA 217:1392, 1971

Herer J: The Emperor Wears No Clothes. Van Nuys, CA, HEMP Publishing, 1992

Hollister LE: Marijuana and immunity. J Psychoactive Drugs 24:159–164, 1992

Institute of Medicine: Marijuana and health. Washington, DC, National Academy Press, 1982

Intermountain Jewish News: Hashish used as medicine. Jewish Telegraphic Agency, June 12, 1992, p 23

Journal of the American Medical Association: Effects of alcohol and cannabis during labor. JAMA 94:1165, 1930

Jones RT: Psychological studies of marijuana and alcohol in man. Psychopharmacologia 18:108–117, 1970

Kaslow RA, Blackwelder WC, Ostrow DG, et al: No evidence for a role of alcohol or other psychoactive drugs in accelerating immunodeficiency in HIV-1-positive individuals. JAMA 261:3424–3429, 1989

Marijuana Tax Act of 1937, Pub L No 238, 75th Congress (1937)

Mattison JB: Cannabis indica as an anodyne and hypnotic. St Louis Medical and Surgical Journal 61:265–271, 1891

Mattison JB: Cannabis indica as an anodyne and hypnotic (1891), in Marijuana: Medical Papers: 1839–1972. Edited by Mikuriya TH. Oakland, CA, Medi-Comp Press, 1973

Mayor's Committee on Marijuana: The Marijuana Problem in the City of New York. Lancaster, PA, Jaques Cattell, 1944

McMeens RR: Report of the committee on cannabis indica, in Transactions of the Fifteenth Annual Meeting of the Ohio State Medical Society. Columbus, OH, Follett, Foster, 1860, pp 75–100

McMeens RR: Report of the committee on cannabis indica (1860), in Marijuana: Medical Papers: 1839–1972, 1st Edition. Edited by Mikuriya TH. Oakland, CA, Medi-Comp Press, 1973, pp 117–140

Meinck HM, Schonle PW, Conrad B: Effect of cannabinoids on spasticity and ataxia in multiple sclerosis. J Neurol 236:120–122, 1989

Merritt JC: Affidavit of John C Merritt MD (1987), in Marijuana, Medicine and the Law: Direct Testimony of Witnesses on Marijuana's Medical Use in the Treatment of Life- and Sense-Threatening Diseases Including Cancer, Glaucoma, Multiple Sclerosis, Para- and Quadriplegia, Chronic Pain, and Skin Disorders in Hearings Before the US Drug Enforcement Administration. Edited by Randall RC. Washington, DC, Galen Press, 1988, pp 469–479

Mikuriya TH: Historical aspects of cannabis sativa in Western medicine. New Physician 18:902–908, 1969

Mikuriya TH (ed): Marijuana: Medical Papers: 1839–1972. Oakland, CA, Medi-Comp Press, 1973

Miller BA, Ries LA, Hankey BF, et al: Cancer statistics review 1973–1989 (NIC-NIH Publ No 92-2789). Bethesda, MD, National Institutes of Health, 1992

Musto DF: The American Disease: Origins of Narcotics Control, Expanded Edition. New York, Oxford University Press, 1987

Nadkarni AK (ed): Indian Materia Medica. Bombay, India, Popular Book Depot, 1945

National Eye Institute: Factsheet: marijuana and glaucoma. Bethesda, MD, National Eye Institute, August 16, 1978

National Eye Institute: Factsheet on the therapeutic use of marijuana for glaucoma. Bethesda, MD, National Eye Institute, 1992

National Institute on Allergy and Infectious Diseases: Factsheet on the therapeutic use of marijuana for patients with HIV-Wasting Syndrome. Bethesda, MD, National Institute on Allergy and Infectious Diseases, 1992

O'Shaughnessy WB: On the preparations of the Indian hemp, or gunjah: the effects on the animal system in health, and their utility in the treatment of tetanus and other convulsive diseases. Transactions of the Medical and Physical Society, Bengal, India (1838–1840), 1842, pp 421–461

Osler W, McCrae T: Principles and Practice of Medicine, 8th Edition. New York, Appleton, 1916

Petro DJ: Marijuana as a therapeutic agent for muscle spasm or spasticity. Psychosomatics 21:81–85, 1980

The Pharmacopeia of the United States of America, 11th Edition. Easton, PA, Mack Printing, 1936, p LXVIII

Randall RC: Affidavit of Robert C Randall (1987), in Marijuana, Medicine and the Law: Direct Testimony of Witnesses on Marijuana's Medical Use in the Treatment of Life- and Sense-Threatening Diseases Including Cancer, Glaucoma, Multiple Sclerosis, Para- and Quadriplegia, Chronic Pain, and Skin Disorders in Hearings Before the US Drug Enforcement Administration. Edited by Randall RC. Washington, DC, Galen Press, 1988, pp 481–502

Randall RC (ed): Marijuana, Medicine and the Law: Direct Testimony of Witnesses on Marijuana's Medical Use in the Treatment of Life- and Sense-Threatening Diseases Including Cancer, Glaucoma, Multiple Sclerosis, Para- and Quadriplegia, Chronic Pain, and Skin Disorders in Hearings Before the US Drug Enforcement Administration. Washington, DC, Galen Press, 1988

Randall RC (ed): Marijuana, Medicine and the Law, Vol 2: Legal Briefs, Oral Arguments and Decision of the Administrative Law Judge on Marijuana's Medical Use in the Treatment of Life- and Sense-Threatening Diseases Including Cancer, Glaucoma, Multiple Sclerosis, Para- and Quadriplegia, Chronic Pain, and Skin Disorders in Hearings Before the US Drug Enforcement Administration. Washington, DC, Galen Press, 1989

Randall RC (ed): Cancer Treatment and Marijuana Therapy: Marijuana's Use in the Reduction of Nausea and Vomiting and for Appetite Stimulation in Cancer Patients: Testimony from Historic Federal Hearings on Marijuana's Medical Use (Marijuana, Medicine and the Law Series). Washington, DC, Galen Press, 1990

Randall RC (ed): Marijuana and AIDS: Pot, Politics and PWAs in America. Washington, DC, Galen Press, 1991a

Randall RC (ed): Muscle Spasm, Pain and Marijuana Therapy: Testimony from Federal and State Court Proceedings on Marijuana's Medical Use in the Treatment of Multiple Sclerosis, Paralysis, and Chronic Pain (Marijuana, Medicine and the Law Series). Washington, DC, Galen Press, 1991b

Randall RC, O'Leary AM: Marijuana as Medicine—Initial Steps: Recommendations for the Clinton Administration. Washington, DC, Galen Press, 1993

Ratnam EV: Cannabis indica. Journal of the Ceylon Branch of the British Medical Association 13:30–33, 1916

Reynolds JR: Therapeutical uses and toxic effects of cannabis indica. Lancet 1:637–638, 1890

Rogers P: Pot charges against epileptic dismissed: Santa Cruz woman had faced prison term. San Jose Mercury News, March 27, 1993, p 5B

Sallan SF, Zinberg NE, Frei E III: Antiemetic effect of delta-nine-tetrahydrocannabinol in patients receiving cancer chemotherapy. N Engl J Med 293:795–797, 1975

Stedman TL: Stedman's Medical Dictionary, 21st Edition. Baltimore, MD, Williams & Wilkins, 1966

Stevens AA: Modern Materia Medica and Therapeutics. Philadelphia, PA, WB Saunders, 1903

Suckling CW: On the therapeutic value of Indian hemp. Br Med J 2:12, 1881

Tashkin DP, Shapiro BJ, Frank IM: Acute effects of smoked marijuana on specific airway conductance in asthmatic subjects. Am Rev Respir Dis 109:420–428, 1974

Tashkin DP, Calvarese BM, Simmons MS, et al: Respiratory status of seventy-four habitual marijuana smokers. Chest 78:699–706, 1980

Thompson LJ, Proctor RC: The use of pyrahexyl in the treatment of alcoholic and drug withdrawal conditions. N C Med J 14:520–523, 1953

Treaster JB: Agency says marijuana is not proven medicine. The New York Times, March 19, 1992, p B11

United States Department of Agriculture: Hemp for Victory [film]. Washington, DC, United States Department of Agriculture, 1942

United States Department of Justice, Drug Enforcement Administration: In the matter of marijuana rescheduling petition: opinion and recommended ruling, findings of fact, conclusions of law and decision of Administrative Law Judge Francis L. Young. September 6, 1988

United States Public Health Service: Untitled statement by Dan Spyker, MD, explaining decision to cancel all legal access to medical marijuana. Contained in fax from USPHS spokesman Bill Grigg, March 8, 1992

US rescinds approval of marijuana as therapy. The New York Times, March 11, 1992, p A21

Vinciguerra V, Moore T, Brennan E: Inhalation marijuana as an antiemetic for cancer chemotherapy. N Y State J Med 88:525–527, 1988

Walton RP: Marijuana: America's New Drug Problem. Philadelphia, PA, JB Lippincott, 1938

Walton RP: Marijuana: America's new drug problem (1938), in Marijuana: Medical Papers: 1839–1972, 1st Edition. Edited by Mikuriya TH. Oakland, CA, Medi-Comp Press, 1973, pp 83–113

Waring EJ: Practical Therapeutics. Philadelphia, PA, Lindsay & Blakiston, 1874

Weil AT: Affidavit of Andrew Thomas Weil MD (1987), in Marijuana, Medicine and the Law: Direct Testimony of Witnesses on Marijuana's Medical Use in the Treatment of Life- and Sense-Threatening Diseases Including Cancer, Glaucoma, Multiple Sclerosis, Para- and Quadriplegia, Chronic Pain, and Skin Disorders in Hearings Before the US Drug Enforcement Administration. Edited by Randall RC. Washington, DC, Galen Press, 1988, pp 429–441

Wu TC, Tashkin DP, Djahed B, et al: Pulmonary hazards of smoking marijuana compared with tobacco. N Engl J Med 318:347–351, 1988

Cost Containment

At the Cost of Quality and Access?

CHAPTER SIX

The Impact of Cost-Containment Measures on Somatic Psychiatry

Harold I. Schwartz, M.D.

The drive to contain cost is reworking the very fabric of the delivery of mental health services. One of the great debates in health care reform revolves around the ability to reduce cost while maintaining the quality of care. The linkage of ever-increasing efficiency with increasing quality has become ubiquitous within the jargon of the continuous quality improvement and health care reform movements. However, many significant reforms in the delivery of health care services and, in particular, in the reform of mental health services are, in fact, large social experiments that have been imposed with little data on their likely impact on patient care. For all of our experience with managed care, for instance, there are little hard data, prospectively acquired, examining objective outcome measures for large populations of psychiatric patients.

Although there are virtually no direct data on the relationship between cost-containment reform and the use of somatic therapies in psychiatry, recent research on drug cost-containment policies does allow for some informed speculation. In a review of such programs, Soumerai and Ross-Degnan (1990) emphasized the need to differentiate the unintended impact of such policies from their intended ones and highlighted the differentiation between the control of inappropriate prescribing behavior and the impact on essential medical care.

Reimbursements Caps

Studies that examine the impact of programs that cap or limit reimbursements for prescription drugs for individual patients indicate that these programs clearly have an impact on the utilization of appropriate and necessary medication. One such study (Soumerai et al. 1987) examined the impact of the imposition of a drug payment cap for Medicaid patients in the state of New Hampshire and compared the impact of the cap program with a copayment program, which ultimately was substituted.

In 1981 New Hampshire began to limit the number of prescriptions that would be reimbursed by the Medicaid program to three per month per patient. The investigators reviewed Medicaid data in an attempt to ascertain the numbers of prescriptions filled, total doses dispensed, and reimbursed drug costs, attempting to differentiate the impact on essential versus nonessential medications. Of note, lithium was among the essential drugs whose use was evaluated. The greatest impact of this program was experienced by patients who were multiple drug recipients and, by implication, the most infirm. This group received an average of 5.2 prescriptions per person per month prior to the implementation of the cap; during the 11 months following implementation, they received an average of only 2.8 prescriptions per month, representing a drop of 46%. Although the percentage decline was greatest for drugs of limited efficacy and smallest for medications considered to be essential, declines in prescriptions for essential medications were notable. For example, among patients continuing to receive insulin through Medicaid, fully one-quarter had decreased their insulin prescriptions by 50% and almost half experienced decreases of more than 25% in their average monthly doses. The impact on utilization of psychotropic medications can be appreciated when we consider that among patients who were the highest users of medication, 27% were long-term recipients (greater than or equal to four prescriptions per year before the cap) of medication for affective disorders and 26% were long-term recipients of medication for psychosis. One might argue that such diminished utilization resulted from decreases in inappropriate use, but a patient-specific analysis indicated this was not the case. When the cap was eliminated 11 months after its implementation, a rapid increase in reimbursed prescriptions was observed, suggesting that prescribing physicians continued to consider the prescribed medications to be necessary.

In a follow-up study, Soumerai and colleagues (1991) examined the impact of the cap on a cohort of chronically ill elderly patients in New Hampshire. They studied the rate of admission to nursing homes and hospitals and compared it with the rates for an equivalent cohort in a state without such a cap. Psychoactive medications (anxiolytic, hypnotic, antipsychotic, and antidepressant drugs) were among the classes of drugs whose use was tracked for this patient group. This study demonstrated significant reductions in the use of medications following the imposition of the three-drug reimbursement limit followed by a moderate trend toward increased hospitalization (which did not reach statistical significance) and a statistically significant increase in the rate of admission to nursing homes. The risk of nursing home admission for the sickest patients in the study cohort more than doubled in comparison with the control group. Of note, rates of institutionalization returned to baseline and control group rates following discontinuation of the cap program. However, most institutionalized patients did not return to the community following removal of the reimbursement limit. Although this is not direct patient outcomes research, the inference appears to be clear. Programs that place arbitrary limits on reimbursement for medications diminish the utilization of essential and effective medications with a negative clinical outcome for patients. This is likely to be true for several classes of psychotropic medications as it is for all other essential medications. To make matters worse, when cost-containment measures produce increases in morbidity and cost shifting, it is likely that overall costs go up. For example, new data from the New Hampshire drug cap study suggest that this policy shifted service use among schizophrenic patients from the federal/state Medicaid program to the state mental health system (Soumerai and McLaughlin 1992).

Cost sharing (e.g., copayments) is another method used by state Medicaid plans to limit reimbursement for medications. Although copayments may have a more moderate impact on the utilization of essential medications, they clearly do have an impact, and there is suggestive evidence that low-income patients are equally likely to eliminate appropriate as well as inappropriate medications when faced with cost-sharing requirements (Soumerai and Ross-Degnan 1990). Given the degree to which mental illness and the use of psychotropic medications remain stigmatized in our society as well as the resistance, denial, and noncompliance seen in many psychiatric patients (Appelbaum and Gutheil 1980; Van Putten et al. 1976), it is likely that the impact of cost sharing on utilization of psychotropic medications will be greater than it is for many other classes of necessary drugs. This issue remains an important subject for further research.

The Omnibus Budget Reconciliation Act of 1990 (OBRA 90)

It is likely that other federal and state cost-containment regulations and hospital policies may, in fact, have adverse impacts on the appropriate utilization of psychotropic medications. OBRA 90 contained a number of provisions that could affect psychotropic utilization. Perhaps the most dramatic of these was a provision that currently allows state Medicaid programs to exclude reimbursement of all benzodiazepines or barbiturates. In 1990 five states excluded reimbursement for benzodiazepines or reimbursed only with prior authorization (Soumerai et al. 1993). The very implication that benzodiazepines are "nonessential" could have an unfortunate influence on their appropriate use.

Still another requirement of OBRA 90 was the establishment of prospective drug use review (DUR) programs to be conducted at the point of sale (by the community-based pharmacist) (Law notes 1991). Prospective review would require the pharmacist to obtain and record information about the patient and the patient's medical history and condition. State DUR boards are required to establish standards for retrospective and prospective review. Although the effects of such programs on prescribing judgments have not yet been adequately studied, one could hypothesize that they might exert an effect similar to that of triplicate prescription programs. As noted by Schwartz and Greenblatt (Chapter 9, this volume), when benzodiazepines were added to the triplicate prescription program in New York, appropriate prescribing of benzodiazepines diminished, at least in part, out of fear of regulatory scrutiny (Schwartz and Blank 1991). In addition, less safe and effective sedative hypnotics and antipsychotics were often substituted for benzodiazepines (Schwartz 1992). Although OBRA 90 required demonstration projects to evaluate the efficiency and cost effectiveness of prospective DUR, substantive data are not yet available. Drug utilization review may ultimately have an even greater impact on practice through its linkage to reimbursement. If insurers reduce or refuse benefit payments for prescriptions that are deemed medically unnecessary, the impact could indeed be great. The likelihood that prospective DUR would produce large numbers of "false positive" prescribing problems might also result in unintended reductions in appropriate medications. Increasingly health maintenance organizations (HMOs) and preferred provider organizations are aggressively seeking to manage the cost of pharmaceutical benefits through the use of preferred pharmacy networks, copayments, restricted formularies, and concurrent DUR. Again, there is a generally unproven assumption that such programs can "maximize cost savings while insuring appropriate drug use and quality of care" (Dichter 1993, p. 37). However, it is likely that some plans with a greater focus on quality of care may be able to achieve this objective, whereas others overemphasize cost saving to the detriment of quality.

Managed Care

A Rand Corporation study (Rogers et al. 1993) that followed 617 depressed patients over 2 years has demonstrated that seriously depressed patients treated by psychiatrists in prepaid plans have worse outcomes than those treated by fee-for-service psychiatrists. The patients treated in prepaid settings developed new limitations in role and physical functioning, whereas those treated in fee-for-service settings did better. Of note, there was a sharp decline in the use of antidepressant medication over the 2-year period for patients in prepaid settings compared with fee-for-service settings. The authors suggested that the nature of the care received was a more likely explanation of these differences than confounding factors such as severity of illness.

Although hard data regarding the impact of managed care practices on the use of somatic therapies in psychiatry are beginning to accumulate, there are much anecdotal data and even more speculation about the impact. Given the notable decline in utilization of inpatient services secondary to utilization review and precertification requirements, it is evident that a certain proportion of psychopharmacology trials previously performed on an inpatient basis have been shifted to the outpatient arena. We, unfortunately, have no data on the increased morbidity that might be hypothesized from undetected medication side effects, drug interactions, or other untoward events that may occur in a less supervised treatment setting.

The impact of the emphasis on reduced length of stay must also be considered. Taking time to assess a patient prior to initiating a treatment plan is now considered a luxury on inpatient psychiatry services. Drug-free periods, which are necessary to allow a period of "washout" of any other substances that may compound the patient's mental state and to allow for direct observation by those responsible for developing the treatment plan, may be more difficult to justify. Although the standard of care for a complete trial of a tricyclic antidepressant continues to require 6 weeks of treatment at a dosage in the therapeutic range, it is almost inconceivable to consider such full courses of treatment in the current inpatient atmosphere. Psychiatrists are pressed to augment treatment or to change antidepressants before trials are complete. As a result, patients may rapidly come to be considered treatment resistant, and their medical records may reflect that they have failed numerous medications (which by implication should not be used again in the future) when in fact they never received an adequate trial. In addition, patients are placed at the added risk of iatrogenic morbidity from agents used for augmentation when such agents may have been unnecessary had the preaugmentation phase of treatment been longer.

Likewise, clinicians may find themselves feeling pressured to choose electroconvulsive therapy (ECT) as the treatment of choice rather than to risk prolonged trials on antidepressants. Although evidence of the effectiveness of this treatment is overwhelming (American Psychiatric Association 1990; Consensus Conference 1985), ECT brings its own set of risks (e.g., those that attach to the use of general anesthesia).

Selecting between the various risks of ECT and antidepressant therapy on the basis of economic considerations may lead to a subtle but nevertheless unconscionable violation of ethical standards of practice and would certainly erode the foundations of informed consent.

As managed care practices move away from a reliance on utilization review and toward a greater reliance on the selection of preferred provider panels, we may find comparable impact on the use of somatic therapies. The establishment of provider panels requires a process that has come to be known as "economic credentialing." Individuals are selected for (or kept on) panels on the basis of their ability to perform efficiently, which is to say, their ability to operate within the principles of managed care. Traditional referral patterns will be further disrupted when, for instance, the psychopharmacologist of choice for your requested consultation turns out to have been excluded from the panel on the basis of economic credentialing. In fact, the limitation of closed provider panels has already reduced the ability to refer to colleagues exclusively on the basis of their expertise. Ultimately, referral patterns could be driven by financial rather than clinical credentials. Economic credentialing is likely to lead to the selection of practitioners who do not become entangled in lengthy psychotherapies. Although the evidence to date indicates that the optimal treatment for moderate to severe depression is a combination of medication and psychotherapy (American Psychiatric Association 1993), the deemphasis on psychotherapy could distort the appropriate use of pharmacotherapy and may lead to increased morbidity and perhaps mortality, particularly for patients requiring lengthy periods of psychotherapeutic treatment. These questions should be examined in future research.

Provider panels will undoubtedly place a heavy emphasis on nonpsychiatric mental health clinicians. At the same time there is likely to be an increased emphasis on nonpsychiatric physician generalists serving as gatekeepers to all specialty care. Although the developments outlined above may lead to an inappropriate overutilization of medication, these developments clearly threaten underutilization. Nonpsychiatrist mental health clinicians may fail to detect conditions that require medication or may have treatment philosophies that lead them to underutilize this approach. It is well established that depression is significantly underdiagnosed and improperly treated by nonpsychiatric physicians (Haggerty et al. 1986; Ketai and Hull 1978). This is especially true in elderly patients and has been shown to lead to significant morbidity and mortality (Rovner et al. 1991). In a review of the subject, Eisenberg (1992) cited the estimated rate of failure by primary care providers to detect psychiatric disorder to be 45%–90%. He concluded that the performance of generalists in the treatment of major depressive disorder is "woefully inadequate."

The American Psychiatric Associations's (APA) managed care hotline has received nearly 8,000 calls in its 3 years of operation. These complaints have provided data that "document significant problems with access to care, denial of safeguards for confidentiality, refusal to publish medical criteria, and other impediments to quality of care for the mentally ill" ("APA's Managed Care . . ." 1993, p. 1). In a letter to the Clinton administration's Task Force on Mental Health Reform, Jay Cutler, the APA's Director of Government Relations, summarized the clinical and administrative problems with managed care documented by the hotline. These included denial of access to care for chronic conditions such as schizophrenia, bipolar disorder, recurrent depression, and autism and arbitrary denial of coverage for conditions such as eating disorders, personality disorders, and chemical dependency. Other clinical findings included the following:

- Disparity among managed care companies in medical necessity and level of care criteria and subsequent disparity in access to care
- Arbitrary restriction of inpatient care, often limiting hospitalization to those who are a "danger to self or others," denying care for patients with medically complex conditions unless they are suicidal or homicidal
- Criteria for "severity" that prohibits prevention, early intervention, and appropriate maintenance treatment
- Denial of access to the full range of effective treatment modalities (e.g., limiting treatment for depression to medication while denying psychotherapy)
- Interruptions in the continuity of care
- Deleterious effects of "gatekeeping" by primary care providers who are untrained in the appropriate detection of and referral for mental illness (Cutler 1993)

Capitation and the Chronic Patient

One study attempted to ascertain the impact of placing chronically mentally ill individuals in capitated systems (Lurie et al. 1992). A cohort of chronic mentally ill Medicaid recipients who were randomly assigned to prepaid plans for mental health services was examined and compared with a group of Medicaid recipient control subjects who remained in a fee-for-service system. Although, overall, no consistent evidence of poorer outcome was detected for the capitated group, individuals with schizophrenia did experience a significantly greater decline in Global Assessment Scale scores in comparison with control subjects. The authors speculated that "attempts to limit utilization may have resulted in some treatment limitations or in a shift from psychiatrists to other providers who would be less likely to use psychotropic medications as an element of treatment" (p. 3304).

In another pilot program, the state of Massachusetts has shifted the mental health and substance abuse components of care for Medicaid patients to a managed care system. The Mental Health Management Administration won a contract in 1992 to manage inpatient and ambulatory services for more than 380,000 individuals on Medicaid. The program includes a waiver of the federal regulation prohibiting the use of Medicaid funds to pay for the hospitalization of adults in psychiatric hospitals, freeing the Mental Health Management Administration to contract with general and psychiatric hospitals alike. Although the Mental Health Management Administration appears to have saved the state Medicaid program $14 million in 1992 with larger savings projected for 1993 (Bass 1993), questions about the impact on the quality of care are being raised by consumers. These include charges of premature discharge from hospitalization of seriously mentally ill patients with a subsequent increase in rehospitalization rates, inadequate inpatient and aftercare services for substance abusers, and insufficient bed availability for children (Bass 1993). However, no objective population-based data are yet available to corroborate these case reports.

Fink and Dubin (1991) highlighted the risks of capitation systems for psychiatric hospital and HMO beneficiaries. Seltzer (1988) argued that the limitations on HMO services for mentally ill patients threaten to redefine chronic mental illness as "any mental illness that cannot be treated in 30 hospital days or 20 outpatient visits" (p. 138–139). He further argued that such service limitations not only redefine but also encourage chronicity, as inadequate treatment may lead to extended or even chronic dependence on medication and treatment down the road.

A final speculation on the relationship of the payment system to the nature of care delivered emerges from a review by Sharfstein and colleagues (1993). They noted that although Medicare has always paid for the evaluation of mental illness in a nondiscriminatory fashion, treatment of mental illness was always subject to more strict limitations than treatment of medical conditions. Although mental health coverage was extended in 1987 to a maximum of $1,100 from the previous maximum of $250, a 50% copayment remained in place. Of note, the modifications to Medicare reimbursement formulated in 1987 for the first time allowed for the *medical management* of mental disorders to be covered on the same basis as all other medical conditions (80% of approved charges). For the first time, physician-patient interactions revolving around the prescribing and monitoring of psychotropic medications would be paid on an equivalent basis with other medical management. This could be claimed as a victory of sorts for psychiatry and psychiatric patients, with a modest movement in the direction of nondiscriminatory reimbursement. However, one must also wonder about the negative influence that discrimination against the psychotherapeutic element of treatment might have. Does the differential reimbursement of the prescribing element of the relationship reinforce prescribing as compared with other therapeutic components? It would be hard to believe otherwise.

Clearly, careful investigation of the impact of cost-containment measures on mental health remains to be done. It is true that, at the time of this writing, as we contemplate national health care reform, we are in fact contemplating the imposition of multiple massive social experiments that will have a large impact on care long before that impact is readily understood. Were we contemplating changes in the scientific components of medical care that might be anticipated to have equivalent results, such changes could never be imposed without large-scale, controlled, experimental evaluation of the potential outcomes and informed consent concerning potential risks and benefits to affected patients.

References

American Psychiatric Association: The Practice of Electroconvulsive Therapy: Recommendations for Treatment, Training and Privileging. Washington, DC, American Psychiatric Press, 1990

American Psychiatric Association: Practice guideline for major depressive disorder in adults. Am J Psychiatry 150 (suppl 4):1–26, 1993

APA's managed care phone complaints to go to Clinton. Psychiatric News, May 7, 1993, pp 1, 16

Appelbaum PS, Gutheil TG: Drug refusal: a study of psychiatric inpatients. Am J Psychiatry 34:669–676, 1980

Bass A: Views mixed on plan for mentally ill. The Boston Globe, April 6, 1993

Consensus Conference: Electroconvulsive therapy. JAMA 254:2103–2108, 1985

Cutler JB: Letter to Mrs. Tipper Gore, Task Force on Mental Health Reform, by Jay B. Cutler, Special Counsel/Director, Division of Government Relations, American Psychiatric Association, May 5, 1993

Dichter E: Managing the drug benefit for cost and quality advantage. Journal of the American Association of Preferred Provider Organizations (AAPPO) 3:37, 41, 1993

Eisenberg L: Treating depression and anxiety in primary care: closing the gap between knowledge and practice. N Engl J Med 326:1080–1084, 1992

Fink PJ, Dubin WR: No free lunch: limitations on psychiatric care in HMO's. Hosp Community Psychiatry 42:363–365, 1991

Haggerty JJ, Evans DL, McCartney CF, et al: Psychotropic prescribing patterns of nonpsychiatric residents in a general hospital in 1973 and 1982. Hosp Community Psychiatry 37:357–361, 1986

Ketai RM, Hull AL: Tricyclic antidepressant prescribing habits: a comparison of family physicians and psychiatrists. J Fam Pract 7:1011–1014, 1978

Law Notes: Summary of 1990 Drug Rebate Legislation. American Journal of Hospital Psychiatry 48:114–117, 1991

Lurie N, Moscovice IS, Finch M, et al: Does capitation affect the health of the chronically mentally ill? JAMA 267:3300–3304, 1992

Omnibus Budget Reconciliation Act of 1990, Pub L No 101-508, 104 Stat 1388, as amended (1990)

Rogers WH, Wells KB, Meredith LS, et al: Outcomes for adult outpatients with depression under prepaid or fee-for-service financing. Arch Gen Psychiatry 50:517–525, 1993

Rovner BW, German PS, Brant LJ, et al: Depression and mortality in nursing homes. JAMA 265:993–996, 1991

Schwartz HI: An empirical review of the impact of triplicate prescription of benzodiazepines. Hosp Community Psychiatry 43:382–385, 1992

Schwartz HI, Blank K: Regulation of benzodiazepine prescribing practices: clinical implications. Gen Hosp Psychiatry 13:219–224, 1991

Seltzer DA: Limitations on HMO services and the emerging redefinition of chronic mental illness. Hosp Community Psychiatry 39:137–139, 1988

Sharfstein SS, Stoline AM, Goldman HH: Psychiatric care and health insurance reform. Am J Psychiatry 150:7–18, 1993

Soumerai SB, McLaughlin T: A case study in research on a state mental health specific policy change (abstract). Presented at The Use of Medicaid Data in Mental Health Services Research, workshop sponsored by the Services Research Branch, Division of Applied and Services Research, National Institute of Mental Health, Bethesda, MD, June 15–16, 1992

Soumerai S, Ross-Degnan D: Experience of state drug benefits programs. Health Aff (Millwood) Fall 1990, pp 36–54

Soumerai SB, Avorn J, Ross-Degnan D, et al: Payment restrictions for prescription drugs under Medicaid: effects on therapy, cost and equity. N Engl J Med 317:550–556, 1987

Soumerai SB, Ross-Degnan D, Avorn J, et al: Effect of Medicaid drug-payment limits on admissions to hospitals and nursing homes. N Engl J Med 325:1072–1077, 1991

Soumerai SB, Ross-Degnan D, Fortess EE, et al: A critical analysis of studies of state drug reimbursement policies: research in need of discipline. Milbank Q 71:217–252, 1993

Van Putten T, Crumpton E, Yale L: Drug refusal in schizophrenia and the wish to be crazy. Arch Gen Psychiatry 33:1443–1446, 1976

CHAPTER SEVEN

The Regulating Effect of the Managed Care Movement

Edward Hanin, M.D.

Few regulatory efforts by government have had the impact on American medicine that has been experienced as a result of "managed care" and "utilization review" instituted by employers and insurance companies in an effort to contain rising costs. Physicians are upset when regulatory requirements appear to interfere with the scientific practice of medicine. It is no surprise that physicians, both individually and through their professional societies, have expressed outrage and dismay about the impact of managed care.

Physicians are unhappy when we either cannot use a treatment that we feel would be effective or when we are forced to treat a patient by following protocols with which we do not agree. We like to believe that medicine is a pragmatic scientific discipline that takes objective research findings, replicates them, and then applies what has been learned to the care of patients who are suffering from a variety of illnesses. All of the other factors are irrelevant, or so we would like to believe.

The eminent historian Gerald N. Grob (1966), in his fascinating work *The State and the Mentally Ill,* provided the following quote from the distinguished physician, Dr. Oliver Wendell Holmes (1891), which is probably much closer to the truth:

> The truth is that medicine, professedly founded on observation, is as sensitive to outside influence, political, religious, philosophical, imaginative, as is the barometer to the changes of atmospheric density. Theoretically, it ought to go on its own straightforward inductive path without regard to changes of government or to fluctuations of public opinion. But . . . [actually there is] a closer relationship between the Medical Sciences and the conditions of Society and the general thought of the time than would at first be suspected. (p. 177)

Holmes' comments would certainly apply to how biological treatments have, over the years, been used in the treatment of mental illness and how factors other than their efficacy have affected their use.

The Proliferation of Mental Health Services and Costs

In psychiatry, although we glibly speak of the biopsychosocial model for the understanding and treatment of our patients, the tensions and splits between the biological, the psychological, and the social or environmental influences have often been more readily apparent than their interactions and mutual dependence. In the professional lives of many of us, we have seen psychiatry move from a discipline that emphasized the biological basis of severe mental illness and whose treatments were predominantly biological and rooted in the mental hospitals to become a field where concerns with environmental and interpersonal factors became dominant (Grob 1986). This change has resulted in a focus on the stresses of everyday life, in efforts directed toward the prevention of mental illness, a move on the part of most psychiatrists out of the hospitals and into office treatment settings, and a decline in interest and involvement with those who are severely mentally ill.

With the recent advances in research, especially in the areas of brain biology and neurophysiology, we have seen a revival of interest in the biology of the mental illnesses and in those illnesses felt to have a strong biological basis. Indeed, some would now encourage a different level of insurance benefit for those illnesses felt to be "biologically based," one that would put them on a par with benefits provided for "other physical illnesses" and be more comprehensive than those provided for "psychologically based" illnesses. Since many of those conditions commonly defined as severe mental disorders (e.g., schizophrenia, bipolar illness, panic disorders) fall into this category, there has been much support for such an approach to provide for broader benefits for those most severely disabled. Indeed such legislation has already been introduced in several state legislatures (e.g., California, Maine), and such a bill was introduced in the United States Senate with strong support from advocacy groups for the mentally ill. Others are unconvinced of the scientific basis for the sharp dichotomy between the biological and psychological factors in mental illnesses and have real concern that such legislation discriminates against care for individuals with significant impairment, even though their disability may not be as profound. American psychiatry continues to wrestle with this issue and is having significant difficulty in reaching consensus. Unquestionably, as interests have shifted, the acceptability and utilization of one form of treatment or another has also shifted.

Certainly in the years before World War II, psychiatry in America was essentially an inpatient specialty. Psychiatrists trained and worked in the large mental hospitals. By 1950, more than 550,000 patients resided in public mental hospitals throughout the country. Although many of these patients suffered from deteriorating organic disorders, and the public mental hospitals had unfortunately become warehouses for many senile elderly patients, those patients with disorders such as schizophrenia or affective disorders who required active care were treated with a range of biological treatments in attempts to control or reverse the symptoms of their illnesses.

Although not all such treatments were successful and not all have remained in our treatment armamentarium, they provided hope in a period when little else was available. Electroconvulsive therapy (ECT), especially for the treatment of severe depression, and the introduction of the antipsychotics in the 1950s certainly fundamentally changed the treatment of severely ill psychiatric patients and made deinstitutionalization and community care possible.

The impact of the experiences of World War II on American psychiatry cannot be overestimated (Grob 1986). The obvious impact of environmental stressors and the symptoms such stress could produce became very obvious as did the efficacy of nonbiological treatments and environmental supports and interventions. The large number of men rejected for military service also pointed to a broader public health issue. Psychiatrists felt that the insights gained in the treatment of patients could provide valuable insights into such global problems as war, violence, poverty, and other social ills.

Treatment moved out of the hospitals and into the community, which now became the locus for most treatment and for training.

Large numbers of nonphysician mental health workers were trained, since there were certainly not a sufficient number of psychiatrists to treat all patients who could use care under this broadened definition of mental illness. Lacking any medical background, the nonphysician mental health workers provided treatments that were much more likely to be psychotherapeutic in nature and directed at a new pool of patients who, although not as severely ill, would nevertheless be more likely to respond to the wide variety of treatment interventions now being offered. Hospitalization, should it be necessary, was much more likely to be accomplished in a community general hospital than in a mental hospital, and a marked shrinkage of the public sector occurred. At the same time, especially in those states where certificate of need requirements were abolished, the proprietary sector moved aggressively to develop private psychiatric hospitals in the community to respond both to the perceived need and to the opportunities provided by insurance benefits for inpatient care. This resulted in considerable "overbedding" in some areas. Despite predictions that this would lower costs through competition, this did not occur.

It is difficult to understand managed mental health care without this background. The care of mentally ill patients was, in many ways, moving into the mainstream of medicine. As such, care was more likely to be covered by the patient's insurance. That coverage more often than not was limited or discriminatory, but at least a portion of treatment was covered. In addition, mental illness was becoming much more broadly defined, with many more conditions included than had been true in the past.

With this broader definition, and with a large number of mental health practitioners entering the field from a variety of backgrounds, treatment approaches proliferated. Unfortunately, no clear-cut, generally accepted practice guidelines were defined or generally accepted by the field. The public's view of psychiatric treatment was often that of unending care, with no end point other than a patient's sense of satisfaction and contentment. The phrase "worried well" began to appear. There is no question that access to care was extended and that this was considered good. The cost implications of such an expansion of services had not yet become paramount.

At the same time, care was becoming far more technological and specific. Computed tomography scans and magnetic resonance imaging became a part of general psychiatric practice. New medications that required blood monitoring appeared. Lithium levels, antidepressant levels, and a variety of other laboratory tests were added to our treatment regimens in psychiatry. With access to care vastly expanded, with quality care becoming considerably more technological and costly, and with the credibility of our treatments often questioned by others, we were poorly prepared to defend ourselves when the growing concerns about the cost of medical care hit all of medicine. Health care had become a major industry accounting for more than 12% of the gross national product. Reports showed that the cost to employers of providing mental health services for employees was rising at an even more rapid rate than general health care. Large employers saw already shrinking profits being used to provide employees with health insurance. Small employers could no longer afford to insure their employees. Federal, state, and local governments sought to control rising costs through regulation and the establishment of expenditure caps. The private sector chose managed care.

What Is Managed Care?

Few people agree totally on any single definition of managed care. Despite this lack of precision, managed care has become, for some, the only way to control runaway health care costs, and for others, a euphemism for a rationing system that reflects all that is wrong with society's efforts to reduce the rate of growth of health care expenditures. An industry description attempts to define managed care as,

> A structured health care financing and delivery system that provides cost-effective care through organized relationships with physicians, hospitals, and other health providers. The goal of managed care programs is to deliver cost savings over traditional insurance programs along with high quality medical care.
> Broadly speaking, managed care programs can include:
>
> > prepaid health plans such as group or staff model health maintenance organizations (HMOs) or independent practice arrangements (IPAs);
> >
> > preferred provider organizations that offer discounts in exchange for incentives to use panel providers;

point of service products (POs) (often referred to as "open ended HMOs") that allow members to select either their primary care "gatekeeper" physician or, at a higher cost, another provider outside of the network; and

conventional indemnity plans that are "managed" in some way, usually by utilization management provisions on their enrollees.

Increasingly, managed care plans have the following common elements: (1) a commitment to appropriate care that is coordinated; (2) arrangements with selected providers to furnish comprehensive services to members; (3) incentives for members to use providers covered by the plan; (4) formal programs for on-going quality assurance; and (5) incentives for participating providers to be cost efficient (e.g., prospective pricing, capitation financing, negotiated fees and/or financial risk sharing). (Blue Cross/Blue Shield Association 1992, pp. 1–2)

The principles of managed care as defined above are being applied not just to psychiatry but to all of medicine. The nature of psychiatric illness and treatments, however, leaves psychiatry more vulnerable than other specialties. Nowhere else in medicine has it raised the storm of concern, anger, and protest that marked its entry into the management of psychiatric care (Hodgkin 1992). Relatively few psychiatrists or other mental health professionals had worked in HMOs or in other organized systems of care. Most, until quite recently, were private practitioners, working alone in an office practice, and not used to having treatment plans questioned, let alone rejected. Suddenly, or so it seemed, practitioners were on the defensive.

The impact was initially felt mostly by those whose practices included the care of patients in inpatient settings. Psychiatrists were asked to estimate length of stay and initiate discharge planning at point of admission. Their judgments as to the need for hospitalization were questioned, frequently by a reviewer with more limited credentials. Utilization reviewers used criteria sets that were not shared with physicians, who were therefore often unclear as to the reasons for adverse judgments. Anecdotal reports abound about inappropriate refusal of admission and pressure to discharge patients hastily. No systematic studies, however, have compared the quality of outcomes.

Unlike the surgical specialties that had developed many practice and procedural guidelines, psychiatry has been slow to do so. Psychiatrists were concerned that such guidelines could stifle creativity and lead to cookbook approaches to patient care. There may or may not have been validity to their concerns, but the absence of such practice parameters certainly encouraged the development of a variety of "utilization review criteria," developed by many different proprietary utilization review firms. These criteria, at the very least, reflected sets of beliefs not necessarily shared by all practitioners and, at their worst, were more concerned with cost reduction than with quality care. The proprietary nature of these criteria and the initial reluctance of many utilization review firms to share them with physicians and other providers have added yet further fuel to the fire and fostered distinctly adversarial relationships (Borenstein 1990; Sharfstein 1990).

It was through utilization review that most mental health practitioners were introduced to managed care, first in requirements for prior approval and ongoing concurrent review of inpatient care and, more recently, with concurrent review extended to ambulatory care as well. The relationship has hardly been a smooth or cordial one. Both sides saw the other as villain. Psychiatrists saw their patients being denied needed care. Outsiders, who did not know the patient and who in the eyes of the practitioners lacked clinical skill, were seen as applying arbitrary criteria in an arbitrary fashion. They were now determining, through control of reimbursement, how long a patient would stay in the hospital or how many sessions in the office would be covered. Physicians felt that, since this new industry of utilization review could be profitable only if costs were cut, cost containment rather than patient need and quality care was the primary objective of this activity. In at least one well-publicized instance these concerns were borne out. A huge volume of complaints against one managed care company led the insurance commissioner in Connecticut to establish a psychiatric review panel to study the complaints. The panel detailed "serious compromises of care" (Bakken 1991, p. 86), which included refusal to pay for necessary care and creation of other impediments to necessary treatment. The panel found the managed care company "was insensitive to and inflexible about continuity of care, confidentiality, coordination of care and differences in treatment approaches" (p. 86). Of note, in responding to these deficiencies, the commissioner mandated that the managed care company share with providers the clinical criteria used in the review process (Bakken 1991).

In response to mounting concern expressed by its members, the American Psychiatric Association opened a "hot line" for the reporting of difficulties and abuses experienced in contacts with the managed care industry. Initially, a large number of calls were received from physicians who were having difficulty with one or another of the utilization review firms. The complaints fell into several quite distinct categories:

1. Inordinate delays in reaching reviewers or in receiving decisions as to whether care was approved or disallowed. These complaints probably resulted from the rapid expansion of utilization review networks with inadequate training of staff and have lessened as more effective systems are installed.
2. Rudeness and hostile remarks by reviewers when challenging the physicians' plans for care. In reviewing the complaints, one often got the impression that diplomacy and tact were in short supply at both ends of the telephone line.
3. Significant differences in treatment philosophy between the treating therapist and the reviewer. When is it appropriate to hospitalize a patient? When can a recently suicidal patient be discharged? What are the indications for long-term intensive therapy?
4. Lack of awareness of the nature of an appeals process or the ineffectiveness of this review process in settling the dispute.

The American Psychiatric Association has used information from hot-line calls in establishing a dialogue with major managed care companies around issues raised by its members. Hopefully, such a dialogue can help address some of the real issues that have made the process of utilization review so adversarial. The American Psychiatric Association has also summarized its findings from the hot line in a letter to the administration's Task Force on Mental Health Reform (Cutler 1993). These findings are summarized by Schwartz (Chapter 6, this volume).

From the point of view of the managed care industry, scarce health care dollars were being wasted, and patients were being kept in hospitals for prolonged stays not because such care was needed but because insurance coverage was there. Miraculous cures that occurred just as the insurance ran out were cited. There had been inadequate use of transitional services, respite care, or crisis intervention, and little motivation to develop such programs. Psychiatric treatment seemed unending, with few guidelines as to when therapy was completed. Patients remained in treatments that fostered dependency on the therapist, rather than moves toward independence. Given the growing concerns about the cost of treatment of mental illness and substance abuse, managed care was seen as an alternative to arbitrary benefit caps or the possible elimination of coverage for mental disorders under health insurance. Employers were concerned that the cost of their mental health benefit was rising even more rapidly than general health costs and looked to "managed care" and "carve outs" as methods to control costs. Indeed, it is clear that utilization management has led to a sharp drop in inpatient stays and that intermediate and long-term inpatient intensive care programs now have major problems in keeping their beds full (Hodgkin 1992). Hospitals are now far from fully occupied, and this has resulted in some creative responses to this new challenge. They have reduced their number of beds, developed a broader range of ambulatory programs, and opened a variety of sheltered living facilities. They have become "health care systems." Unfortunately, the resultant decline in inpatient census has led to some questionable practices on the part of some facilities and hospital chains, which have tarnished the image of psychiatry and further weakened our credibility with employers, with insurance companies, and with the general public. Reports of unnecessary hospitalizations, "bounty hunters," and patient diagnosis to maximize reimbursement have harmed the reputation of all of psychiatry.

The Evolution of Managed Care

Utilization review and management is a costly activity. It requires a large staff of trained individuals to do the initial reviews and a sizable cadre of physicians either to approve questionable stays or to deny care. Such a system is required so long as the patient has free choice of physician and treatment by any professional is covered. Since no one physician treats that many patients, it is difficult to establish physician profiles of care, except for the most unusual circumstances. As long as every provider is in the system, a great deal of review has to be done. It is so much simpler if a smaller, closed pool of practitioners provides the care. One could rather quickly see who could work within the protocols developed and who could not. The latter could be dropped from the network. An appropriate mix of mental health providers could be established and a cadre of therapists developed, depending on the size and need of the group requiring treatment.

The development of preferred provider panels has been just such a development and is a second stage in the development of a managed care approach to psychiatric care. How such provider panels are selected is, of course, critical to whether quality care and the elimination of wasteful practices, or pure cost containment is the dominant factor. Providers and hospitals are willing to discount their rates and become part of the network because they are promised significant volume that will keep beds and practice hours filled. Facilities themselves have developed managed care programs and market their services directly to the insurance companies and to major employers. Many hospitals go into competition with their own voluntary attending staffs through the development of faculty practice panels and networks of providers in the community.

Increasingly, facilities and practitioners are agreeing to accept some of the risk by accepting a capitated or case rate for significant groups of patients. Some are developing their own managed care entities. With the development of selective provider networks, we are beginning to see a broader willingness to "flex the benefit," allow for exceptions, and provide for alternatives not necessarily covered in the policy. For example, day treatment services, ordinarily not covered under the patient's insurance, is substituted for unused inpatient days, speeding the patient's discharge, or perhaps preventing an admission altogether. There are also economic incentives for employees to choose such a limited provider panel over general indemnity coverage. Treatment within the "network" may be without the copayments or deductibles that would be required of an employee who wished to receive care outside of the closed panel. Access to membership on such panels has thus become a critical issue for many therapists. Issues such as how panels are selected, the criteria for admission or exclusion from panels, and the governance of such panels may well eclipse concerns about utilization management in the future.

Although there is debate as to whether managed care has been successful at holding down the overall cost of care (as opposed to cost shifting), certainly employers are convinced that creating integrated networks of care to manage the benefit produces savings (Washington Business Group On Health 1992). There has been a tremendous growth in the number of employees covered under a managed benefit, either by an HMO or through a preferred provider network. For example, in 1976, 40% of United States residents were covered through some form of Blue Cross/Blue Shield indemnity coverage and less than 5% received their care through an HMO. Preferred provider groups did not then exist. By contrast, in 1990 Blue Cross/Blue Shield coverage accounted for less than 30% of insured; the percentage of persons covered by HMOs had risen to almost 15%; and individuals served through preferred provider agreements now represented almost 35% of all insured (Snowden et al. 1992). This represents a fundamental shift in the way Americans receive their medical care and will have a profound effect on how psychiatry is practiced.

The Impact on Utilization of Somatic Therapies

A review of the criteria for care applied throughout the managed care industry allows us to identify a set of clinical principles that appear to drive the managed care approach. It is important to understand these principles if we are to assess the impact that managed care has had on traditional standards of care.

These principles include the following:

1. Most mental illness is episodic in nature, and the patient's need for treatment is episodic. Even in patients with chronic mental illness, the need for care may be episodic.
2. Treatment should be directed at restoring an individual who has been compromised by mental illness to functioning. Other goals such as personality enhancement are laudable but are not a covered service under managed care.

3. Treatment should be individualized and provided in a milieu as close to the patient's usual context as possible. Inpatient care should be avoided whenever possible and its use restricted to severe situations in which the health of the patient or others would be endangered by treatment in a less-restrictive setting.
4. If inpatient care is required, it should be limited to crisis intervention and be considered a phase in treatment with a clear goal of moving the patient to a less-restrictive milieu as rapidly as is consistent with good patient care. Care should be oriented to restoring the patient to function in the home or work environment or both as soon as possible.
5. There are few areas of consensus concerning the efficacy of psychiatric treatments. The existence of a credible treatment approach does not necessarily mean that such treatment will be reimbursed if shorter-term, more cost-effective treatments are available. Unless there is clear-cut evidence that a more costly and prolonged treatment is required and is more efficacious, such care will not be covered under managed care.
6. There are many different mental health providers with considerable overlap in what they do for patients. Especially in ambulatory care, and for those patients treated in psychotherapy, the use of costly psychiatric services should be reserved for those patients whose severity of illness demands that level of expertise. Others will be cared for by less costly mental health practitioners.
7. Benefits can be made "flexible" to provide for less-intensive services not necessarily covered under the patient's policy, which could reduce inpatient stays. This is defined as "case management" or "managing the benefit."

These principles are quite different from the traditional principles that have governed the care of psychiatric patients in the past. This is especially true in the area of inpatient treatment. In certain regards the impact is obvious. Patients are moved rapidly through the system, often with little time for a full assessment of the patient's condition, which is a necessary prelude to good treatment. Too little attention may be paid to patients whose response to treatment is a bit slower or whose physical condition or age requires a more gradual progression of therapies. The physician is pushed to make rapid changes in treatment without taking time to see if a treatment is effective or not.

When inpatient care is to be used only briefly and primarily for crisis intervention, the utilization of somatic therapies will be effected. As Schwartz (Chapter 6, this volume) highlights, provision of a prolonged assessment period has largely been eliminated. Assessment periods have long been viewed as an integral component of rational pharmacotherapy. They allow observation of the patient over 24–72 hours to diminish the requirement to make major treatment decisions prematurely. Further, such periods (optimally drug free) allow for the washout of psychoactive substances (prescribed or otherwise) that may be confounding the diagnostic picture. When inpatient days are strictly limited, the "luxury" of adequate assessment periods is threatened.

Another area of concern is the length of time allowed for trials of medication, particularly antidepressants. It remains the scientific standard that a full trial of tricyclic antidepressants takes 6 weeks. It is already true that, with the exception of patients on funded research units, virtually no patient can be so treated on an inpatient unit. Increasingly, psychiatrists are pressured to switch antidepressants or add augmenting agents. One negative result is the growing number of patients with histories of having failed various antidepressants who, in fact, have never received complete trials on these agents. Clearly, moving to an augmentation strategy sooner than necessary exposes the patient to an additional side-effect burden for the sake of cost savings, as does inappropriately rapid dosage escalation, driven by the same factors.

Psychiatrists have reported pressure by utilization managers to eliminate the 2-week washout period between treatment with a monoamine oxidase inhibitor and initiation of ECT, thus increasing the risk of anesthesia. Indeed, psychiatrists may find themselves pressured to choose ECT sooner to avoid hospitalizations that are lengthened by drug trial failures.

The impact of such negative outcome factors have yet to be systematically studied, and the impact that such concerns may have on the evolution of managed care is unknown.

It does not matter that the literature speaks to the efficacy of prolonged inpatient treatment for, say, the borderline patient. Absenting evidence that such treatment is the only way to treat such a patient, such care would be deemed inappropriate under managed care guidelines. Treatment plans are expected to be developed quickly, and discharge planning begins no later than the time of admission. Inpatient care for long-standing personality disorders or for the purpose of achieving major personality changes are out. If appropriate aftercare services do not exist, then it is up to the provider community to be sure they are developed. This includes many levels of supportive housing, transitional day treatment programs, respite care, and rehabilitation services, when appropriate. As new preferred provider networks are developed, those facilities and practitioners who cannot adapt to this new treatment environment will be dropped from the panel and will no longer receive referrals.

Impact of Managed Care on the Public Sector

Employers are not the only ones who have looked favorably on the apparent savings generated by managed care arrangements. The public sector too has been watching. Attempts to control the costs of the public mental health system through regulation and other means have not been successful. They are now looking to bring managed care (case management, limited provider networks, and utilization review) into the public sector to help control costs. Many questions remain to be answered about how such a system would operate given the multiple social and rehabilitative needs required by patients in the public sector. We do have a model in how psychiatric patients are handled in HMOs, as to how such a public system might operate (Dorwart and Epstein 1992).

HMOs have been around for a long time, with their greatest period of growth occurring recently. In a grossly oversimplified description, they have combined the elements of prepayment, capitation, and group practice in a delivery system that, proponents believe, offers quality cost-effective care (Feldman 1992). Such systems operate with primary care "gatekeepers" who provide the bulk of medical services and limit referrals to specialists. For most plans, the medical model has been the primary one, used with services restricted to inpatient care or outpatient visits. Mental health coverage has generally been restricted, often to the minimums required by federal regulation, although some plans do offer a broader menu of benefits. One of the reasons for the restrictive mental health benefit package has been to exclude patients with illnesses that would require longer-term care and would be costly for the plan. Stelovich (1992) described well the limitations of many HMO plans. Certainly, if this typical model is applied to public sector care and to the treatment of severe and persistently ill patients, who comprise many of the patients in the system, this would be disastrous to their care. This is not to say that the HMO model must be limited to such a restricted package of services. There is no reason that, with clearly defined populations and with a closed panel of providers selected to serve such a population, a much richer package of benefits could not be developed, one tailored to the population covered. However, the model would need considerable revision and broadening beyond traditional inpatient and outpatient services before it could be applied. There would need to be some way to support programs and services that would cut back on costly inpatient care and to pay for the nonmedical services that are so crucial to this population's survival in the community (Sharfstein and Stoline 1992; Surles et al. 1992).

A rising concern as the care of more and more patients is "managed" is that patients who could have been cared for by the private sector, but whose need for care exceeds the more limited availability of benefits, will now be pushed into the already overloaded public sector for care. One could certainly see that the potential is there, if the ratcheting down of benefits is guided only by economics and not by concerns for quality. This would not represent any reduction of the cost of care, but rather the shifting of such costs directly to the taxpayer. Although anecdotal reports of this phenomenon abound, it too remains to be systematically studied.

What About the Future?

Managed care is certainly here to stay. It is moving from pure utilization review functions to the development of selective networks of providers and to more complex interrelationships with groups of providers. Many employers continue to carve out mental health benefits and assign the management of that benefit to outside companies that provide the service for a fee. Increasingly, the larger employers and insurance companies, as they gain expertise and experience, are bringing that function back in-house. Although impressed with cost savings, major employers are concerned about the health of their employees and their ability to function well on the job. There is evidence that these concerns are beginning to balance overaggressive cost cutting by some managed care companies.

The managed care industry has been very concerned about governmental regulation, especially at the state level, seeing such regulation as attempts to limit their ability to operate in a cost-effective fashion. The industry, with the support of the American Medical Association, the American Psychiatric Association, the American Hospital Association, and other provider, insurance, and consumer groups has attempted to develop self-imposed voluntary accreditation standards through the formation of the Utilization Review Accreditation Commission (URAC). Minimal accreditation standards are now in place, and a process of voluntary accreditation has begun. These standards cover such areas as availability and credentials of reviewers, presence of a true appeals process, and rapid notification to providers of especially adverse decisions. A number of utilization review firms have sought and been granted this accreditation. However, an ever-increasing number of states, responding to concerns raised by both patients and providers, are developing regulatory statutes to govern the performance of managed care companies that serve their residents. Several states are requiring URAC accreditation for companies to operate. In an ironic twist, the existence of such a voluntary accrediting agency, with its own set of standards, has been used to prevent the imposition of more stringent regulation in the state of Connecticut.

The URAC also demonstrates how dialogue between managed care entities and providers has, to some extent, replaced purely adversarial relationships. No one group dominates, and all are at the table. All are involved both in the development of standards and in the accreditation process itself. However, URAC accreditation is, and should be, a voluntary process. Unless state regulations require or employers demand that utilization review companies acquire such accreditation, many firms see no need to do so. In addition, as utilization review functions are subsumed into larger managed care systems, the viability of an accreditation process that reviews only that aspect of a managed care network's activity is questionable. We are seeing a system in evolution whose final form and impact have not yet been determined.

At first glance, it would appear that the push for shorter lengths of stay, crisis intervention, and brief focused treatments will continue to encourage the use of somatic therapies, at least in inpatient settings. If the goal of an inpatient stay is to stabilize an acutely ill patient as rapidly as possible and return that individual to a functioning status as quickly as possible, then the use of antipsychotic and antidepressant medications would clearly be indicated. One would simply not have the time for the more gradual response to psychotherapy and counseling that has, in the past, been such an important factor in inpatient care, especially in the treatment of the character and personality disorders. However, as mentioned earlier, the push for rapid discharge can have a distorting effect on how medications and other somatic treatments are to be used and their effects assessed.

The rapidity with which ECT can end a severe, even suicidal depression, points to an increasing emphasis on this modality. If anything, physicians may be pushed to begin such somatic treatments too quickly, before their assessment and understanding of the patient is complete.

Inpatient care will now truly be directed to those conditions defined as severe mental illness, primarily the psychoses. These are also the conditions for which expanded health insurance coverage is being sought, in part through defining them as "biologically based illnesses." Being a biologically based illness does not mean that all treatment for that condition should be purely biological, but there is no doubt that reductionistic thinking threatens to lead to the equation of biological illness with biological treatment. We are far from objective, scientific evidence that severe mental illnesses, or the less severe mental disorders, are purely biological or psychological in nature, or that a treatment regimen should be purely biological or psychological. However, medicine is not a pure science, and one can readily see some of the pressures that drive managed care pushing us in that direction.

The picture is not that clear nor the issues that simple. The answer to the question as to how managed care will regulate the use of somatic treatment approaches in the future is unknown. Certainly for new treatments, some outcome studies that demonstrate efficacy (effectiveness plus reasonable cost) will need to be present before such treatments are accepted. As with so many other conditions in medicine, the cost-benefit ratio will be an increasingly prominent factor in decisions regarding care. The field will need to develop a much larger group of practice parameters and guidelines related both to the treatments of psychiatric disorder and to the appropriate use of a variety of somatic therapies, such as medications, ECT, and biofeedback. As with the rest of medicine, costly procedures and tests will need to be justified. To the extent that providers will be sharing both the cost and the risk with the various payers, there will now be institutional and personal provider incentives to control the costs of unnecessary tests. Again, practice parameters will be needed to define when, for example, magnetic resonance imaging with contrast is appropriate and when its use (and cost) cannot be justified. We psychiatric physicians have not always used resources in cost-effective ways. Treatment planning has not always been sharply focused. Tests and treatments have, at times, been unnecessarily delayed. Patients have been kept in hospitals beyond the point of maximum therapeutic effectiveness. We have not been blameless in the sharp rise in the cost of medical care. We will no longer be able to plan treatment without taking economic considerations into account.

The newer models of managed care will involve facilities and groups of providers in a fundamentally different way in decisions as to how patients under their care will be treated. To the extent that providers will go equally at risk for cost overruns or suffer financially if their contract assumptions were faulty, a new element will have entered into managed care, but one that will very directly affect practice patterns. Provider groups will be cost effective, or will fail. To the extent that somatic therapies are cost effective, they will have a friend in managed care. If their use raises the cost of care substantially, and there are any cost-effective alternatives, they will find diminished support in the managed care environment. It is safe to assume that the problems in the early utilization of clozapine and the impact of cost on utilization, for example, would have been the same whether managed care or Medicaid regulations were in place.

Who Will Provide Care? The Impact of Discipline, Specialty, and Training

A significant question remains. Who will care for mentally ill patients in this new world of managed medicine? How this question is answered will have a significant impact on how somatic treatments will be utilized in this new environment. Klerman and colleagues (1992) pointed out that two broad strategies have been advanced to reduce the unmet need for mental health care. One emphasizes the role of the general medical sector; the other the role of the specialty psychiatric sector. Depending on which approach is used, the implications for service planning and utilization are profoundly different. If the responsibility for the bulk of care is to be given to the primary care physician, with specialized mental health personnel called on only in special circumstances, then unless the training of such primary care physicians is vastly expanded and improved, we are very likely to see underdiagnosis of mental illness and inappropriate use of psychotropic medication.

From one point of view such an approach may be not an unreasonable way to deal with the issue of broadening access to care. Patients whose illnesses are currently unrecognized or untreated would receive care without the tremendous rise in the cost of that care that would result from treatment by highly trained specialists. Highly trained psychiatrists would be reserved for the difficult, treatment-resistant cases. Health care planning is clearly moving in the direction of the expansion of primary care and limitations on specialists. How this will play out and what its impact will be is of considerable interest to psychiatrists. As physicians, they would be open to the use of somatic therapies by primary care physicians. However, unless their training is expanded, generalists are likely to continue to use such treatments inappropriately and inadequately.

If mental health services are to be primarily provided by mental health specialists, then who are these specialists to be? What is the appropriate ratio of psychiatrist, psychologist, social worker, counselor, and so on, and who will decide to whom to refer the patient? Psychiatrists see themselves as being in the best position to provide the broadest service to patients and therefore most critical in any system. However, closed networks of care will find them a costly option. The questions will not arise with the profoundly depressed and suicidal patient. That patient will be referred to the psychiatrist and will in all probability be admitted to the hospital and be treated vigorously with either medication or ECT. But what about those patients whose dysthymic disorder makes them apprehensive and anxious, robs them of energy to function on the job or with their family, ends any pleasure in their accomplishments, and poisons their relationships with others? Will these patients be referred to a psychiatrist for treatment with medication and psychotherapy, or to a psychotherapist, or to a family or marital counselor? The key is, of course, the training and orientation of the person doing the triage, the gatekeeper. Whether primary care physician or mental health worker, that person's orientation, beliefs, and skills will have significant impact as to where such patients will be referred and what kind of treatment they will receive. Whether appropriate somatic treatments will be considered may depend in large part on the training of such individuals and on the training and expertise of the therapists to which they refer. Differences in discipline, training, and consequent treatment philosophy have been the source of a significant number of complaints to date to the American Psychiatric Association's managed care hot line.

Another important factor in what treatments survive will depend on the training of practitioners. For example, if treatment with ECT is limited to a few specialized programs, and most psychiatric residents neither see the response of patients treated with ECT nor gain any experience in administering the treatment, it will not be a treatment they are likely to use or recommend. Managed care will have a profound effect on medical education. As cost shifting and the expenses of training are eliminated from reimbursement and as major contractors eliminate their employees from the pools of patients used to train students, a rethinking of how medical education is to be funded will have to occur.

The impact of managed care on the use of somatic therapies is just a small part of its total impact on health care. We are looking at fundamental changes in the way in which health care is going to be organized, funded, and delivered in the future. Health care has become a major item in the national agenda, and calling the changes that are being proposed revolutionary is not an exaggeration. The impact of mandated health care services on governmental budgets is profound and is seen as out of control. Demands for access to care by those currently not able to use our health care system are growing, and the pressure to respond through reform is great. Employers are looking for ways to trim the cost of health care for their employees and are no longer willing to tolerate the cost shifting that allowed hospitals to provide "free" care to the uninsured and to support training programs in medicine and allied disciplines. The traditional financial supports for medical education are likely to crumble.

In mental health, we have probably already seen the major financial benefits that will come from strict utilization review of broad indemnity coverage using a wide range of physicians and others. The costs of such programs will no longer be matched by the savings they generate. Organized, selective networks of care utilizing principles of active case management seem to be the wave of the present and the future. Significant questions are being raised as to how solo practitioners, let alone groups and facilities, will operate in such networks. Several models are now moving forward, not all of them equally friendly to psychiatry and to the range of therapies that a psychiatrist can provide. Which practitioners are to be permitted in the network and what proportion of them are to be psychiatrists? What is the appropriate ratio of psychiatric physicians to other mental health professionals in the network? How we, as a profession, will be able to ensure that our patients receive quality care, somatic and otherwise, provided in an ethical and appropriate fashion in this time of great change will surely be one of the major challenges of the next decade.

References

Bakken E: Cigna Subsidiary Denied Payments for Needed Care Panel Finds, The Psychiatric Times-Medicine and Behavior, September 1991

Blue Cross/Blue Shield Association: State Barriers to Managed Care: Results of a National Survey of Blue Cross and Blue Shield Plans, 2nd Edition. Blue Cross/Blue Shield Association, July 1992

Borenstein DB: Managed care: a means of rationing psychiatric treatment. Hosp Community Psychiatry 41:1095–1098, 1990

Cutler JB: Letter to Mrs. Tipper Gore, Task Force on Mental Health Reform, by Jay B. Butler, Special Counsel/Director, Division of Government Relations, American Psychiatric Association, May 5, 1993

Dorwart RA, Epstein SS: Economics and managed mental health care: the HMO as a crucible for cost effective care, in Managed Mental Health Care: Administrative and Clinical Issues. Edited by Feldman J, Fitzpatrick R. Washington, DC, American Psychiatric Press, 1992, pp 11–27

Feldman J: The managed care setting and the patient-therapist relationship, in Managed Mental Health Care: Administrative and Clinical Issues. Edited by Feldman J, Fitzpatrick R. Washington, DC, American Psychiatric Press, 1992, pp 219–229

Grob GN: The State and the Mentally Ill. Chapel Hill, University of North Carolina Press, 1966

Grob GN: Psychiatry and social activism: the politics of a specialty in postwar America. Bull Hist Medicine 60:477–501, 1986

Hodgkin D: The impact of private utilization management on psychiatric care: a review of the literature. Journal of Mental Health Administration 19:143–157, 1992

Holmes OW: Medical Essays 1842–1882. Boston, MA, Houghton Mifflin, 1891

Klerman GL, Olfson M, Leon AC, et al: Measuring the need for mental health care. Health Aff (Millwood) 11:23–33, 1992

Sharfstein SS: Utilization management: managed or mangled psychiatric care. Am J Psychiatry 147:965–966, 1990

Sharfstein SS, Stoline AM: Reform issues for insuring mental health care. Health Aff (Millwood) 11:84–97, 1992

Snowden K, Feeley F, Jacobsen L: Background Paper on Strategic Planning. Psychiatrist Purchasing Group, 1992

Stelovich S: Managed care and major mental illness: an overview, in Managed Mental Health Care: Administrative and Clinical Issues. Edited by Feldman J, Fitzpatrick R. Washington, DC, American Psychiatric Press, 1992, pp 249–260

Surles RC, Blanch AK, Stern DL, et al: Case management strategy for systems change. Health Aff (Millwood) 11:151–163, 1992

Washington Business Group on Health: A Vision of the Future Health Care Delivery System: Organized Systems of Care. Prepared for Washington Business Group on Health Invitational Meeting: "A Dialogue on the Future of Health Care Delivery," May 1992

Regulation of Controlled Substances and New Drug Development

Law and Scientific Practice at the Crossroads

CHAPTER EIGHT

Controlled Substances, Medical Practice, and the Law

David E. Joranson, M.S.S.W.
Aaron Gilson, M.S.

The development of drug control policy in the United States has been characterized by vacillation between tolerance and intolerance toward drugs (Musto 1987). Today's war on drugs is distinguished by intense media coverage of drug-related crime, new antidrug laws, and efforts to educate schoolchildren and the public to "just say no" to drugs. The message is clear: Drugs are dangerous and must be avoided. The United States continues to have significant drug abuse problems that must be addressed, but we should be careful not to reject the medical benefits of drugs or restrict the ability of physicians to care for patients.

Antidrug efforts are directed not only at the illegal controlled substances such as marijuana, heroin, and cocaine, but also at the legal controlled substances that have important medical uses: the opioids (narcotics), stimulants, and sedative hypnotics. These efforts involve media campaigns against perceived overprescribing (Safer and Krager 1992), vigorous enforcement efforts against suspect prescribers (Benton 1993; Hill 1989; McIntosh 1991a, 1991b; Nowak 1992), regulations to increase restrictions on prescribing (Weintraub et al. 1991), and federal proposals to monitor all prescribing to patients of all controlled substances (Stark 1990).

When controlled substances are used for medical purposes, they can provide great improvements in the quality of life for millions of people with debilitating diseases and conditions, including pain, severe anxiety, narcolepsy, and epilepsy. However, when diverted from the

Assistance from Heather Horn in preparing the manuscript is gratefully acknowledged.

legitimate distribution system, the nonmedical use of controlled substances can lead to serious public health problems. For example, there are a small percentage of practitioners who abuse their privilege to prescribe and are a source of drugs for addicts and the illicit market. Consequently, it is in the public interest to protect the medical uses of controlled substances while at the same time preventing their diversion and abuse. Public policy should recognize the dual effect of controlled substances on public health to obtain the broadest medical benefit while reducing the risks of diversion and abuse.

There is troubling evidence that some controlled substances laws and regulations and their enforcement interfere with medical practice and patient care. In this chapter we explore whether controlled substances laws and regulations achieve an appropriate balance between controlling abuse and protecting medical use. The primary focus is on the opioids (narcotics) that are used in the somatic treatment of pain, in particular pain due to cancer.

Tragically, cancer pain is often undertreated. Several factors impede pain management, including inadequate preparation of health care professionals, the low priority given to pain management, and the effects of antidrug policies. Although most, if not all, cancer pain can be relieved (Foley 1985; Takeda 1987), it is estimated that one-half to three-quarters of cancer patients with pain are inadequately treated and that nearly 25% die with severe unrelieved pain (Daut and Cleeland 1982). The mainstay of cancer pain management is opioid therapy (World Health Organization 1986). Efforts to improve pain management and eradicate misuse and abuse of prescription controlled substances take place in a medical and regulatory environment characterized by misinformation about opioids. Misinformation about opioids and exaggerated fears of addiction are prevalent among the professions and medical regulators and are partly responsible for the undertreatment of pain (Ferrell et al. 1992; Jaffe 1989; Jasinski 1989; Joranson et al. 1992; Morgan 1986).

The Framework of Controlled Substances Policy

Three tiers of law establish the policy framework that governs the medical use and diversion of controlled substances: 1) international treaties, 2) federal laws and regulations, and 3) state laws and regulations. As will be seen, international and federal laws clearly recognize the principle that a balance should be maintained between controlling drug abuse and ensuring that controlled substances are available for medical use. However, most state laws do not achieve this balance and, in some instances, interfere with medical practice.

International Treaties, Drug Control, and Medical Use

Treaties provide the basic legal framework for controlling international and domestic production and distribution of drugs that have been determined to have an abuse liability. The principal treaties recognize that many controlled substances are *indispensable* to public health and that their availability for legitimate medical and scientific purposes must be ensured. These treaties are the Single Convention on Narcotic Drugs, 1961 (United Nations 1977b), and the Convention on Psychotropic Substances, 1971 (United Nations 1977a). In becoming a party to a treaty, a government agrees to ensure the availability of controlled substances for medical purposes. Most, but not all, of the governments of the world have acceded to these treaties (International Narcotics Control Board 1991).

The International Narcotics Control Board, the United Nations agency responsible for monitoring governments' compliance with the treaties, has reported that opioids are not sufficiently available for legitimate medical purposes throughout the world and that this is due in part to antidrug abuse laws and regulations that unduly restrict the availability of opioids for medical use (International Narcotics Control Board 1989).

A World Health Organization expert committee has also expressed concern that the fear of drug abuse has curtailed appropriate medical use of opioids, particularly for the treatment of cancer pain (World Health Organization 1990); laws are so strict in some countries that physicians cannot prescribe morphine for cancer pain. The expert committee commented on "multiple copy prescription programs" that are used in several countries as well as in several states in the United States.

> The extent to which these programmes restrict or inhibit the prescribing of opioids to patients who need them should be questioned. . . . Health care workers may be reluctant to prescribe, stock or dispense opioids if they feel that there is a possibility of their professional licenses being suspended or revoked by the governing authority in cases where large quantities of opioids are provided to an individual, even though the medical need for such drugs can be proved. (World Health Organization 1990, p. 39)

Thus, although the purpose of the international treaties is to ensure availability of drugs for medical use, restrictive laws in some countries limit the use of opioids for the treatment of pain. To what extent do laws and regulations in the United States maintain a balance between the control of drug abuse and the appropriate medical use of opioid analgesics or other controlled substances?

Federal Law and Medical Practice

THE FEDERAL FOOD, DRUG, AND COSMETIC ACT

The Food and Drug Administration (FDA) has approved opioids, stimulants, and sedative hypnotics as safe and effective for medical use and commercial marketing under the Federal Food, Drug, and Cosmetic Act of 1962. This act does not restrict a physician's prescribing either to labeled indications or to recommended doses. This policy is clearly stated in the foreword to the *Physician's Desk Reference* (1993). Once a product has been approved under the Federal Food, Drug, and Cosmetic Act for marketing, a physician may prescribe it for uses, in treatment regimens, or in patient populations that are not included in the approved labeling (Federal Register 1983). Appropriate medical practice and patient interest require that physicians be free to administer drugs according to their best knowledge and judgment (Federal Register 1975).

> New uses for drugs are often discovered, reported in medical journals and at medical meetings, and subsequently may be widely used by the medical profession. . . . When physicians go beyond the directions given in the package insert it does not mean they are acting illegally or unethically, and Congress does not intend to empower the FDA to interfere with medical practice by limiting the ability of physicians to prescribe according to their best judgment. (*United States v. Evers* 1981)

In addition, the federal courts have supported the principle that the FDA does not regulate medical practice (*United States v. Evers* 1981). It is generally recognized that the states, not the federal government, regulate the practice of medicine and that federal law generally defers to state law in areas where there is not a direct conflict (see amendments to the Federal Food, Drug, and Cosmetic Act 1962).

THE CONTROLLED SUBSTANCES ACT

Opioids, stimulants, and sedative hypnotics are additionally subject to controlled substances laws because of their abuse liability. The federal Controlled Substances Act (CSA) (1970) parallels the international treaties, by regulating production and distribution and prohibiting nonmedical use of controlled substances, while clearly recognizing their medical value to public health. The CSA states that "many of the drugs included within this title have a useful and legitimate medical purpose and are necessary to maintain the health and general welfare of the American people" (p. 834).

Controlled substances are placed in five schedules. Drugs with no accepted medical use are placed in Schedule I and are available only for scientific research. Drugs that have been approved for medical use are placed in Schedules II–V according to potential for abuse, with drugs having the highest potential for abuse assigned to Schedule II. Although prescriptions for certain controlled substances must be in writing, and refills are limited, the fact that a drug has been approved for medical use does not change when it becomes a controlled substance.

Today's medical and psychiatric practitioners are probably more familiar with legal restrictions over controlled substances prescribing than they are with the legal provisions that were included in the CSA to ensure that drug law enforcement does not interfere with medical practice. For many years prior to the adoption of the CSA in 1970, narcotic prescribing was marked by controversy between drug law enforcers and physicians (Musto 1987). This controversy reached its pinnacle in 1970 during congressional consideration of the new Controlled Substances Act. Congress was considering legislation drafted by the Bureau of Narcotics and Dangerous Drugs in the Department of Justice. The bill proposed that the Department of

Justice and an advisory committee appointed by the attorney general would be solely responsible for making the scientific and medical findings necessary to place a drug under the control of the CSA (Committee on Ways and Means 1970). There was deep concern in the scientific and medical community when it was learned that this bill would give law enforcement complete authority over scientific and medical decisions (Committee on Ways and Means 1970). Following testimony from numerous physicians, the American Medical Association, and the American Psychiatric Association, Congress adopted a different bill that placed the responsibility for medical and scientific determinations in the Department of Health, Education, and Welfare (now the Department of Health and Human Services) and specified that its determinations were binding on drug control decisions made by the attorney general (Controlled Substances Act 1970). Other provisions of law and legislative history make it clear that the CSA is not intended to interfere either with medical practice or the availability of these drugs for patient care (Joranson 1990a; United States House of Representatives 1970).

The Availability of controlled substances for medical purposes is ensured. In an effort to control diversion from excessive manufacture of drugs, the CSA gives the Drug Enforcement Administration (DEA) authority to set production quotas for a number of opioids, stimulants, and sedative hypnotics. Quotas must accommodate all legitimate medical and scientific needs (Controlled Substances Act 1970). In one instance, however, the DEA tried to stop diversion of methylphenidate at the retail level by setting a very low production quota. This action led to an official statement of the principle of "undisputed proposition of drug availability":

> The CSA requirement for a determination of legitimate medical need is based on the *undisputed proposition* that patients and pharmacies should be able to obtain sufficient quantities of methylphenidate, or of any Schedule II drug, to fill prescriptions. A therapeutic drug should be available to patients when they need it. . . . The harshest impact of actual and threatened shortages falls on the patients who must take methylphenidate, not on the manufacturers to whom the quotas directly apply. Actual drug shortages, or even threatened ones, can seriously interfere with patients' lives and those of their families. (Federal Register 1988, pp. 50593–50594; italics added)

In addition to recalculating the quotas for methylphenidate, the DEA has expressed willingness to grant additional quotas for opioids to respond to improvements in the treatment of cancer pain (Max 1989).

Medical practice is not regulated by the CSA. The states, not the federal government, have the authority to regulate medical practice. This authority is based on the police power in state constitutions and underlies the medical practice acts that are designed to protect the public health and safety (Parmet 1989). The CSA was not intended to supersede the authority of the Federal Food, Drug, and Cosmetic Act (United States House of Representatives 1970) and provides no authority for the DEA to regulate medical decisions such as the indications for which a drug may be prescribed and the amount or the duration of therapy.

However, the DEA promulgated a regulation in 1986 that could negatively affect medical practice in the care of cancer patients. The regulation placed the new synthetic tetrahydrocannabinol product (THC) into Schedule II following its approval for medical use by the FDA (Federal Register 1986). Because of the drug's chemical relation to marijuana, the regulation stated that physicians who choose to prescribe the drug for other than the specifically labeled use (for the treatment of cancer chemotherapy-induced nausea and vomiting that is unresponsive to other modalities) may subject themselves to investigation for possible violation of the CSA. The DEA argued that the policy was necessary to comply with United States treaty obligations governing marijuana and THC under the Convention on Psychotropic Drugs. Many medical organizations objected to this interference in medical decisions and in FDA policy that allows off-label prescribing. Any rationale for the DEA policy disappeared when THC's international classification was changed to reflect its medical use, but the regulation has not been repealed.

Further, the *Pharmacist's Manual* (United States Department of Justice 1986) lists indications "which may indicate that a purported prescription order was not issued for a legitimate medical purpose in the course of the physician's professional practice" (p. 31), including "Does the purported prescription order contain an indication other than one found in the package insert?" (p. 32).

The DEA's enforcement authority is intended to be concentrated on those practitioners who engage in unlawful use of controlled substances outside of medical practice. Indeed, it is unlawful for a practitioner to prescribe a controlled substance except in the course of professional practice. The phrase *in the course of professional practice* defines the boundaries of practitioner investigations and prosecutions for the DEA.

> It matters not that such acts might constitute terrible medicine or malpractice. They may reflect the grossest form of medical misconduct or negligence. They are nevertheless legal. On the other hand, any act of prescribing, dispensing or distributing of a controlled substance other than in the course of the registrant's professional practice is an illegal distribution of that controlled substance, subject to the same penalties as if the drug were sold by the lowest pusher on the street. (Stone 1983, p. 23)

The intent of the CSA to avoid interference with medical practice was reaffirmed in 1978 when Congress enacted a law to satisfy United States obligations under the Convention on Psychotropic Substances. In so doing, Congress determined that control of psychotropic substances (e.g., tetrahydrocannabinol, benzodiazepines) in the United States should be accomplished within the framework of the CSA to ensure that their availability "for useful and legitimate medical and scientific purposes will not be unduly restricted" (Controlled Substances Act 1970, p. 836). Further, the law stated that nothing in the treaties was to "interfere with ethical medical practice in this country as determined by the secretary of Health and Human Services on the basis of a consensus of the American medical and scientific community" (p. 836).

Treatment of addiction is distinguished from treatment of intractable pain. It is essential to differentiate between prescribing opioids for intractable pain and prescribing them for addiction. When Congress adopted the new CSA, it also settled a long controversy between drug law enforcement and health officials about the lengths a physician could go in prescribing opioids to narcotic addicts (United States House of Representatives 1970). Congress decided that prescribing opioids for narcotic addiction was outside of professional practice and, therefore, unlawful under the CSA, unless the physician was specifically registered in the Narcotic Treatment Program to use methadone to maintain or detoxify narcotic addicts. Consequently, the definition of *addict* becomes critically important, particularly in view of long-standing problems in defining terms associated with drug abuse phenomena. The CSA defines *addict* as a person who "habitually uses any narcotic drug so as to endanger the public morals, health, safety, or who is so far addicted to the use of narcotic drugs as to have lost power of self-control with reference to his addiction" (Controlled Substances Act 1970, p. 836).

The CSA definition of *addict* is imprecise and does not parallel the definition of *drug dependence* of the World Health Organization (1969) or the DSM-IV (American Psychiatric Association 1994). The definition does not distinguish an addict from a patient who is simply physically dependent on an opioid for pain management. However, controlled substances regulations promulgated by the DEA make it clear that a physician who prescribes opioids to treat intractable pain over an extended period is considered to be acting within the professional practice of medicine.

> This section is not intended to impose any limitation on a physician or authorized hospital staff to . . . administer or dispense (including prescribe) narcotic drugs to persons with intractable pain in which no relief or cure is possible or none has been found after reasonable efforts. (Code of Federal Regulations, Title 21 Part 1306.07 [c], April 1988)

State Laws and Prescribing of Controlled Substances

Like federal law, state controlled substances laws prohibit nonmedical use of controlled substances. Unlike federal law, most state controlled substances laws, although they permit prescribing, do not explicitly recognize either the public health benefits of controlled substances or the need to balance their control by ensuring availability for medical purposes. In fact, some state laws and regulations that have been enacted to deal with drug abuse and diversion clearly interfere with medical practice and patient care.

Today's state controlled substances laws are based on a 1970 model law called the Uniform Controlled Substances Act (UCSA). The purpose of the 1970 UCSA was to repeal a plethora of antidrug laws that individual states had adopted since the turn of the century and replace them with a single unified framework to achieve consistency in national drug control policy (National Conference of Commissioners on Uniform State Laws 1970). But instead of establishing a federal-like balance of power between law enforcement and medical science, the UCSA only mentioned in a prefatory note that states could consider establishing an advisory committee to the regulatory agency, an alternative that was rejected by the Congress. The UCSA did not mention the importance of ensuring the availability of controlled substances. A definition of *addict* was also not included, leaving the states without a uniform definition, such as had been developed by the World Health Organization (1969). The UCSA, like the CSA, did not regulate medical decisions such as the quantity of a drug that may be prescribed at one time.

Although the UCSA was adopted in some form in most states, a number of states did not repeal old laws. In addition, some states have adopted new laws and regulations that restrict prescribing and dispensing of FDA-approved drugs. For example, South Carolina's controlled substances law prohibits the prescribing of any controlled substance for a use other than approved by the FDA, and the use of methadone as an analgesic is restricted to patients in hospitals (South Carolina Health Code 1984). A review of state-controlled substances law reveals additional examples of nonuniform provisions that interfere with the use of controlled substances in medical practice (Joranson 1990a). The following are several examples:

Pain Patients May Be Confused With Addicts

It should be recalled that federal law, which is applicable in every state, defines *addict* as an individual who is a danger to society, whose need for opioids can be legally provided for only by specially registered narcotic treatment programs, and for whom a physician may not prescribe opioids unless for pain. A number of state definitions allow confusion of an *addict* with a pain patient who is only physically dependent on an opioid (Joranson 1990a). However, physical dependence is a common physiologic consequence of using opioids to treat chronic pain and should not be confused with *addiction* (American

Pain Society 1992). For example, the New York State Controlled Substances Act defines *addict* as "a person who habitually uses a narcotic drug and who by reason of such use is dependent thereon" (New York State Controlled Substances Act, Sect 3302.1, p. 467). A companion provision states that controlled substances may not be prescribed for an addict, unless he or she is a "bona fide patient suffering from an incurable and fatal disease such as cancer or advanced tuberculosis" (New York State Controlled Substances Act, Sect 3351 [b], p. 524). Some states require physicians to report to the government those patients who have been treated longer than several months with a Schedule II controlled substance. New York requires these people to be reported on a special state form *as addicts* (Joranson 1990a). These laws are similar to one in California that was enacted many years ago, apparently as an alternative to "the removal of abusable Schedule II drugs from the commercial market" (Tennant 1981, p. 193). The law required physicians to report habitués to the state's Bureau of Narcotic Enforcement. Before repeal, the largest single category of habitués to opioids that had been reported were individuals with diagnoses of cancer (Joranson 1990a).

THE QUANTITY PRESCRIBED MAY BE LIMITED TO LESS THAN MEDICALLY INDICATED

Although federal law does not limit the amount that can be prescribed, a number of states have restricted the number of dosage units that can be dispensed to as little as 100 dosage units or a 5-day supply (Joranson 1990a) (see Table 8–1). Since it is not uncommon for a cancer patient to take 30–50 pills a day for pain management, prescriptions must be dated every 2 or 3 days. Restricting the prescription amount to less than the medical needs of the patient can result in greater expense to obtain more frequent prescriptions as well as additional dispensing fees. Unfortunately, pain management may also be affected. One Indiana physician has a number of cancer pain patients who need large quantities of opioids and whose insurance plan requires the use of a mail-order pharmacy in New Jersey (which limits dispensing to 120 dosage units per prescription). This physician, whose prescriptions are mailed to New Jersey every few days, reports that his patients ration their medication because of delays in delivery (Joranson 1990a). As a result, these patients experience pain that could be relieved if they had a predictable and sufficient supply of medication.

In Wisconsin, the Controlled Substances Board found that the "120 dosage units or a 34-day supply whichever is less" rule was confusing and unnecessarily limited prescribing of controlled substances, especially in the treatment of cancer pain. Further, the rule was not useful in preventing diversion (Joranson and Bachman 1988). In cooperation with the Pharmacy Examining Board, the rule was amended in 1991

Table 8–1. Examples of state restrictions for Schedule II controlled substances

State	Restriction
Missouri	30-day supply (may be increased up to 6 months if medical reason is described on prescription)
New Hampshire	34-day supply or 100 dosage units, whichever is less (C-III also) (up to 60-day supply for amphetamine or methylphenidate if for ADD or narcolepsy)
New Jersey	30-day supply or 120 dosage forms, whichever is less
New York	30-day supply for C-II (triplicate) (except up to 3 months if for relief of pain in patients 65 years of age or over and suffering from diseases known to be chronic and incurable; minimal brain dysfunction in patients not more than 16 years of age; convulsive disorders, narcolepsy, or panic disorders). Same if for written Rx for C-III, IV, and V; if an oral Rx for C-III or V, up to a 5-day supply; if an oral Rx for C-IV, up to 30 days or 100 dosage units, whichever is less
Rhode Island	100 dosage units per prescription; no more than 100 dosage units may be dispensed at one time (C-II, III, IV)
South Carolina	30-day supply or 120 dosage units, whichever is less
Utah	1-month supply
Wisconsin	34-day supply (except up to a 90-day supply for C-III or IV anticonvulsant substance)

to delete the 120 dosage unit restriction.

Limitations on the number of dosage units for controlled substance prescriptions are not confined to laws and regulations. Mail-order pharmacy members of the American Managed Care Pharmacy Association have guidelines that specify that dispensing of Schedule II controlled substances must be limited to the amount necessary to meet the legitimate medical needs of the patient.

> The dispensing of Schedule II substances should be limited to a 30 day supply, or 120 dosage units, whichever is less. . . . These maximum quantity limitations enable the patient to obtain a reasonable quantity of controlled substances to assist in an established medical regimen. (American Managed Care Pharmacy Association, undated, p. 3)

American Managed Care Pharmacy Association materials state that these guidelines are consistent with the policies of the DEA, although as stated previously, neither federal law nor the DEA regulations limit the quantity of a Schedule II prescription. Nevertheless, the DEA wrote to the American Managed Care Pharmacy Association in 1990: "The DEA commends the efforts your members have made to the implementation of the Guidelines. The Office of Diversion Control is pleased to offer our continued support of your Association" (American Managed Care Pharmacy Association, undated, p. 3).

PRESCRIPTION MONITORING PROGRAMS
INTERFERE WITH MEDICAL PRACTICE

Multiple copy prescription programs (MCPPs), or "triplicate" prescription programs, began in the United States with the New York program in 1913 (see Table 8–2). These programs are established to curtail diversion of Schedule II drugs "without adversely affecting the supply of medication to the legitimate user" (United States Department of Justice 1987, p. 4). MCPPs typically require physicians and pharmacists to use a special multipart government prescription form so that prescribing and dispensing of certain drugs to patients can be monitored by a designated state regulatory or enforcement agency. MCPPs differ from state to state. For example, the New York law provides that prescriptions for all drugs subject to the triplicate program must be written and are not refillable; these are controls that are reserved for Schedule II drugs under the CSA and UCSA. The result is that Schedule II prescription controls were imposed on the benzodiazepines (Schedule IV) when New York added these drugs to the triplicate prescription program in 1989.

The DEA reports that implementation of MCPPs results in prescription decreases of 50% or more in the period following implementation, reduction in the state's per capita consumption of the substances, and significant reduction in physician requests for triplicate forms in successive years. Administrators of MCPPs insist that these programs do not compromise the quality of medical care; indeed, they claim that medical practice has been improved because practitioners tend to examine more closely their reasons for prescribing and often choose a less potent analgesic or a smaller quantity (United States Department of Justice 1987). The DEA strongly supports implementation of legislation to adopt these programs in all states (United States Department of Justice 1987, 1990).

The Risk of Regulatory Scrutiny

Researchers, clinicians, and policy specialists have expressed concern that strict prescription monitoring can interfere with appropriate prescribing and limit patient care (Angarola and Wray 1989; Foley

Table 8–2.   Multiple copy prescription programs

Year	State
1913–1915; 1972	New York
1940	California
1943	Hawaii (duplicate)
1961	Illinois
1967	Idaho
1978	Rhode Island (duplicate)
1982	Texas
1989	Michigan
1989	Indiana

1989; Hill 1989; Joranson 1990a; Max 1990; Portenoy 1990). Indeed, researchers have reported that an MCPP hampered the prescribing of Schedule II opioids for terminally ill patients with chronic pain (Berina et al. 1985). The substitution of weaker opioids in lower schedules for more potent opioids was encouraged by an MCPP (Sigler et al. 1984). Furthermore, factors such as "excessive regulation" and "reluctance to prescribe" were identified as significantly greater barriers to pain management by physicians who treat cancer patients in states with MCPPs than by physicians in states without these programs (Von Roenn et al. 1993). Of the physician members of the American Pain Society who responded to a survey, 40% agreed that their prescribing of opioids for chronic nonmalignant pain was influenced by legal concerns (D. C. Turk, personal communication to D. E. Joranson, December 1992; Turk and Brody 1992). A pilot study found that more than one-half of physicians surveyed reported that they would reduce the dose or quantity, reduce the number of refills, or choose a drug in a lower schedule because of concern about regulatory scrutiny (Weissman et al. 1991).

Although documented, these concerns are not necessarily recognized as valid by regulatory agencies:

> Nothing in the multiple copy program limits or restricts medical judgement as to which drug or amount to prescribe. They must simply write the prescription on a different form. . . . Physicians do not abandon their professional training, oath, and duty to their patients because a prescription for a specific drug requires a state-issued prescription blank. . . . The concern about MCPPs interfering in the management of pain is frequently raised in reference to, specifically, cancer pain. The word cancer evokes an emotional, fearful response in most people, and this fear and emotion have been exploited by MCPP opponents. . . . The management of pain is not influenced by MCPPs, rather, it is a function of physician education. (United States Department of Justice 1990, pp. 40–42)

To explore further whether there is valid cause for physicians to perceive risk associated with investigation by regulatory agencies, we studied a sample of the members of state medical examining boards throughout the United States (Joranson et al. 1992). State medical boards administer medical practice laws and have the duty to protect the public health from substandard, incompetent, and unlawful practices. These boards determine what constitutes unprofessional conduct and have the authority to grant, suspend, deny, limit, or revoke a license to practice medicine.

A total of 627 medical board members were surveyed in 1991 with the cooperation of the Federation of State Medical Boards of the United States. We obtained a 49% response rate. The mean age of the respondents was 55, and they had received their medical degrees between 1926 and 1987; the median year was 1961. The physician board members were asked to rank the opioid analgesics they would and would not recommend for management of moderate to severe cancer pain. These regulator-physicians tended to prefer drugs like aspirin and acetaminophen alone or in combination with codeine instead of the potent opioids like morphine and hydromorphone that are preferred for moderate to severe pain. This may be an example of the customary prescribing patterns that have been discussed by Morgan (1986) in his treatise on "opiophobia." Further, most of the board members indicated that "addiction" includes physical dependence. Only 10% chose psychological dependence alone.

Board members were also asked to give their opinion on the legality of prescribing opioids for more than several months to chronic pain patients with and without cancer. Only 75% of medical board members were confident that prescribing opioids for chronic cancer pain was both legal and acceptable medical practice; 14% felt it was legal but would discourage it; and 5% believed the practice to be illegal. If the patient's chronic pain was from a nonmalignant source, only 12% were confident that the practice was both legal and medically acceptable; 47% would discourage it; and nearly 33% would investigate the practice as illegal. If the patient had a history of drug abuse, the perception that prescribing opioids was illegal greatly increased. The fact that 80% of the medical board members stated that their medical board was the agency most likely to investigate improper prescribing of controlled substances in their state underscores the significance of these data.

Overall, the survey suggested that medical board members lack knowledge about the use of opioids and other controlled substances to manage pain. To varying degrees they would also discourage or investigate the prescribing of opioid analgesics for intractable pain, particularly if the patient does not have cancer but especially if the patient had a history of drug abuse. It is important to recognize that the presenting problem in each scenario was pain, not addiction. There was also confusion about the definition of addiction. Addiction is not established by the presence of physical dependence or tolerance, but rather by psychological dependence (American Pain Society 1992). Given these results, it is not hard to understand why physicians might avoid extended opioid prescribing for a patient with pain. In fact, concerns have been expressed about vigorous investigations of physicians for what was considered to be appropriate prescribing of opioids for pain (Benton 1993; Hill 1989; McIntosh 1991a, 1991b; Nowak 1992).

Conclusions and Future Directions

If it is in the public interest that drugs meet rigorous standards of effectiveness and safety, it should be of equal interest to public health that drug laws and regulations be held to the same standards (Woods 1990). In fact, efforts are emerging to examine controlled substances policy as it relates to the prescribing of opioids for pain and to take appropriate action (Joranson 1990a). The Federation of State Medical Boards and the American Pain Society have sponsored educational symposia for medical regulators, and some medical boards are issuing new prescribing policies in the area of pain management (Joranson et al. 1992). The DEA has issued a statement that controlled substances should be prescribed when there is a legitimate medical need (United States Department of Justice 1990). Ultimately, if state and federal agencies have reasonable policies that are communicated to physicians, it may be possible to reach the ideal circumstance in which physicians will not view as a threat inquiries from these agencies about their prescribing.

A revised UCSA was given to the states in 1990 in an effort to help bring state controlled substances laws up to date with many new drug control provisions in the federal CSA and to improve the balance between drug control and medical use of controlled substances (National Conference of Commissioners on Uniform State Laws 1990). The 1990 UCSA 1) gives modest recognition to the medical value of controlled substances—alternative language has been suggested to emphasize this key principle (Joranson 1990b); 2) urges states to ensure that their definition of terms does not allow patients who are physically dependent on opioids for the treatment of pain to be confused with addicts; 3) clarifies that opioid treatment of intractable pain is part of medical practice and thus outside the scope of controlled substances violations; and 4) establishes a model interagency diversion control program to coordinate the use of existing information, authority, and resources to identify and prosecute individuals who are responsible for diverting controlled substances to illicit uses. The progress to balance state-controlled substances laws could be facilitated if professional organizations were to take an interest in adoption of the 1990 UCSA in their respective state legislatures.

As we pass through another cycle of intense concern about drugs, we must take care not to discard medical and scientific knowledge nor to ignore or stigmatize those among us, especially those with chronic illnesses, who benefit from the essential medical uses of controlled substances. Controlled substances are essential to the quality of life of millions of patients. A balanced drug policy should provide ample authority to address diversion problems without interfering in the use of controlled substances in the medical care of patients. Drug laws have a dual purpose; achieving both ends must be emphasized, for only in this way will the greatest health benefit be realized.

References

American Managed Care Pharmacy Association: Voluntary guidelines, controlled substances. Arlington, VA, American Managed Care Pharmacy Association

American Pain Society: Principles of Analgesic Use in the Treatment of Cancer Pain, 3rd Edition. Skokie, IL, American Pain Society, 1992

American Psychiatric Association: Diagnostic and Statistical Manual of Mental Disorders, 4th Edition. Washington, DC, American Psychiatric Association, 1994

Angarola RT, Wray SD: Legal impediments to cancer pain treatment, in Advances in Pain Research and Therapy, Vol 11. Edited by Hill CS, Fields WS. New York, Raven, 1989, pp 213–231

Benton O: Innocent victims of the drug war? APS Bulletin 3:17–19, 1993

Berina LF, Guernsey BG, Hokanson JA, et al: Physician perception of a triplicate prescription law. Am J Hosp Pharm 42:857–859, 1985

Code of Federal Regulations Title 21 Part 1306.07 (c), April 1, 1988

Committee on Ways and Means: Controlled Dangerous Substances, Narcotic and Drug Control Laws: Hearings before the U.S. House of Representatives Committee on Ways and Means. Washington, DC, U.S. Government Printing Office, 1970

Controlled Substances Act of 1970, Pub L No 91-513, 84 Stat 1242 (1970)

Daut RL, Cleeland CS: The prevalence of severity of pain in cancer. Cancer 50:1913–1918, 1982

Federal Register 15393-94, 1975

Federal Register 2673, 1983

Federal Register 1746-8, 1986

Federal Register 50591-97, 1988

Ferrell BR, McCaffery M, Rhiner M: Pain and addiction: an urgent need for change in nursing education. Journal of Pain and Symptom Management 7:117–124, 1992

Foley KM: Treatment of cancer pain. N Engl J Med 313:84–95, 1985

Foley KM: The "decriminalization" of cancer pain, in Advances in Pain Research and Therapy, Vol 11. Edited by Hills CS, Fields WS. New York, Raven, 1989, pp 5–18

Food, Drug, and Cosmetic Act of 1962, Pub L No 87-871, 76 Stat 780, Sec 202 (1962) (amended by Act of 1962, Pub L No 87-871, 76 Stat 780, Sec 202 [1962])

Hill CS: The negative effect of regulatory agencies on adequate pain control. Primary Care and Cancer, November 1989, pp 47–53

International Narcotics Control Board: Demand For and Supply of Opiates for Medical and Scientific Needs. New York, United Nations, 1989, pp 1–21

International Narcotics Control Board: Report of the International Narcotics Control Board for 1991. New York, United Nations, 1991

Jaffe JH: Misinformation: euphoria and addiction, in Advances in Pain Research and Therapy, Vol 11. Edited by Hills CS, Fields WS. New York, Raven, 1989, pp 163–174

Jasinski DR: Pharmacological misinformation that prevents optimum pain control with narcotic analgesics, in Advances in Pain Research and Therapy, Vol 11. Edited by Hills CS, Fields WS. New York, Raven, 1989, pp 139–143

Joranson DE: Federal and state regulation of opioids. Journal of Pain and Symptom Management 5 (suppl 1):S12–S23, 1990a

Joranson DE: A new drug law for the states: an opportunity to affirm the role of opioids in cancer pain relief. Journal of Pain and Symptom Management 5:333–336, 1990b

Joranson DE, Bachman A: Option paper. Madison, WI, Wisconsin Department of Health and Social Services Controlled Substances Board, 1988

Joranson DE, Cleeland CS, Weissman DH, et al: Opioids for chronic cancer and non-cancer pain: a survey of state medical board members. Federation Bulletin 79:15–49, 1992

Max MB: Pain relief and the control of drug abuse: conflicting or complementary goals?, in Advances in Pain Research and Therapy, Vol 11. Edited by Hills CS, Fields WS. New York, Raven, 1989, pp 241–245

Max MB: Improving outcomes of analgesic treatment: is education enough? Ann Intern Med 113:885–889, 1990

McIntosh H: How physicians handle drug investigations. J Natl Cancer Inst 83:1282–1284, 1991a

McIntosh H: Regulatory barriers take some blame for pain undertreatment. J Natl Cancer Inst 83:1202–1204, 1991b

Morgan JP: American opiophobia: customary underutilization of opioid analgesics. Alcohol and Substance Abuse 5:163–173, 1986

Musto DF: The American Disease: Origins of Narcotic Control. New York, Oxford University Press, 1987

National Conference of Commissioners on Uniform State Laws: Uniform Controlled Substances Act. St. Louis, MO, August 1–7, 1970

National Conference of Commissioners on Uniform State Laws: Uniform Controlled Substances Act. Milwaukee, WI, July 13–20, 1990

New York State Controlled Substances Act, Public Health Law, Article 33, Title I

Nowak R: Cops and doctors: drug busts hamper pain therapy. The Journal of NIH Research 4:27–28, 1992

Parmet WE: Legal rights and communicable diseases: AIDS, the police power and individual liberty. J Health Polit Policy Law 14:741–771, 1989

Physician's Desk Reference, 47th Edition. Montvale, NJ, Medical Economics Company, 1993

Portenoy RK: Chronic opioid therapy in nonmalignant pain. Journal of Pain and Symptom Management 5:S46–S62, 1990

Safer DJ, Krager JM: Effects of a media blitz and a threatened lawsuit on stimulant treatment. JAMA 268:1004–1007, 1992

Sigler KA, Guernsey BG, Ingrim NB, et al: Effect of a triplicate prescription law on prescribing of Schedule II drugs. Am J Hosp Pharm 41:108–111, 1984

South Carolina Health Code, Sec 44-53-360(c) (1984)

Stark P: Introduction of the Medicare Controlled Substances Accountability Act of 1990. Special Order of Remarks in the House of Representatives. Washington, DC, House of Representatives, 1990

Stone SE: The investigation and prosecution of professional practice cases under the Controlled Substances Act: introduction to professional practice case law. Drug Enforcement, Spring 1983, pp 21–26

Takeda F: Results of field-testing of the WHO draft interim guidelines on relief of cancer pain in Japanese cancer patients, in 1986 Symposium on Pain Control (International Congress and Symposium Series No 123). Edited by Doyle D. London, Royal Society of Medicine, 1987, pp 109–117

Tennant F: The California registration system for habitués to Schedule II drugs, in Problems of Drug Dependence: Proceedings of the 42nd Annual Scientific Meeting of the Committee on Problems of Drug Dependence (Publ No ADM 81-1058). Edited by Harris LS. Washington, DC, U.S. Government Printing Office, 1981, pp 193–198

Turk DC, Brody MC: What position do APS's physician members take on chronic opioid therapy? APS Bulletin 2:1–5, 1992

United Nations: Convention on Psychotropic Substances, 1971. New York, United Nations, 1977a

United Nations: Single Convention on Narcotic Drugs, 1961. New York, United Nations, 1977b

United States Department of Justice, Drug Enforcement Administration: Pharmacist's manual: an informational outline of the Controlled Substances Act of 1970. Washington, DC, U.S. Department of Justice, 1986

United States Department of Justice, Drug Enforcement Administration: Multiple copy prescription programs resource guide. Washington, DC, U.S. Government Printing Office, 1987

United States Department of Justice, Drug Enforcement Administration: Multiple copy prescription programs resource guide, revised. Washington, DC, U.S. Government Printing Office, 1990

United States House of Representatives, Comprehensive Drug Abuse Prevention and Control Act of 1970, House Report No 91-1444, September 10, 1970

United States v Evers, 643 F2d 1043 5th Circuit (1981)

Von Roenn JH, Cleeland CS, Gonin R, et al: Physician attitudes and practice in cancer pain management: a survey from the Eastern Cooperative Oncology Group. Ann Intern Med 119:121–126, 1993

Weintraub M, Singh S, Byrne L, et al: Consequences of the 1991 New York State triplicate benzodiazepine regulations. JAMA 266:2392–2397, 1991

Weissman DE, Joranson DE, Hopwood MB: Wisconsin physicians' knowledge and attitudes about opioid analgesic regulations. Wis Med J December:671–675, 1991

Woods J: Abuse liability and the regulatory control of therapeutic drugs: untested assumptions. Drug Alcohol Depend 25:229–233, 1990

World Health Organization: WHO Expert Committee on drug dependence: 16th report. Geneva, World Health Organization, 1969

World Health Organization: Cancer pain relief. Geneva, World Health Organization, 1986

World Health Organization: Cancer pain relief and palliative care: report of a WHO Expert Committee. Geneva, World Health Organization, 1990

CHAPTER NINE

The Misapplication of Controlled Substance Regulation to Benzodiazepines

Harold I. Schwartz, M.D.
David J. Greenblatt, M.D.

As a class of medication whose use is subject to the influence of negative media reports, public and professional misperceptions, and now inappropriate regulation, benzodiazepines may be second only to the opioid analgesics. As Gelenberg (1992) noted in the closing remarks of a special *Journal of Clinical Psychiatry* supplement devoted to benzodiazepine sedative hypnotics: "Agents that can save and improve lives if used properly have been attacked by the misled and malevolent for varied but ominous reasons" (p. 87). This has not always been the case.

Trends in Benzodiazepine Use

The benzodiazepines were introduced in the 1960s with the arrival of chlordiazepoxide. They were rapidly accepted for the treatment of anxiety and insomnia. Prior to development of the benzodiazepines, barbiturates accounted for the majority of hypnotic prescriptions along with glutethimide, chloral hydrate, ethchlorvynol, and methyprylon (Walsh and Englhardt 1992). In a short time, data began to emerge about the relative safety and efficacy of these drugs, matching the growing clinical consensus. They were noted to be effective in the treatment of anxiety and, in some studies, more effective than barbiturates or meprobamate (Greenblatt and Shader 1974). Their reported effectiveness was matched by reports on their relative safety with regard to overdose (Greenblatt et al. 1977, 1978) and drug interactions (Greenblatt and Shader 1974). By the 1970s benzodiazepines had replaced barbiturates and meprobamate as the most widely prescribed pharmacologic agents for the treatment of insomnia and anxiety (Shader et al. 1991).

Benzodiazepines rapidly became among the most widely prescribed drugs in the world (American Psychiatric Association 1990; Woods et al. 1992). Shader and colleagues (1991) reported that during the years 1973–1975, the peak years of benzodiazepine prescribing, more than 80 million prescriptions per year were dispensed in American pharmacies. Approximately 1.5 billion prescriptions were dispensed in America between 1965 and 1985 (Woods et al. 1987).

The phenomenal growth in benzodiazepine acceptance and use was soon met by a backlash. The public's perception of anxiety and sleep disorders has always been colored by a conservative moralism, which attributes these conditions to a failure of will. Manheimer and colleagues (1973) reported that 87% of Americans surveyed agreed that "it is better to use willpower to solve problems than it is to use tranquilizers" (p. 1248); 40% believed tranquilizer use to be a sign of weakness. Anecdotal reports of benzodiazepine abuse, dependence, and withdrawal syndromes began to appear (Shader et al. 1991), beginning what Taylor (1989) has called "the damnation of benzodiazepines" (p. 697) by the media. Media reports highlighted anecdotal autobiographical accounts of lives disrupted by benzodiazepine "addiction" and fueled the belief that benzodiazepines were being significantly overprescribed and widely abused.

Although problems of overuse, drug dependence, and abuse of the benzodiazepines do exist (American Psychiatric Association 1990), the perception of these problems and the public and regulatory response to them have negatively influenced the appropriate use of these medications. The clinical and epidemiologic data support the conclusion that the benzodiazepines are generally prescribed appropriately for legitimate indications (Woods et al. 1987, 1988, 1992) and that the risks of abuse and dependence are low in relation to the overall volume of their use (Uhlenhuth et al. 1988). Woods and colleagues (1988) attributed these discrepant perceptions of the benzodiazepines to the very different "abuse" and "therapeutic use" models that have been advocated by investigators who approach the benzodiazepines through very distinct patient populations and with differing agendas. These differing models are rarely melded into a complete and accurate view of the use and abuse of these drugs. The authors' review of the epidemiologic data lead them to the conclusion that the abuse model, which hypothesizes that a significant proportion of benzodiazepine use is for purposes other than those for which the drugs have been prescribed, is not sustained by the data. The authors noted that such abuse of benzodiazepines occurs almost exclusively among individuals who are involved in abusing other psychoactive substances. To the contrary, the authors concluded that the "therapeutic use model" is indeed supported by the epidemiologic data, which argue that "benzodiazepines are generally prescribed appropriately and that the vast majority of people actually taking these drugs do manifest the conditions for which benzodiazepine treatment is indicated and efficacious" (p. 3476).

If anything, the data suggest that both anxiolytics (Nagy 1987) and hypnotics (Balter and Uhlenhuth 1992) are underprescribed to populations in need of treatment.

Trends in the use of benzodiazepine hypnotics seem to be especially to the point. In a review of the use of benzodiazepines for insomnia, Walsh and Englhardt (1992) reported that although overall pharmacologic treatment for insomnia showed a decline of 10% from 1987 to 1991, the use of benzodiazepine hypnotics fell by about 30% during this period. Remarkably, the use of antidepressants in the treatment of insomnia increased by approximately 100% during the period studied. They attributed the drop-off in benzodiazepine use to negative media reports about triazolam, which began in 1988. In October of 1991 triazolam was removed from the market in the United Kingdom. Several other countries followed suit, although most have reinstated the drug, and the United States Food and Drug Administration refused to require the withdrawal of triazolam from the market following extensive hearings. Of course, these developments all postdate the period of study reported by Walsh and Englhardt. They concluded that the influence of the media in determining medical practice may be greater than that of scientific data, and they noted that the effect may well be harmful as in the substitution of drugs such as tricyclic antidepressants with greater toxicity and worrisome side-effect profiles for the safer benzodiazepines (Walsh and Englhardt 1992). Rothschild (1992), reviewing the data on triazolam, concluded that there is little scientific evidence to support the adverse reports in the lay press that triazolam is associated with adverse reactions, particularly violent disinhibition, with any greater frequency than any other benzodiazepine.

Although we have yet to document the overall cost to society of untreated insomnia, we have reason to believe the cost may be great (Dement and Mitler 1993). Balter and Uhlenhuth (1992) estimated that 6% of the adult population suffer from chronic insomnia that is untreated with hypnotic medication. Kupfer (1992) suggested that "this major public health problem is costing billions of dollars and leading to a variety of other morbidity and perhaps even mortality outcomes" (p. 85).

Triplicate Prescription of Benzodiazepines

The clash between the "therapeutic use" and "abuse" models elaborated by Woods and colleagues (1988) has been highlighted dramatically by the imposition of a requirement that benzodiazepines be prescribed by triplicate prescription form in New York State. To understand the ramifications of this regulatory development one needs to understand the concept of multiple copy prescription programs.

Multiple copy prescription programs are, as of this writing, in operation in nine states—accounting for 38% of all pharmacies and physicians in the United States (United States Department of Justice 1990). These programs require that prescriptions for Schedule II controlled substances be written on special prescription forms that must be purchased from the state. Two states require that prescriptions be written on duplicate forms; seven require triplicate forms. (A 10th state, Washington, requires the use of multiple-copy prescriptions for a small group of physicians who are already under scrutiny.) The physician keeps one copy for his or her own records; the pharmacy keeps another and sends a third copy to the state agency monitoring controlled substance use. The data base established by the state can then be used for a variety of purposes. The Drug Enforcement Administration (United States Department of Justice 1990) promotes the use of these data to diminish drug diversion via outright diversion by health care professionals, indiscriminate prescribing and over-prescribing and dispensing, and forgery and theft. The Drug Enforcement Administration and various state agencies have defended multiple copy prescription programs at all costs and in the face of evidence that argues that they are ineffective in their goals and have a negative impact on the appropriate use of controlled substances. Although the Drug Enforcement Administration argues that legitimate medical care is unimpeded by such programs, as we shall see, the experience of adding benzodiazepines to the triplicate program in New York State argues otherwise.

Before examining the impact of triplicate prescriptions on benzodiazepines, it is worth noting some of the data that challenge the effectiveness of multiple copy prescription programs in controlling drug diversion of any kind. Applying data from the Epidemiologic Catchment Area study, Weissman and Johnson (1991) compared the rates of drug use, abuse, dependence, and diversion in five cities, only one of which had a multiple copy prescription program in effect (Los Angeles, California). They noted that the rates of drug use, abuse, and dependence were significantly higher in that one city than in the others in the study and that the vast majority of those abusing prescription drugs obtained their drugs from a source other than their physician. In a review of national data on emergency room visits related to drug use, Jacob (1990) concluded that there is no evidence that multiple copy prescription programs effect a lower incidence of abuse of Schedule II drugs. The author noted that although reduction in prescription volume may occur, reduction does not necessarily correlate with a reduction in drug abuse. Indeed, it is the differentiation between overall reduction in prescription volume, reductions in drug abuse, and reductions in appropriate prescribing that is central to the evaluation of the impact of New York State's imposition of a triplicate requirement for benzodiazepines.

In imposing the benzodiazepine regulation, the New York State Department of Health (1989) argued that benzodiazepines were

widely abused, were being diverted into illicit use by some practitioners, and contributed to high levels of overdose emergency room
admissions. There is no question that benzodiazepine prescribing
declined sharply following the imposition of the triplicate program on
January 1, 1989. In fact, in the first year total benzodiazepine prescriptions from all sources fell from 5.3 million to 2.96 million, a decline
of 44%. Prescriptions for benzodiazepines filled through the Medicaid
program fell from 1.5 million to 600,000, a decline of 60% (Weintraub
et al. 1991). The Department of Health was quick to claim success for
the program, including huge reductions in dispensing by pharmacies
suspected of being "Medicaid mills" and significant reductions in
emergency room admissions involving overdose by benzodiazepines
(New York State Department of Health 1989, 1990a, 1990b). It is
also important to note that approximately 18 million dollars in savings
were realized via reduced benzodiazepine prescribing in the Medicaid,
Elderly Pharmaceutical, and Empire plan prescription programs
(Brahams 1990). The most contentious claim of the Department of
Health has been that appropriate use of benzodiazepines has been
unaffected (New York State Department of Health 1989). Certainly
this assertion has not been documented by anything approaching
rigorous investigation. However, the contrary assertion, that appropriate utilization of benzodiazepines has been significantly diminished,
has been supported by a number of important findings.

   A powerful argument in this regard has been the data that indicate
that there has been a significant substitution of other medications,
usually less effective and more toxic, for the benzodiazepines that have
not been prescribed. Weintraub and associates (1991) compared the
rates of prescription of various substitute medications in New York
with national trends for the 1 year before and the 1 year after
implementation of the benzodiazepine triplicate prescription regulation. Reviewing data from the National Prescription Audit, the New
York State Medicaid program, and Blue Cross/Blue Shield, they noted
significant discrepancies in the prescribing patterns in New York State
as compared with the rest of the nation for older and less safe
alternatives to the benzodiazepines. For example, whereas prescriptions for ethchlorvynol decreased by 18% nationally, they increased by
29% in New York State. Meprobamate use declined by 9% nationally

but increased by 125% in New York. Methyprylon prescriptions decreased by 15% nationally, whereas they grew by 84% in New York State. Likewise, butabarbital use decreased 15% nationally, whereas it increased 31% in New York. Chloral hydrate, which decreased by .4% nationally, increased by 136% in New York during this period. Although the actual patterns of substitution differed somewhat in the Medicaid program as compared with the Blue Cross/Blue Shield program, significant declines in the Blue Cross/Blue Shield program argue that the impact of the triplicate program extended beyond the closing of "Medicaid mills." Working from the same data, Shader and colleagues (1991) calculated that the triplicate prescription program "was responsible for some 168,000 prescriptions of meprobamate and almost 30,000 prescriptions for various barbiturates that would not otherwise have been written in 1989" (p. 783). They argued that the increased prescribing of these older, less effective, and more toxic substitutes represents a kind of "unlearning" of appropriate clinical and scientific experience as a direct result of the benzodiazepine regulation. Another of their findings highlights the clearly dangerous impact that the triplicate program has had in one respect.

> In the category of "benzodiazepine anticonvulsants," the reduction in New York State was only 3%; the DOH [Department of Health] interprets this as indicating "not all benzodiazepines are affected equally." However, in the context of the corresponding 48% *increase* in the rest of the nation, the 3% reduction in New York State in fact represents a substantial blunting of an otherwise national increase in prescribing, attributable to the rising recognition of the potential value of one benzodiazepine, officially classified as an anticonvulsant, for the treatment of panic disorder. (Shader et al. 1991, p. 783)

Inappropriate substitution of less safe and effective medications for benzodiazepines was reported by Zullich and colleagues (1992) in a review of prescribing practices in 10 nursing homes following implementation of the regulation. Of 155 patients receiving benzodiazepines at the time the regulation went into effect, 108 (70%) had at least one benzodiazepine discontinued following the regulation. Of these, 74 (47.7%) were placed on a substitute psychoactive medication. These included haloperidol (21%), buspirone (8%), and phenobarbital (8%) as a substitute for an anxiolytic benzodiazepine and chloral hydrate (26%), diphenhydramine (14%), and phenobarbital (12%) as a substitution for a sedative-hypnotic benzodiazepine. A significant number of patients were withdrawn from their benzodiazepine precipitously, and 14% experienced withdrawal symptoms.

Abrupt cessation of benzodiazepine therapy was not an uncommon response to the regulation. Schwartz and Blank (1991) reviewed all benzodiazepine-related psychiatric emergency room and walk-in visits in one New York hospital for a 3-month period following implementation of the regulation. The authors identified 59 cases in which benzodiazepine use appeared to be related to the presenting problem. Of these cases, 24 (41%) were believed to be directly related to the new triplicate prescription program. In the typical case, patients presented with a benzodiazepine withdrawal syndrome following the abrupt discontinuation of their medication or with the unmasking of a previously treated anxiety disorder. Two examples, which were previously reported in *General Hospital Psychiatry,* [1] are illustrated below.

Case 1. Mr. V. is a 52-year-old married man with a long history of panic attacks with varying degrees of agoraphobia as well as moderate obsessive-compulsive disorder. He was referred to a group for panic disorder after his symptoms worsened following the death of his mother and his second myocardial infarction 6 years ago. He had been medicated with alprazolam 0.5 mg tid. On this regimen he was less anxious and suffered no panic attacks, however, he often had exacerbations of severe anticipatory anxiety as when his wife and various siblings have been hospitalized.

For the last several years Mr. V. has had his medications monitored at a neighboring municipal hospital where he also received his alprazolam at no cost. In January 1989 he reported that his alprazolam had been decreased to 0.5 mg po bid even though his anxiety was high at the time. He reported that his psychiatrist told him that "she is not allowed to write for as much alprazolam because of changes by the State of New York." His alprazolam has not been readjusted despite his protest and his increased level of anxiety surrounding additional stresses in his life. (p. 221)

---

[1] Reprinted by permission of the publisher from Schwartz HI, Blank K: "Regulation of Benzodiazepine Prescribing Practices: Clinical Implications." *General Hospital Psychiatry* 13:219–224, 1991. Copyright 1991 by Elsevier Science Inc.

Case 2. Mrs. O. is a 56-year-old Hispanic woman who presented to our walk-in clinic complaining of feelings of nervousness, irritability, difficulty sleeping, muscle twitching and muscle tension. Four weeks prior to presentation her physician had abruptly discontinued prescribing the lorazepam (4 mg total per day) which he had been prescribing for several years. Her condition had deteriorated from that time to the point that she now felt too anxious to shop, cook or clean. Mrs. O. had first been placed on benzodiazepines 10 years earlier when she felt "jumpy and nervous all the time" following the onset of menopause. On examination she was observed to be tense, anxious, irritable, strident and preoccupied with obtaining lorazepam. The impression on evaluation was that the patient had a generalized anxiety disorder which had been successfully managed with lorazepam and that she was now suffering from her previously treated anxiety and secondarily from lorazepam withdrawal. (p. 221)

Evidence that concerns about confidentiality in triplicate prescription programs extend beyond those raised by the physicians who write the prescriptions came from one patient in the series who presented to the walk-in clinic seeking help after refusing to accept a renewal of her benzodiazepine out of concern about being "registered as a drug user" by the state.

Surveys of primary care physicians and psychiatrists document the negative impact of the triplicate program from the physician's point of view. Approximately half of the physicians surveyed in two studies reported decreased benzodiazepine prescribing and substitution with less satisfactory medications (Rodriguez 1991; Schwartz 1991). Perhaps one of the most alarming findings regarding drug substitution comes from the New York Poison Control Center. A modest (2%) reduction in calls relating to exposure to benzodiazepines between 1988 and 1989 was more than compensated for by a 30% increase in calls relating to exposure to sedative hypnotics such as chloral hydrate, ethchlorvynol, glutethimide, meprobamate, and methaqualone. Even more alarming, reductions in benzodiazepine overdose emergency room visits were balanced by an equivalent increase in overdoses on meprobamate and chloral hydrate, agents with a notoriously higher lethality (Hoffman et al. 1991).

The use of benzodiazepines, indeed the use of all psychotropic agents, is influenced by our cultural acceptance of mental illness as a reality rather than a reflection of personal weakness and by our cultural position on the use of psychoactive substances of any kind for any purpose. The decline in benzodiazepine prescribing following the media attention devoted to dependency and "addiction" is powerful testimony to the influence of public perception and attitude on the use of medication. The inclusion of benzodiazepines in New York State's triplicate prescription program is evidence of a much more formal regulatory mechanism that confuses drug abuse policy and goals with the legitimate regulation of medical practice.

A number of premises underlying the triplicate benzodiazepine program are subject to challenge. These include the following:

1. *Triplicate programs are effective in reducing drug abuse.* The very premise of the utility and effectiveness of triplicate programs in reducing drug abuse of any kind is an open question. Although such programs probably do reduce some kinds of diversion, there is no convincing evidence that they reduce overall drug abuse rates. Furthermore, no systematic attempts have been made by the Drug Enforcement Administration or any state agency promoting such programs to differentiate reductions in illegitimate medication use from reductions in legitimate use.

2. *Triplicate prescription programs have no impact on the legitimate use of medication.* An underlying presumption here is that doctors would not change legitimate prescribing patterns without compelling reasons. However, there is ample evidence that doctors have legitimate reason to be concerned when regulatory agencies set standards of care, scrutinize practice, and impose sanctions. Triplicate prescriptions have been described as having a "chilling effect" on prescribers (Watry 1988). Reports in the literature highlight the damaging impact on individual practitioners of misguided investigations based on triplicate prescription data (Carlova 1984; Goldman 1990). Various state multiple copy prescription programs routinely generate practitioner-based reports that are used as the basis for investigations of the highest volume prescribers. For example, in 1978 New York used its triplicate program to identify for investigation 46 physicians who were prescribing high volumes of amphetamine. Many prosecutions followed (Eadie 1993). The underutilization of opiates in the treatment of pain provides striking evidence that multiple copy prescription pro-

grams and other regulatory mechanisms have an adverse impact on legitimate practice stemming, at least in part, from fear of regulatory agencies. The growing evidence regarding benzodiazepine prescribing supports this view.

3. *Greater controls are necessary for benzodiazepines than for other Schedule IV substances because they represent a public health hazard.* New York State's extension of the triplicate program to benzodiazepines in effect implies that the potential for abuse and misuse of benzodiazepines is equivalent to that of other substances on Schedule II. This view has been discredited by the scientific community as reflected in the positions of the National Institute of Drug Abuse (1990) and the American College of Neuropsychopharmacology (1991), and in numerous other published reviews (e.g., Woods et al. 1987, 1988, 1992).

The requirement that triplicate prescriptions be used in the prescription of benzodiazepines in New York is a regulatory *experiment* in medical practice. It reflects the degree to which regulatory requirements that have an extraordinary impact on practice can be imposed without any of the scientific controls that otherwise dictate the evolution of standards of medical care. Regulations are generally not imposed in pilot settings with the use of controls so that studies of their impact can be performed before the regulation is imposed on the public at large. Thus, it is incumbent on the medical and scientific communities to examine rigorously the impact of regulations that affect medical practice and to challenge the premises of new regulations when possible before they are implemented. Congressional initiatives to replace triplicate prescription programs with an electronic data transfer system exemplify regulatory programs that could have a huge impact on legitimate prescribing practices (Prescription Accountability Act 1990). Such a program would link dispensing pharmacies to computerized centralized data bases and require that prescriptions for all controlled substances be entered into these data banks at the point of sale. Certainly the impact of such a program on legitimate practice should be studied before the concept is imposed on a large scale.

Regulatory policy influencing the use of psychotropic medication is driven by a set of varied goals that are not always synchronous. Indeed, although the control of drug abuse and the promotion of good medical practice and cost effectiveness are all worthy public policy goals, they may lead to policies with contradictory results. Patterns of use of benzodiazepines, and all psychotropic medications, should be driven by standards of care derived from clinical experience and scientific research. The medical and scientific communities must resist non-scientifically driven influences on practice patterns if patients are not to be deprived of effective and appropriate treatments.

References

American College of Neuropsychopharmacology: Multiple copy prescriptions for benzodiazepines. Accepted as a consensus statement by ACNP Council, March 22, 1991. Neuropsychopharmacology 4:285–287, 1991

American Psychiatric Association: Benzodiazepine Dependence, Toxicity and Abuse: A Task Force Report of the American Psychiatric Association. Washington, DC, American Psychiatric Association, 1990

Balter MB, Uhlenhuth EH: New epidemiologic findings about insomnia and its treatment. J Clin Psychiatry 53 (suppl):34–39, 1992

Brahams D: Benzodiazepine overprescribing: successful initiative in New York State. Lancet 336:1372–1373, 1990

Carlova J: Patients in pain can put you in jail. Medical Economics 61:195–206, 1984

Dement WC, Mitler MM: It's time to wake up to the importance of sleep disorders. JAMA 269:1548–1550, 1993

Eadie JL: New York State's triplicate prescription program, in Prescription Drug Diversion Control Systems, Medical Practice and Patient Care: A Review and Research Agenda. Edited by Cooper J, Czechowicz D, Molinari SP, et al. Rockville, MD, National Institute on Drug Abuse, 1993, pp 176–193

Gelenberg AJ: The use of benzodiazepine hypnotics: a scientific examination of a clinical controversy: closing remarks. J Clin Psychiatry 53 (suppl):87, 1992

Goldman B: Politics of pain: are U.S. drug laws too tough on patients? American College of Physicians Observer 10:1, 10–11, 1990

Greenblatt DH, Shader R: Benzodiazepines in Clinical Practice. New York, Raven, 1974

Greenblatt DJ, Allen MD, Noel BJ, et al: Acute overdosage with benzodiazepine derivatives. Clin Pharmacol Ther 21:497–514, 1977

Greenblatt DJ, Woo E, Divoll Allen M, et al: Rapid recovery from massive diazepam overdose. JAMA 240:1872–1874, 1978

Hoffman RS, Wipfler MG, Maddaloni MA, et al: Has the triplicate benzodiazepine regulation influenced sedative-hypnotic overdoses? N Y State J Med 91:436–439, 1991

Jacob TR: Multiple copy prescription regulation and drug abuse: evidence from the DAWN Network, in Balancing the Response to Prescription Drug Abuse: Report of a National Symposium on Medicine and Public Policy. Edited by Wilford B. Chicago, IL, American Medical Association, 1990, pp 205–216

Kupfer DJ: The use of benzodiazepine hypnotics: a scientific examination of a clinical controversy: closing remarks. J Clin Psychiatry 53 (suppl):84–85, 1992

Manheimer DI, Davidson ST, Balter MB, et al: Popular attitudes and beliefs about tranquilizers. Am J Psychiatry 130:1246–1253, 1973

Nagy A: Long-term treatment with benzodiazepines: theoretical, ideological and practical aspects. Acta Psychiatr Scand (suppl 756):47–55, 1987

National Institute of Drug Abuse, Office of Policy and External Affairs: NIDA position on triplicate prescriptions (memorandum). Rockville, MD, National Institute on Drug Abuse, March 29, 1990

New York State Department of Health: Benzodiazepines: prescribing declines under triplicate program. New York State Department of Health Epidemiology Notes 4:1–4, 1989

New York State Department of Health: Benzodiazepines: additional effects of the triplicate program. New York State Department of Health Epidemiology Notes 5:1–3, 1990a

New York State Department of Health: New York State's Regulation Placing Benzodiazepines on Triplicate Prescriptions: The First Year, 1989. Albany, New York State Department of Health, Division of Public Health Protection, May 1990b

Prescription Accountability Act of 1990, HR5530 101st Congress, 2nd session, 1990

Rodriguez RF: The impact of the New York triplicate prescription program on the Hispanic community. N Y State J Med 91 (suppl):24s–27s, 1991

Rothschild AJ: Disinhibition amnestic reactions and other adverse reactions secondary to triazolam: a review of the literature. J Clin Psychiatry 53 (suppl):69–79, 1992

Schwartz HI: Negative clinical consequences of triplicate prescription regulation of benzodiazepines. N Y State J Med 91 (suppl):9s–12s, 1991

Schwartz HI, Blank K: Regulation of benzodiazepine prescribing practices: clinical implications. Gen Hosp Psychiatry 13:219–224, 1991

Shader R, Greenblatt DJ, Balter MB: Appropriate use and regulatory control of benzodiazepines. J Clin Pharmacol 31:718–784, 1991

Taylor FK: The damnation of benzodiazepines. Br J Psychiatry 154:697–704, 1989

Uhlenhuth EH, DeWit H, Balter MB, et al: Risks and benefits of long-term benzodiazepine use. J Clin Psychopharmacol 8:161–167, 1988

United States Department of Justice, Drug Enforcement Administration: Multiple Copy Prescription Programs Resource Guide, Revised. Washington, DC, U.S. Government Printing Office, 1990

Walsh JK, Englhardt CL: Trends in the pharmacologic treatment of insomnia. J Clin Psychiatry 53 (suppl):10–17, 1992

Watry A: Innovations enhancing board effectiveness: triplicate prescriptions. Federal Bulletin 75:150–154, 1988

Weintraub M, Singh S, Byrne L, et al: Consequences of the 1989 New York State triplicate benzodiazepine prescribing regulations. JAMA 226:2392–2397, 1991

Weissman MM, Johnson J: Drug use and abuse in five U.S. communities. N Y State J Med 91 (suppl):19s–23s, 1991

Woods JH, Katz JL, Winger G: Abuse liability of benzodiazepines. Pharmacol Rev 39:251–419, 1987

Woods JH, Katz JL, Winger G: Use and abuse of benzodiazepines: issues relevant to prescribing. JAMA 260:3476–3480, 1988

Woods JH, Katz JL, Winger G: Benzodiazepines: use, abuse, and consequences. Pharmacol Rev 44:151–347, 1992

Zullich SG, Grasela TH Jr, Fiedler-Kelly JB, et al: Impact of triplicate prescription program on psychotropic prescribing patterns in long-term care facilities. Annals of Pharmacotherapy 26:539–546, 1992

The Impact of Prescription Drug Diversion Control Systems and State Regulations on the Use of Psychoactive Medications

James R. Cooper, M.D.
Dorynne J. Czechowicz, M.D.

Concern about the nature and extent of abuse and diversion of prescription drugs has resulted in development of international treaties and federal and state statutes as preventative measures. International treaties and federal laws primarily focus on controls related to import, export, manufacture, and wholesale distribution of prescription drugs. With few exceptions, the oversight of dispensers and prescribers of these medications is the purview of state jurisdictions. Over the last 30 years, states have developed various methods to monitor prescribing or dispensing of various psychoactive medications of interest and to investigate or regulate exceptional prescribing or dispensing. These drug diversion control methods have been discussed in detail elsewhere (Gitchel 1993; Horgan et al. 1991; Wilford 1991). In general, these state-operated systems have a common purpose of monitoring the drug distribution chain from the wholesaler to the consumer. Although these systems are the jurisdiction of individual states, many have received technical and financial support from the Drug Enforcement Administration (DEA), which has for many years supported various efforts to monitor drug distribution from the manufacturer to the patient.

Drug investigational units were originally a federally sponsored diversion control effort administered by the DEA. These units consisted of a coordinated group of law enforcement and regulatory representatives organized to target and investigate drug diversion. Between 1972 and 1979, 20 states implemented drug investigational units. The methods used for investigating pharmacists' and practitioners' behavior varied among states. Some state investigators actually performed random or routine pharmacy audits. Others monitored triplicate prescription data to identify suspicious prescribing behavior. With few exceptions (e.g., North Carolina), most drug investigational units have either been abandoned or reorganized into state regulatory diversion control offices when federal funding ceased.

The Medicaid Abusable Drug Audit System is a software system designed by the Office of the Inspector General, Department of Health and Human Services, in conjunction with the DEA (Roslewicz 1993). This system is capable of analyzing all prescription drugs in Schedules II through V that are prescribed for or dispensed through the Medicaid claims system. As of this writing, 18 states use this system.

The multiple copy prescription programs are currently the most frequently used drug diversion control system. As of this writing, they are used in nine states. One additional state, Washington, requires the use of multiple copy prescriptions for physicians whose prescribing practices are under scrutiny. The scope of these systems varies among states, but there are some similarities. In general, the prescriber writes a prescription for a controlled medication on a preprinted and numbered prescription form in either duplicate or triplicate format. The prescriber and dispenser each maintain a copy of the prescription. In most situations the dispenser forwards a copy of the prescription to a state regulatory agency. The scope of the drugs included in each state system varies.

The electronic data transfer system is a computerized diversion control system that requires pharmacists and dispensing physicians to submit various patient and medication information electronically to a central data bank. As of this writing, three states have implemented such a system. The medications reported and the related information provided to the central data bank vary. Unique to this system is that it does not require the prescriber to use specialized prescription pads.

Several years ago, the White House Office of National Drug Control Policy was evaluating the merits of the triplicate prescription system, already implemented in nine states (and in Washington for a limited number of physicians). Their interest was in determining whether the Office of National Drug Control Policy should encourage other states to develop similar prescription drug diversion control systems. In 1988, a White House conference report had supported this method as a means to reduce prescription drug diversion (The White House 1988). Hence, the Office of National Drug Control Policy sought the advice and counsel of both the Department of Health and Human Services and the Department of Justice regarding the relative risk and benefits of the triplicate prescription system.

At the beginning of this review process, a preliminary literature search revealed a dearth of published scientific data on the effectiveness of the various drug diversion control systems in reducing prescription drug diversion or their relative cost or impact on medical practice and patient care. Nonetheless, reasonable people, using identical data bases, made sharply differing interpretations of the same data to argue for or against the magnitude of prescription drug diversion, the effectiveness of a particular drug diversion control system, or the impact of these systems on medical practice and patient care. Likewise, definitions of accepted medical use, therapeutic usefulness, and drug abuse varied and often were ill defined. For example, some considered the use of certain narcotics, stimulants, or sedative hypnotics for unapproved indications or for chronic therapeutic use in general a measure of "inappropriate prescribing" or retail diversion. Others included intentional use of psychoactive medicines in successful or unsuccessful suicide attempts as a measure of prescription drug abuse. Without an agreement on these definitions, individual interpretation and therapeutic bias affect one's perception of the nature and extent of prescription drug abuse and retail diversion and the effect of drug control systems on patient care. The authors subsequently consulted with various professional, enforcement, regulatory, and patient advocacy groups and administered a government-funded independent evaluation of the existing data on the impact of drug diversion control systems on medical practice and patient care (Cooper et al. 1993). Subsequently, the Department of Health and Human Services declined to support or recommend to states the use of any specific drug control program because of the paucity of research data on which to determine the risks, benefits, or superiority of any particular drug diversion control system.

In this chapter we summarize the findings from the evaluation of the impact of these control systems on medical practice and patient care. We also outline our concerns about the possible future effects these control systems may have on medical practice and patient care given the current sentiment on regulating medical practice and the current influence of law enforcement to affect the availability of these medications for therapeutic use in an attempt to prevent retail diversion for illicit use.

Impact of Drug Diversion Control Systems on Medical Practice

Evidence of the impact of these systems on medical practice and patient care is also usually anecdotal or, when data-based, difficult to interpret. The electronic point-of-sale computer reporting systems recently instituted in Oklahoma, Hawaii, and Massachusetts are too new to have been systematically evaluated. Most of the limited research in this area involves the multiple copy prescription programs already in operation. These programs usually require that prescriptions for Schedule II drugs be written on special forms with one copy going to the state. Several studies have shown changes in prescription rates that may suggest adverse effects. The earliest of these studies (Sigler et al. 1984) found that Schedule II outpatient medication prescribing in a 1,200-bed Texas teaching hospital decreased by 60.4% within 6 months after the regulatory change—a decline from 3,870 prescriptions to 1,534. Although the therapeutic appropriateness of this change was not studied, house staff physicians believed the new law interfered with medically appropriate prescribing. However, this change in prescribing was attributed to the inconvenience of using the special prescription form rather than increased government surveillance (Berina et al. 1985).

More recent studies are primarily based on New York State's

multiple copy prescription program, which was modified in January of 1989 to include benzodiazepines. These studies are thoroughly reviewed by Schwartz and Greenblatt (Chapter 9, this volume) and are not presented here. Our review of the data suggests that there is a basis for concern that regulatory changes may have unanticipated effects on physicians' willingness to prescribe psychoactive medications despite appropriate medical indications for their use. In addition, there is evidence of substitution of less safe and effective medications following more restrictive regulatory changes. What is so obviously missing is any systematic clinical study of the impact of these control systems. Furthermore, there is no current consensus on the most appropriate design or methodologies for evaluating the impact of these various drug diversion control systems on drug abuse prevalence or on medical practice and patient care. Most studies have had serious weaknesses in design. Many fail to consider alternative factors that might affect abuse or prescribing practices. Likewise, no consensus was reached on defining accepted medical use, particularly as it relates to prescribing psychoactive medicines for unapproved indications or for long-term use. However, we now have a basis on which to design a research program to answer some of these questions. Several states have recently implemented an electronic data transfer system. These changes in regulatory systems provide a "natural laboratory" in which prospective studies to evaluate the impact on medical practice and patient care as well as diversion can be done. The National Institute on Drug Abuse is funding a multiyear prospective study of the Massachusetts electronic data transfer system that will include a population-based clinical study that captures patients' histories and diagnoses to evaluate the impact of the system on medical practice.

Discussion

The increasing use of computers to maintain pharmacy records, the expansion of drug utilization reviews of all medications by third-party payers, and the availability of software systems such as the Medicaid Abusable Drug Audit System portend the growth of centralized prescription data banks. Presumably, some states will establish more comprehensive drug-monitoring systems before the research results are available. Undoubtedly, many law enforcement and regulatory officials will actively support the implementation of surveillance systems that readily identify physicians and patients who prescribe or consume large quantities of drugs. It is also reasonable to assume that such a system would simplify their enforcement task of identifying unscrupulous practitioners and pharmacists and reduce diversion sources to thefts, forgeries, illicit synthesis, and importation.

The availability of statewide prescription data is likely to resurrect a long-standing controversy that emerges each time governments attempt to control access to potentially abusable medications for various approved and unapproved indications. This controversy is in large part due to the intrinsic properties of these medications and the differing opinions regarding their benefit and harm and is often based on individual experiences and perceptions. For many years, the differences in emphasis have been sharply delineated by health and enforcement officials and account for the periodic disagreements between health and enforcement departments over drug abuse control recommendations. The legislative history of the current federal drug control legislation illustrates this issue and explains why Congress delegated separate drug control functions to the Health Department (United States House of Representatives 1970).

In a previous publication (Cooper et al. 1992), a considerable body of literature was reviewed suggesting that these analgesics, stimulants, and tranquilizers are effective for a variety of approved and unapproved indications notwithstanding their abuse potential. Although claims of overutilization are frequently made, significant underutilization occurs, particularly with regard to the effective use of medications to treat large subpopulations of patients with anxiety disorders or pain (Dahl 1993; Mellinger et al. 1984; Morgan 1986; Nagy 1987; Portenoy 1990; Shapiro et al. 1984; Uhlenhuth et al. 1984). Some of these prevalent illnesses are associated with serious morbidity and mortality, and many of us are witness to the personal harm and suffering when access to these medications is either denied or made difficult (France et al. 1984; Hash 1984; Hill 1987; Markowitz et al. 1989). Furthermore, subpopulations of patients derive continued benefit from the chronic use of tranquilizers, analgesics, and stimulants for illnesses such as anxiety disorders, malignant and nonmalignant pain, attention-deficit hyperactivity disorder, obesity, treatment-resistant depression, and adjunctively in cancer pain management (Chiarello and Cole 1987; Green and Coyle 1989; Portenoy 1990; Rickels and Schweizer 1993; Satel and Nelson 1989; Tennant and Uelmen 1983; Uhlenhuth et al. 1988; Weintraub 1992). Several medical professional associations have formally acknowledged the appropriateness of chronic use of stimulants (American Academy of Child and Adolescent Psychiatry 1991) and benzodiazepines (American Psychiatric Association 1990) in subpopulations of patients. Although chronic use may result in drug dependence, most patients do not escalate their dose once stabilized or abuse their medication (Balmer et al. 1981; Garvey and Tollefson 1986; Hechtman et al. 1984; Loney 1988; Perry and Heidrich 1982; Portenoy 1990; Porter and Jick 1980; Uhlenhuth et al. 1988). Existing research indicates that there is little overlap between the population taking prescribed psychoactive medications and abuser populations (Cole and Chiarello 1990; Dupont 1988; Woods et al. 1988). National population-based surveys support many of these findings. Thus, from a health perspective, the therapeutic benefit of these medications far outweighs their potential risk of harm, which is primarily limited to a subpopulation of polydrug and alcohol abusers and is dwarfed in comparison with the prevalence of abuse and consequences of cocaine, heroin, marijuana, and alcohol.

In contrast, these same medications are viewed by others with an emphasis on their abuse potential. Based on their experience, regulatory and enforcement officials emphasize the dangerousness of the drug and the greed and evil of the practitioner and the pharmaceutical company that benefits from supplying these addictive "street drugs" (Haislip 1993). Isolated accounts of practitioner criminal prescribing or dispensing and inflated estimates of drug abuse and its consequences are dramatic and make good sound bites on the evening news. Advocates for the use of these medications for long-term therapeutic use or unapproved indications are often dismissed simplistically as proxies for the financial interests of industry or are "soft" on drug abuse, or both. Such views are not limited to enforcement or regulatory officials. Drug abuse treatment program physicians, profoundly influenced by the consequences of the abuse potential of these drugs, will frequently support various enforcement or regulatory activities aimed at reducing their availability for therapeutic use (O'Connor 1993; Sanders 1989). The dangerousness of these medications was a major consideration in the finding by the United States Supreme Court that the needs of law enforcement to collect prescription data to curtail diversion takes precedence over patients' rights to privacy (*Whalen v. Roe* 1977).

The perception of the severity of the various illnesses or indications for which these medications are used also influences public policy. Many of these medications are used to treat medical and psychiatric disorders that a large segment of our society views unfavorably. Unfortunately many believe that fear, depression, pain syndromes, and compulsive or attention disorders are a result of or accompany a "weak will" and that effective recovery efforts are limited to those drug-free interventions aimed at strengthening "willpower" and discipline. Stigmatization, shame, and trivialization of the illnesses often go hand in hand with these biased attitudes. The use of psychoactive medicines is antithetical to these philosophical and ideological biases regarding symptoms of mental illness. The difference in attitude concerning the use of benzodiazepines for seizure disorders or muscle spasms in contrast with anxiety illustrates the point. Many of those who emphasize the dangerousness of these drugs also trivialize the illnesses or indications for which they are used or minimize their effectiveness. Opposition is more intense to the long-term use of these medications. Concern about the development of iatrogenic addiction when prescribing psychoactive medications compounds the problem. Not infrequently, both doctors and patients are confused about the differences between physical dependence and addiction. Thus, the fears and prejudices surrounding the nature and treatment of these disorders are important reasons for underutilization (Bray 1991; Safer and Krager 1992), ineffective use of these medications (Cooper 1992), and the relative ease with which regulators restrict prescribing and patient access to these medications.

The balance that individual states achieve will depend, to a large extent, on the conclusions reached on the risks and benefits of these medications to the individual and the public. Presently the pendulum on this public policy issue is heavily weighted on the risk side as measured by the trend among many states to restrict the use and availability of these medications irrespective of their documented efficacy.

Contrary to the intent of the Food and Drug Administration (FDA), the FDA-approved drug labeling is fast becoming the standard by which accepted medical use is defined. The FDA label enumerates, among other things, the indications, dosages, and duration of treatment for which each medication has been proven effective. These findings are conservative, based on expensive controlled research for finite time periods. Nonetheless, for many years the medical community has had the autonomy to use these various medications in individual patients for unapproved indications and at higher doses and for a longer duration of time than those officially recommended or approved by the FDA. Unapproved uses often appear in the research literature, and their therapeutic benefit is recognized for some subpopulations. For example, although the use of stimulants in treating depression is not an FDA-approved therapeutic indication, clinical studies indicate that for some depressed patients they are highly effective (Chiarello and Cole 1987; Cole et al. 1993; Goff 1986; Rickels et al. 1972; Salzman 1991; Satel and Nelson 1989). Thus current federal health policy recognizes that this use of approved drugs for unapproved indications is medically desirable, leaving the decisions regarding the appropriateness of treatment to local medical standards (Edwards 1972; Nightingale 1992).

Some legislators, health care administrators, medical licensing boards, physicians, and federal law enforcement officials favor limiting psychoactive drug prescribing to well-defined therapeutic indications and to doses, frequencies, and durations of treatment sanctioned by FDA-approved labeling (Federal Register 1985, 1986). The simplicity of these restrictive policies reduces the burden of having to consider and evaluate the complexities of medical practice, the cost of patient care, and the likelihood of diversion by registrants or patients. South Carolina already has such restrictions for all state-controlled substances. Other states have either limited the indications for use of one drug class (analgesics) or have prohibited some FDA-approved indications for use of a specific drug (e.g., amphetamines) (Policy Statement 1989; Richard and Lasagna 1988). A few states limit the number of dosage units of controlled drugs that can be prescribed at one time, or require practitioners to report those patients for whom they chronically prescribe certain controlled drugs for therapeutic indications (Joranson 1990). In a survey of state medical examiners, board members were asked their opinion about the use of narcotics for chronic nonmalignant pain; 47% of those surveyed discouraged such practice, and 32% believed the practice illegal and that physicians engaged in such prescribing behavior should be investigated (Joranson et al. 1992).

At the federal level, for years the DEA has proposed or advocated various regulatory measures, in the name of drug abuse prevention, which would limit existing prescribing autonomy and flexibility. Proposals to prohibit the use of "take as directed" as a valid prescription and to limit use for all unapproved indications are examples. Most recently the DEA has informed Congress of its intent to seek federal legislation that would further limit prescription refills to the duration of treatment approved in the FDA label. In addition the DEA continues to support various state drug regulatory initiatives that restrict prescribing autonomy and local physicians who share their conservative definition of accepted medical practice. The United States General Accounting Office has determined that claims of patient harm resulting from drug diversion control systems "have not been substantiated" (Comptroller General of the United States 1992, p. 2). In this same report, they noted that the DEA is "not aware of any documented evidence that supports these allegations or shows that physicians deny their patients proper medical care because they are afraid of being held accountable for their prescriptions" (p. 11).

These are but a few examples of the effectiveness of the enforcement approach advocates. From their perspective, a closed drug distribution system from the wholesaler to the patient significantly reduces the potential for diversion from pharmacists and practitioners. Their position is well articulated, persuasive, and well received in a political climate of zero tolerance for drug abuse or among those who want to restrict practitioner autonomy for reasons other than reducing retail diversion (e.g., lower health care costs). Unfortunately, this position devalues the substantial benefit of psychotropic medications to the many individuals whose lives are affected by medical conditions that are often dramatically helped by these medications and ignores the diagnostic and therapeutic complexities associated with treating these subpopulations of patients.

Conclusion

Limiting prescribing of psychoactive medications only to approved indications or to certain dosage units or durations of treatment will adversely affect the quality of patients' lives, especially those with treatment-resistant or chronic illnesses. Unquestionably, some patients have been denied access to these medications as a result of some existing drug diversion control systems. The extent to which this will continue once statewide computerized prescription data are analyzed and "suspicious" practitioners and patients are investigated is by no means clear. Notwithstanding the current evidence presented earlier in this chapter, the establishment of these recent less-intrusive prescription drug-monitoring systems does not necessarily allow one to conclude that medical practice and patient care will always be adversely affected.

The manner in which the data are reviewed by state authorities and the methods used for investigating exceptional prescribing will be crucial. Physicians who prescribe large quantities of drugs inappropriately or illicitly must be distinguished from those who prescribe similar quantities for legitimate medical purposes. The same physician may be viewed as an angel of mercy by the patient and as a "drug dealer" by a state investigator. Similar distinctions must be made between patients in need of these medications for acute and chronic use and people acquiring drugs for personal abuse or diversion. The presumption of guilt or innocence will affect the spirit of the investigations of these practitioners and patients. If the objective is limited to stopping the illegal prescription mills and patient scams, then the task is relatively easy and short-lived, since it is difficult to conceive that such illegal prescribing will continue in such a monitoring system. If these same systems permit practitioners to prescribe tranquilizers, narcotics, or stimulants to patients for unapproved indications and for chronic use (in the absence of evidence of diversion) without intimidation, threat of criminal prosecution, or requiring frequent time-consuming justifications of their behavior, then it is possible that such systems will have little effect on medical practice and patient care. Such a situation is more likely to occur when there are broadly defined practice parameters developed by expert clinicians and when peer review is done by physicians knowledgeable about the various diagnoses and associated pharmacotherapeutic complexities often encountered in treatment-resistant or chronically ill subpopulations. Having such a regulatory system in place that includes these "safeguards" may prevent attempts to expand the scope of investigation to doctors and patients who prescribe or take these drugs for unapproved or long-term use in the absence of evidence of drug diversion or drug abuse.

State regulation of this aspect of medical practice and patient care will be dependent on policymakers' perception of the severity of the various illnesses and indications for which these medications are used, the perceived usefulness of the medications and harm when used nonmedically, and the perceived magnitude of retail drug diversion. In addition, the attitudes, biases, and therapeutic acumen of the peer reviewers and state administrators will most likely influence operational definitions of accepted medical use for both acute and long-term use and the spirit and tone of practitioner and patient investigations. The size of the prescription drug control program created to administer and manage the data analysis, peer review, and practitioner investigations will be determined by their perceptions of the nature and magnitude of the problem.

The availability of statewide prescription data is likely to generate political discussion and debate within state legislatures. Given the current influence and effectiveness of a well-organized enforcement effort with highly articulate spokespersons in support of more regulation, and the existing intolerance by sizable segments of our population of drug dependence of any kind, we are not optimistic about continued physician autonomy to prescribe these medications, especially for long-term therapeutic use or for indications or dosages outside the approved FDA label. Patients who have suffered as a result of being denied or threatened the loss of access to these medications, in the absence of any evidence of drug abuse or diversion, along with organized medical societies and associations (Ambre 1993; Rock

1993; Webb 1993) who support such approved and unapproved use, need to make a concerted effort to educate state policymakers and their members and remain vigilant if prescribing autonomy for their physicians and the quality of patients' lives are to be preserved during these various drug abuse prevention efforts.

References

Ambre JJ: Evaluation of the impact of prescription drug diversion control systems on medical practice and patient care: perspective of the American Medical Association, in Prescription Drug Diversion Control Systems, Medical Practice and Patient Care: A Review and Research Agenda. Edited by Cooper J, Czechowicz D, Petersen RC, et al. Rockville, MD, National Institute on Drug Abuse, 1993, pp 141–144

American Academy of Child and Adolescent Psychiatry: Practice parameters for the assessment and treatment of attention-deficit hyperactivity disorder. J Am Acad Child Adolesc Psychiatry 30:I–III, 1991

American Psychiatric Association: Benzodiazepine Dependence, Toxicity, and Abuse. Washington, DC, American Psychiatric Press, 1990

Balmer R, Battergay R, Von Marschall R: Long-term treatment with diazepam: investigation of consumption habits and the interaction between psychotherapy and psychopharmacotherapy: a prospective study. International Pharmacopsychiatry 16:221–234, 1981

Berina LF, Guernsey BG, Hokangon JA, et al: Physician perception of a triplicate prescription law. Am J Hosp Pharm 42:857–859, 1985

Bray GA: Barriers to the treatment of obesity. Ann Intern Med 115:152–153, 1991

Chiarello RJ, Cole JO: The use of psychostimulants in general psychiatry. Arch Gen Psychiatry 44:286–295, 1987

Cole JO, Bolling LA, Peake BJ: Stimulant drugs—medical needs, alternative indications and related problems, in Prescription Drug Diversion Control Systems, Medical Practice and Patient Care: A Review and Research Agenda. Edited by Cooper JR, Czechowicz D, Petersen RC, et al. Rockville, MD, National Institute on Drug Abuse, 1993, pp 89–108

Cole JO, Chiarello RJ: The benzodiazepines as drugs of abuse. J Psychiatr Res 24:135–144, 1990

Comptroller General of the United States: Prescription Drug Monitoring: States Can Readily Identify Illegal Sales and Use of Controlled Substances (Publ No GAO/HRD-92-115). Washington, DC, General Accounting Office, 1992

Cooper JR: Ineffective use of psychoactive drugs. JAMA 267:281–282, 1992

Cooper JR, Czechowicz DJ, Petersen RC, et al: Prescription drug diversion control and medical practice. JAMA 268:1306–1310, 1992

Cooper JR, Czechowicz D, Petersen RC, et al (eds): Prescription Drug Diversion Control Systems, Medical Practice and Patient Care: A Review and Research Agenda. Rockville, MD, National Institute on Drug Abuse, 1993

Dahl J: Cancer pain initiatives, in Prescription Drug Diversion Control Systems, Medical Practice and Patient Care: A Review and Research Agenda. Edited by Cooper JR, Czechowicz D, Petersen RC, et al. Rockville, MD, National Institute on Drug Abuse, 1993, pp 260–265

Dupont RL: Abuse of benzodiazepines: the problems and the solutions. Am J Drug Alcohol Abuse 14 (suppl 1):1–69, 1988

Edwards CC: Legal status of approved labeling for prescription drugs: prescribing for uses unapproved by the Food and Drug Administration. Federal Register 37:16503–16505, 1972

Federal Register: Changes in protocol requirements for researchers and prescription requirements for practitioners. Federal Register 50:42184–42187, 1985

Federal Register: Schedules of controlled substances: rescheduling of synthetic dronabinol in sesame oil and encapsulated in soft gelatin capsules from Schedule I to Schedule II: statement of policy. Federal Register 51:17476–17478, 1986

France RD, Urban BJ, Keefe FJ: Long-term use of narcotic analgesics in chronic pain. Soc Sci Med 19:1379–1382, 1984

Garvey MJ, Tollefson GD: Prevalence of misuse of prescribed benzodiazepines in patients with primary anxiety disorder or major depression. Am J Psychiatry 143:1601–1603, 1986

Gitchel GT: Existing methods to identify retail drug diversion, in Prescription Drug Diversion Control Systems, Medical Practice and Patient Care: A Review and Research Agenda. Edited by Cooper JR, Czechowicz D, Petersen RC, et al. Rockville, MD, National Institute on Drug Abuse, 1993, pp 132–140

Goff DC: The stimulant challenge test in depression. Psychiatry 47:538–554, 1986

Green J, Coyle M: Methadone use in the control of nonmalignant chronic pain. Pain Management 2:241–246, 1989

Haislip GR: Drug diversion control systems, medical practice, and patient care, in Prescription Drug Diversion Control Systems, Medical Practice and Patient Care: A Review and Research Agenda. Edited by Cooper J, Czechowicz D, Petersen RC, et al. Rockville, MD, National Institute on Drug Abuse, 1993, pp 120–131

Hash BM: A personal account of Valium use. J Clin Psychopharmacol 4:298, 1984

Hechtman L, Weiss G, Perlman T: Hyperactives as young adults: past and current substance abuse and antisocial behavior. Am J Orthopsychiatry 54:415–425, 1984

Hill CS: Painful prescriptions. JAMA 257:2081, 1987

Horgan C, Prottas J, Tompkins C, et al: A Review of Prescription Drug Diversion Control Methods (Report of the Center for Drug Abuse Services Research). Waltham, MA, Bigel Institute for Health Policy, Brandeis University, 1991

Joranson DE: Federal and state regulation of opioids. Journal of Pain and Symptom Management 5:S12–S23, 1990

Joranson DE, Cleeland CS, Weissman DE, et al: Opioids for chronic cancer and non-cancer pain: a survey of state medical board members. Federation Bulletin: The Medical Journal Licensure and Discipline 79:15–49, 1992

Loney J: Substance abuse in adolescents: diagnostic issues derived from studies of attention deficit disorder with hyperactivity, in Adolescent Drug Abuse: Analysis of Treatment Research. Edited by Rahdert ER, Grabowski J. Rockville, MD, National Institute on Drug Abuse, 1988, pp 19–26

Markowitz JS, Weissman MM, Quellete R, et al: Quality of life in panic disorder. Arch Gen Psychiatry 46:984–992, 1989

Mellinger GD, Balter MB, Uhlenhuth EH: Prevalence and correlates of the long-term regular use of anxiolytics. JAMA 251:375–379, 1984

Morgan JP: American opiophobia: customary underutilization of opioid analgesics, in Advances in Alcohol and Substance Abuse. Edited by Stimmel B. New York, Haworth, 1986, pp 163–173

Nagy A: Long-term treatment with benzodiazepines: theoretical, ideological and practical aspects. Acta Psychiatr Scand 76S:47–55, 1987

Nightingale SL: Unlabeled uses of approved drugs. Drug Information Journal 26:141–147, 1992

O'Connor RD: Benzodiazepine dependence—a treatment program perspective, in Prescription Drug Diversion Control Systems, Medical Practice and Patient Care: A Review and Research Agenda. Edited by Cooper J, Czechowicz D, Petersen RC, et al. Rockville, MD, National Institute on Drug Abuse, 1993, pp 266–269

Perry S, Heidrich G: Management of pain during debridement: a survey of U.S. burn units. Pain 13:267–280, 1982

Policy Statement, Washington State Medical Disciplinary Board, August 18, 1989

Portenoy RK: Chronic opioid therapy in nonmalignant pain. Journal of Pain and Symptom Management 5:S46–S62, 1990

Porter J, Jick H: Addiction rare in patients treated with narcotics. N Engl J Med 302:123, 1980

Richard BW, Lasagna L: Anorectic drugs: drug policy making at the state level. J Clin Pharmacol 28:395–400, 1988

Rickels K, Schweizer E: Anxiolytics—indications, benefits and risks of short and long term benzodiazepine therapy: current evaluation of the research data, in Prescription Drug Diversion Control Systems, Medical Practice and Patient Care: A Review and Research Agenda. Edited by Cooper JR, Czechowicz D, Petersen RC, et al. Rockville, MD, National Institute on Drug Abuse, 1993, pp 51–67

Rickels K, Gingrich RL, McLaughlin FW, et al: Methylphenidate in mildly depressed outpatients. Clin Pharmacol Ther 13:595–601, 1972

Rock N: Evaluation of the impact of prescription drug diversion control systems on medical practice and patient care: American Academy of Child and Adolescent Psychiatry, in Prescription Drug Diversion Control Systems, Medical Practice and Patient Care: A Review and Research Agenda. Edited by Cooper JR, Czechowicz D, Petersen RC, et al. Rockville, MD, National Institute on Drug Abuse, 1993, pp 246–248

Roslewicz T: The Medicaid prescription drug initiative, in Prescription Drug Diversion Control Systems, Medical Practice and Patient Care: A Review and Research Agenda. Edited by Cooper JR, Czechowicz D, Petersen RC, et al. Rockville, MD, National Institute on Drug Abuse, 1993, pp 200–205

Safer DJ, Krager JM: Effect of a media blitz and a threatened lawsuit on stimulant treatment. JAMA 268:1004–1007, 1992

Salzman C: Pharmacological treatment of depression in the elderly. Paper presented at NIH Consensus Development Conference on the Diagnosis and Treatment of Depression in Late Life, Bethesda, MD, National Institutes of Health, November 1991

Sanders JH: Prescribing addictive medications. N C Med J 50:105, 1989

Satel SS, Nelson JC: Stimulants in the treatment of depression: a critical overview. J Clin Psychiatry 50:241–245, 1989

Shapiro S, Skinner EA, Kessler LG, et al: Utilization of health and mental health services: three epidemiologic catchment area sites. Arch Gen Psychiatry 41:971–978, 1984

Sigler KA, Guernsey BG, Ingrim NB, et al: Effect of a triplicate prescription law on prescribing of Schedule II drugs. Am J Hosp Pharm 41:108–111, 1984

Tennant FS, Uelmen GF: Narcotic maintenance for chronic pain medical and legal guidelines. Postgrad Med 73:81–94, 1983

Uhlenhuth EH, Balter MB, Mellinger GD, et al: Anxiety disorders: prevalence and treatment. Curr Med Res Opin 8S:37–46, 1984

Uhlenhuth EH, DeWitt H, Balter MB, et al: Risks and benefits of long-term benzodiazepine use. J Clin Psychopharmacol 8:161–167, 1988

United States House of Representatives, Committee on Interstate and Foreign Commerce Report: Comprehensive Drug Abuse Prevention and Control Act of 1970 (Report No 91-1444). Washington, DC, U.S. Government Printing Office, 1970

Webb CE: Prescription drug diversion control systems: perspective of the American Pharmaceutical Association, in Prescription Drug Diversion Control Systems, Medical Practice and Patient Care: A Review and Research Agenda. Edited by Cooper J, Czechowicz D, Petersen RC, et al. Rockville, MD, National Institute on Drug Abuse, 1993, pp 235–238

Weintraub M: Long-term weight control study: conclusions. Clin Pharmacol Ther 51 (suppl):642–646, 1992

Whalen v Richard Roe, 429 US 589 (1977)

The White House: The White House Conference for a Drug Free America: Final Report. Washington, DC, June 1988

Wilford BB: Prescription Drug Abuse: some considerations in evaluating policy responses. J Psychoactive Drugs 23:343–348, 1991

Woods JH, Katz JL, Winger G: Use and abuse of benzodiazepines: issues relevant to prescribing. JAMA 260:3476–3479, 1988

CHAPTER ELEVEN

The Negative Influence of Licensing and Disciplinary Boards on Pain Treatment With Controlled Substances

C. Stratton Hill, Jr., M.D.

The medical literature substantiates the inadequate treatment of both acute and chronic pain, regardless of cause (Edwards 1990; Foley 1985; R. M. Marks and Sachar 1973; Morgan 1986; Sriwatanakul et al. 1983). Pain is most likely to be undertreated when relief requires the use of strong opioids because physicians are generally reluctant to prescribe them, particularly if the doses required to effect relief are considered outside the "usual" or "recommended" range, as defined by standard pharmacology texts, and if prolonged use is necessary (Hill 1991). Similarly, pharmacists have reservations about dispensing opioids under these circumstances. Three basic reasons have been proposed to account for the undertreatment of pain: 1) cultural and societal barriers to adequate and appropriate use of narcotics; 2) knowledge deficits about the pharmacology of narcotics among health care professionals; and 3) influence of disciplinary boards and drug enforcement agencies, both state and federal, on the prescribing practices of physicians and dispensing practices of pharmacists (Hill 1990b).

Government restrictions on controlled substances are authorized by

This chapter was adapted from Hill CS Jr: "The Negative Influence of Licensing and Disciplinary Boards and Drug Enforcement Agencies on Pain Treatment With Opioid Analgesics." *Journal of Pharmaceutical Care in Pain and Symptom Control* 1:43–62, 1993.

two legislative sources: health care practice acts (HPAs) (e.g., medical, nursing, pharmacy, dental), which set standards of practice for the use of controlled substances as well as standards for all professional practice; and controlled substances laws, which mandate how such substances are to be handled when used for medical purposes. States exert influence on health care practice through enactment of HPAs, whereas federal influence is primarily through controlled substances laws.

In this chapter I explore how licensing and disciplinary (regulatory) boards and drug enforcement agencies significantly influence the treatment of pain, as well as other medical conditions such as psychological illnesses. These boards and agencies exert a subtle, and sometimes not so subtle, influence on treatment of pain and other symptoms through the real or perceived threat of loss of license or criminal prosecution felt by practitioners who prescribe, dispense, or administer controlled substances. Even if an accused practitioner is eventually exonerated, the defense against the charges is expensive. Thus the possibility of losing one's license or of criminal prosecution—although only one of the three reasons cited above for inadequate pain and symptom treatment—has a profound, and disproportionate, influence on patient care.

This analysis of problems with regulatory agencies is based on my experience with reviewing regulatory acts in the states of Texas, Louisiana, Florida, and Washington and on my personal experience providing advice and testimony for physicians charged with violations of acts in these states.

Regulatory acts are administered and interpreted by persons who are appointed to regulatory boards. Variations in knowledge and attitudes of these persons (regulators) exist among the 50 states. Some boards have lay, or so-called public, members who not only have no technical medical knowledge but specifically are presumed to have no knowledge of pain and symptom treatment or use of controlled substances. This variation in technical knowledge and societal-based attitudes about opioids obviously influences the boards' disciplinary practices; thus the issues discussed here do not uniformly apply to all states. To obtain data regarding medical board members' knowledge about pain and its treatment with opioids, Joranson and colleagues (1992), under the aegis of the Federation of State Medical Boards, conducted a survey of regulatory board members in all states about their perception of the legality and appropriateness of opioid use for treatment of pain of both malignant and nonmalignant origin (see Hanin, Chapter 7, this volume). The survey also assessed board members' opioid preferences for pain treatment. Of significance is the high percentage of regulators having a negative view of the use of opioids, particularly strong opioids, for treatment of pain in situations for which most practitioners would consider strong opioid use an accepted standard of practice. These findings validate the fear of potential disciplinary action that essentially all practitioners have when prescribing opioids and that significantly contributes to the overall inadequate use of opioids, particularly strong opioids, for pain control.

Health Care Practice Acts

State legislative bodies are responsible for crafting HPAs, which create administrative bodies (e.g., examining boards for medicine, nursing, pharmacy) responsible for enforcing the acts. Such acts protect the public interest in matters of health care by licensing only qualified practitioners and monitoring their continued practice. Practice is monitored by comparing practitioners' actions with the standards of practice set forth in the acts and interpreted according to community standards of practice. Standards must be maintained that will, at the least, prevent practitioners from inflicting harm on their patients. However, it is in the public interest that standards go beyond this negative requirement and ensure that active, modern, high-quality medical care is provided to all citizens of the jurisdiction. High-quality medical care should be measured against a standard that reasonable minds would agree is appropriate for qualified practitioners offering their proposed services, and supported by the purported quality of the facilities where the treatment is offered, and not merely by customary practice in the community unrelated to any other applicable standard. A prevailing philosophy behind HPAs is that they should set only minimum standards and that anything beyond this would be considered quality control, which should be left to local quality assurance boards. However, public interest may require more than minimum standards.

In structuring the wording for practice standards, legislative writers try to avoid language that may inadvertently impede the highest standard of medical practice. However, since it is also desirable that the standards be flexible to apply to myriad practice situations, the language contained in guidelines for determining standards is broad and general and therefore subject to interpretation.

The regulatory boards' function is to define standards of practice by interpreting the language of the acts. It is in this process of interpretation that impediments to proper use of controlled substances may arise. An examination of the process that boards use to carry out the functions with which they are charged reveals why practitioners feel they are vulnerable to possible license loss when prescribing, dispensing, or administering controlled substances for legitimate pain control.

Members of boards are usually appointed by the governor of the state. The composition of the board and qualifications for membership are contained in the HPA. The composition is typically a mix of laypersons and persons who are licensed to practice the discipline the board regulates. The qualifications for members who are licensed to practice the discipline are usually broad. Lay members are not required to have any knowledge of the field. The rationale for including lay members on the board is that their presence will instill confidence in the public that the board is functioning in an impartial manner and not allowing licensees to escape discipline when a violation of the act occurs or when there has been misconduct. The quality of a board's actions is directly related to the quality of the members chosen by the governor.

A distinction should be made between appointed board members and the administrative staff of the board. Most licensees of boards have more contact with the administrative staff than with the board members. Unfortunately, the image of the board may be a reflection of the administrative staff rather than of board members. This can occur if there is an uncritical overreliance by board members on the administrative staff. If board members fail to exercise proper supervision of the administrative staff, the administrative staff can determine what comes before the board and thus essentially control the board by default. Persons who accept appointments by government officials to serve on these boards are usually busy, productive people who may find it difficult to devote the time needed to be an effective member. However, proper functioning of a health care board is not possible if appointed members do not involve themselves in the overall supervision of the staff. Members of boards should be certain that what the administrative staff presents to them, and how it is presented, reflects the actual policy of the board. Licensees should also try to make such a determination. If a procedure seems to be overbearing or frustrating, an effort should be made to contact a board member directly for confirmation of the procedure or a member of the legislative body that supervises the board.

Determining and Applying Practice Standards

For practice standards to be flexible, the language must be broad in scope, not rigid, directive, or prescriptive. This permits interpretation in light of a variety of clinical situations. Examples from the Medical Practice Acts of Texas and Florida illustrate the wide latitude for interpretation these guidelines afford. The Texas act proscribes "prescribing or administering a drug or treatment that is *nontherapeutic in nature or nontherapeutic in the manner the drug or treatment is administered or prescribed*" (Texas Medical Practice Act 1989, Section 3.08[4][E]; italics added), "prescribing, administering, or dispensing in a manner *not consistent with public health and welfare* dangerous drugs as defined by Chapter 425," (Section 3.08[4][F]; italics added), and "professional failure to practice medicine in an *acceptable manner consistent with public health and welfare*" (Section 3.08[18], italics added).

The Florida act states the following:

> The following acts shall constitute grounds for which disciplinary actions specified in subsection (2) may be taken: prescribing, dispensing, administering, mixing, or otherwise preparing a legend drug, including any controlled substance, other than in the course of the physician's professional practice. For the purposes of this paragraph, *it shall be legally presumed* that prescribing, dispensing, administering, mixing, or otherwise preparing legend drugs, including all controlled substances, *inappropriately or in excessive or inappropriate quantities is not in the best interest of the patient and is not in the course of the physician's professional practice, without regard to his intent*. (Florida Statute; italics added)

The Louisiana and Washington statutes contain similar phrases.

The phrases in italics require interpretation or contain a legal presumption. Interpretation of them is strictly the prerogative of the respective boards, and guidelines for interpreting such phrases as "nontherapeutic," "not consistent with public health and welfare," "acceptable manner consistent with public health and welfare," and "inappropriately or in excessive quantities" are not provided in the acts.

The following is an allegation against a Texas physician taken verbatim from the charges of the Board of Medical Examiners:

> Treatment using injectable Demerol and Phenergan continued through March 23, 1987.
> Between January 1986 and March 23, 1987 the patient received prescriptions for approximately 7,800 mg. of injectable Demerol in addition to prescriptions for Percodan, Robaxin, ergotrate, Tuinal, and Fiorinal #3.

This is an example of the emphasis on quantity without consideration for the clinical reason the medication was prescribed. The medical record showed a diagnosis and a justification for narcotic use, but the total dose of meperidine (Demerol) over a 15-month period was the important factor to the investigator. In this case, the patient had experienced severe migraine headaches for more than 20 years. She had severe "breakthrough" headaches for which she required meperidine in larger than usual doses for relief. Had the investigator properly related the patient's history and current clinical condition to the physician's prescribing practice, it would have been obvious that no improper prescribing or diversion was taking place. This physician was exonerated of all charges, but his legal defense cost approximately $50,000.

Health care professionals must make treatment decisions regarding controlled substances despite not knowing how a board will ultimately interpret these phrases in a given clinical situation. Unfortunately, such a decision will be judged by the board after the fact. At some point during the process of judging a practice decision already made, the board will interpret the uncertain terms and phrases and apply them to the particular situation the practitioner faced. Only the board is privy to the guidelines they use in interpretation.

Basing evaluation of treatment decisions on vague guidelines is valid only as long as the interpretation is based on sound scientific principles and is free from the influence of biases, prejudices, myths, and misinformation. Similarly, it is satisfactory only as long as competing public interests are balanced. Unfortunately, however, interpretation of how opioids should be used is vulnerable to influence by societal biases, prejudices, myths, and misinformation about their attributes and uses. Charles Schuster (1989), Director of the National Institute on Drug Abuse, stated, "We have been so effective in warning the medical establishment and the public in general about the inappropriate use of opiates that we have endowed these drugs with a mysterious power to enslave that is overrated" (p. 2). Indeed, it is unlikely that societal prejudices and confusion about the difference between legitimate and illegitimate uses of narcotics can be removed and therefore not influence boards' interpretations of current guidelines. Therefore, boards need guidelines that prevent interpretations based on nonscientific principles of pain management and misinformation about narcotics and their use in pain treatment.

Failure to Recognize Competing Public Interests

It is in the public interest to prevent diversion of legal drugs from legitimate to illegitimate use. It is also in the public interest to ensure that all citizens who suffer from painful medical conditions are relieved of their pain. Boards almost invariably fail to recognize competition between these public interests. When legal opioids are indicated for pain relief, they should be available to the patient requiring them at the appropriate time and in appropriate quantities. However, this medical need competes with the police function of preventing diversion and the board's perception of its role in preventing addiction. It is obviously in the public interest that the antisocial behavior of addicts be prevented. Boards often equate physiological dependence on opioids with psychological dependence on them. The person who is psychologically dependent on a drug has a compulsion to take the drug despite its causing harm, and this person is considered an "addict." Patients who are physiologically dependent on a drug to relieve their pain are not addicts. Boards frequently fail to make this distinction.

Regulatory boards and drug enforcement agencies must ensure that a balance is achieved between medical needs requiring an adequate supply of opioids and the police function of preventing diversion (Hill 1990a). Unfortunately, complaints filed against practitioners in which I have served as an expert witness indicate that boards are preoccupied with the police function and do not recognize their responsibility to ensure adequate treatment of pain. This may be explained by the usual practice of a board's uncritical reliance on its investigative staff's presentation of the case. Investigators are usually persons with a police orientation. They are likely not to understand or to be sensitive to issues of medical practice.

Determining Customary Community Practice

Customary community practice is the usual criterion used by boards to determine standards of health care practice. This method almost universally results in prescribing inadequate doses for intervals that exceed the drug's period of effectiveness and of restricting supplies of medications to patients. Practitioners who prescribe adequate doses for proper time intervals and who provide adequate quantities of opioids to the patient for a reasonable length of time are often considered prima facie outside the standard of practice and are charged with violations of the act, such as "overprescribing," "nontherapeutic prescribing," and "failing to practice medicine in an acceptable manner consistent with public health and welfare." The patient's need for the opioid to treat a targeted symptom and the outcome of pain treatment are not considered vital parts of the community standard.

When interpreting the validity of practitioners' actions, decisions about dosing should be based on current, scientific information de- rived from studies of opioid pharmacology in patients experiencing pain. The cancer patient in pain has provided a new model for studying opioid pharmacology and new knowledge about opioids. Principal among this new knowledge is that pain itself influences the dose of drug required to relieve it (Foley 1989). The more intense the pain, the higher the dose of analgesic needed for relief. A "proper" dose, therefore, is whatever dose is required to relieve the pain and, of necessity, includes a wide range. Recommended or usual starting doses found in pharmacology texts, and other generally accepted authoritative sources, are merely guidelines and should be abandoned quickly if they are inadequate. Doses recommended as "usual" in most sources of dose information were determined by using an older pain model, the postoperative pain patient, and single-dose studies (Twycross 1988). The intensity of pain in patients suffering chronic pain, of both malignant and nonmalignant origin, is usually greater than that of patients experiencing postoperative pain, and doses must be adjusted accordingly. For example, in a multicenter study of cancer pain treatment, the mean daily dose of morphine was 240 mg, with a range of 60–1,800 mg/day (Kaiko et al. 1989).

Determining community standards for the indications for opioids and psychoactive drugs, especially on an outpatient basis, is highly problematic. The use of opioids for pain of nonmalignant origin is controversial, and no consensus exists among experts (Portenoy 1991; Turk and Brody 1991, 1992). This is especially true of back pain with no demonstrable cause (Portenoy 1989) and chronic headaches (Diamond 1991). Recommendations range from an emphatic rejection of the use of opioids under any circumstances to their use for both types of patients in selected cases. These patients frequently have multiple consultations resulting in many different treatment approaches, including, for back pain patients, multiple surgical procedures. For many patients, symptoms either persist as they were or worsen. Almost invariably, these patients are ultimately cared for by a generalist, such as a family practitioner or an internist. For a certain subpopulation of these patients, the only effective option remaining for pain relief is systemic opioid therapy. Because of the frustrating and debilitating nature of their symptoms, these patients frequently exhibit emotional traits that also require the use of psychoactive drugs. Practitioners who use opioids and psychoactive drugs to treat these patients for what they consider legitimate medical complaints are often accused by boards of perpetuating an "addict's" drug habits. The confusion about these two conditions among experts in the respective fields makes determining a community standard extremely difficult. Indeed, the standard is likely to be determined based on prejudices and misinformation about the drugs involved and about patients experiencing these problems. If the doses of opioids and psychoactive drugs required to control the patient's symptoms are outside of the usual range, the physician prescribing them is likely to be charged with "excessive" prescribing in violation of the HPA. Physicians faced with treating these patients are reluctant to risk this possibility, and the result is undertreatment or refusal to treat the patient effectively.

Boards should not rely uncritically on community standards for determining use of these drugs in a given community. Targeted symptoms and outcome of treatment are valid substitutes. Community standards should not be allowed to perpetuate inadequate treatment of valid medical complaints. In some instances, it may be necessary to establish appropriate community standards for treatment of pain by statute.

Failure to Appreciate Pharmacokinetics and Pharmacodynamics

Investigators for boards and agencies are unlikely to have an adequate understanding of the pharmacokinetics of opioids. For example, biotransformation in the liver reduces the amount of active analgesic of an oral dose prior to its reaching the opioid binding sites in the central nervous system; therefore, oral doses must be "larger" than parenteral ones to compensate for this first-pass effect. With equianalgesic doses, essentially the same amount of opioid reaches the opioid binding sites in the central nervous system. However, the "larger" oral doses are frequently considered outside the standard of practice and therefore a violation of them, whereas the "smaller" parenteral doses are considered to be within the standard of practice.

Being unaware of or ignoring pharmacokinetics commonly causes regulators to consider only the absolute number associated with the dose without regard for clinical circumstances. Practitioners who use opioids intraspinally are rarely investigated because investigators consider the "smaller" dose required by this route not only acceptable but desirable compared with equianalgesic oral doses. In contrast, physicians who must treat patients with oral opioids because intraspinal administration has failed or cannot be used are vulnerable to charges of violating the standard of practice for opioid use because the oral dose is considered "excessive" even though the ultimate, effective dose is essentially identical.

Faulty Definition of Addiction
Resulting in Unjust Discipline

The common societal definition of addiction is physiological dependence on a drug resulting from the chronic taking of it, regardless of the reason for taking it. Unfortunately, many regulators accept this definition without critical evaluation. Because of this, practitioners who prescribe opioids for patients with chronic painful conditions over the protracted course of their diseases consider themselves vulnerable to discipline because regulators may judge them to be creating drug addicts, a practice that is not in the public interest and therefore a violation of the practice act. Although the physician believes he or she is treating a patient with a legitimate medical problem, the board may believe the physician is not able to detect a manipulating drug seeker and is feeding his or her addiction.

Discipline under these circumstances is unjust because the physician is *not* creating an addict. Patients who must take opioids chronically for a painful medical condition become physically dependent on them—that is, they will experience an abstinence (withdrawal) reaction if the drug is abruptly stopped; but this can be avoided if the dose is gradually decreased until it is discontinued. Physical dependence is an expected pharmacological result of taking an opioid and is different from psychological dependence, in which the person has a compulsive craving for the drug and takes it despite predictable and consistent harm (Goodman 1990; Jaffe 1990; I. Marks 1990; Rinaldi et al. 1988). Most patients taking opioids to relieve pain have none of these latter characteristics. Thus, it is necessary for boards to have a proper definition of *addiction* and *an addict.*

Another popular misconception about the addictive potential of these drugs is that mere exposure to them will cause addiction. Studies in patients who must take narcotics over prolonged periods for relief of painful medical conditions that eventually heal do not become psychologically dependent on (addicted to) them (Perry and Heidrich 1982; Porter and Jick 1980). Similarly, experience with veterans of the Vietnam War who returned home psychologically dependent on heroin (addicted) revealed that only 25% remained psychologically dependent (addicted) on it after 2 years (Peele 1989; Robins et al. 1974).

Treating patients with opioids for chronic pain is not a threat to the public interest but instead is in the best interest of the public health and welfare of the citizens of the jurisdiction.

Inequitable Enforcement Practices

Health care professionals may be reported to boards and agencies by anonymous complainants. Most boards and agencies are obligated to investigate such complaints regardless of their apparent merit. In some instances, the same patient has been treated with opioids, psychoactive drugs, and other categories of drugs by a succession of practitioners, all of whom have prescribed in essentially the same way, but the complainant, who may be a disgruntled patient or a colleague who is prejudiced against these drugs or disagrees with how the treating physician is using them, charges only one of the practitioners with a violation.

Another inequitable enforcement practice arises from the treatment of chronic back pain, the most common chronic pain of nonmalignant origin. Surgical correction of the cause is possible in some patients; however, in others, severe, chronic pain persists and indeed may worsen after multiple surgical attempts to treat the alleged cause. The indications and justification for multiple surgical procedures may be vague and problematic, and after these multiple surgeries, many patients are nonfunctional because of pain. Opioids are useful in controlling pain and restoring functional status to a selected sub-population of these patients. However, physicians who prescribe opioids for these patients are vulnerable to charges of "non-therapeutic" opioid use and therefore in violation of the standard of practice. In contrast, the surgeon who performed the multiple "non-therapeutic" surgeries is seldom, if ever, vulnerable to being charged with violating the standard of practice. In applying the term *non-therapeutic* to opioid use in this context, there is confusion between the pharmacological and social definitions of *nontherapeutic*. Certainly the use of an analgesic to treat pain is pharmacologically therapeutic. However, society is reluctant to consider the use of opioids in the treatment of chronic noncancer pain, and it labels such use as being *nontherapeutic*.

Questionable Disciplinary Techniques Used by Boards

The following disciplinary actions of boards are some examples of the confusion regarding both the legitimate and illegitimate uses of opioids.

Required courses in narcotics use. A physician who has been charged with a violation of the HPA because of inappropriate use of opioids may be required to enroll in an educational course to learn how "properly" to use them. "Proper" use is characteristically defined as not using opioids at all for the clinical condition the practitioner was treating. Although pain relief may be impossible without using an opioid, the undesirable outcome of unrelieved pain seems irrelevant to the board. Indeed, most courses have no relevance to the realities of the medical situation the charged physician was treating, nor is the faculty for such a course likely to have had experience with clinical situations similar to those the charged physician faced. When practitioners hear of competent professionals being subjected to such irrational discipline, they become reluctant, and indeed unwilling, to use opioids, even when they feel these drugs are indicated, because of fear of being subjected to a similar, or worse, fate.

Required use of all alternative treatments. Regulators assume that if opioids are to be used at all for the treatment of pain, that they must be used only for brief periods or used only as a last resort. Boards therefore require a practitioner to subject a patient to all alternative modalities of treatment before considering opioid use, often regardless of whether these modalities are medically indicated and often despite evidence that multiple attempts to remove the cause of the pain have already been made. Psychiatric consultation for all patients is usually a minimum requirement before treatment. The presumption seems to be that any patient who potentially requires extended treatment with opioids for pain relief has a psychiatric disorder until it has been proven otherwise.

The requirement that all alternative modalities to opioids be tried before opioids are used is based on a belief, or assertion, that alternative modalities are unquestionably effective and that all the physician must do is "learn" what they are and when they should be used. However, there are no data to support such a premise. The evidence from reports of behavioral and other nonpharmacological pain management modalities suggests that patients accepted into these treatment programs are highly selected to ensure that they will indeed respond to this treatment approach. Despite this selection, the long-term success rate in adequately controlling pain is relatively low. Requiring patients to undergo such an arbitrary and problematic succession of treatment modalities is degrading, irrational, and expensive. Additionally, it represents an arbitrary, nonproductive intrusion into the doctor-patient relationship by disciplinary boards.

Medical Indication Restrictions Imposed Either by HPA or Controlled Substance Acts

Medical indications for prescribing controlled substances may also be limited by regulatory boards. For example, until recently, prescribing central nervous system stimulants to counteract the sedation caused by opioids prescribed for pain treatment was prohibited in Wisconsin. Thanks to efforts by the Wisconsin Cancer Pain Initiative, this restrictive rule was changed (*Cancer Pain Update* 1991). Many states have laws and rules that arbitrarily limit medical indications for controlled substances that are out of touch with clinical reality. For example, laws may summarily prohibit persons who are psychologically dependent on (addicted to) controlled substances, or who have a history of drug abuse, from having these drugs prescribed regardless of a current, legitimate medical indication for their use. Clinical reality is that persons falling into these categories may develop chronic painful medical conditions such as cancer. It is inhumane to deny pain relief to such individuals. Admittedly, such patients are likely to be more difficult to manage, but health care professionals have an obligation to provide care. To judge morally these persons as inferior human beings not worthy of pain relief is unconscionable, and laws based on such a judgment, and justified further as protecting the public interest, are irrational and not in the best interest of the health and welfare of the citizens of the state.

Actions Required to Remove Negative Influences of Licensing and Disciplinary Boards

Practitioners' fear of unwarranted discipline by regulatory boards must be removed, and state-controlled substances acts should be amended to reflect realistic clinical needs. Achieving these goals requires a societal reorientation toward pain and psychological illness and the use of controlled substances for their treatment. The first step toward this reorientation will be to make a clear, unequivocal distinction between the legal and illegal uses of controlled substances. Accomplishing reorientation in the short term is unlikely. However, instituting the following changes could help improve treatment in a relatively short period of time.

Action by Regulatory and Disciplinary Boards

- Regulatory and disciplinary boards should actively encourage the use of controlled substances for medical conditions for which they are indicated while monitoring for abuses and diversion by licensees.
- Boards should clearly distinguish between physical dependence, a normal response to taking opioids over a period of time, and psychological dependence (addiction), the compulsive use of a substance despite its causing harm to the user, and define addiction in terms of psychological dependence.
- Outcome of treatment should be a criterion in judging appropriate use of controlled substances for the treatment of pain. This recognizes that dosing varies widely for different patients and that the number of dose units used to treat a patient is, for the most part, irrelevant. Currently, the prescribing process is the major criterion for determining appropriate use of controlled substances. Outcome as a criterion requires that a judgment be based on the humaneness of the patient's treatment rather than the likelihood of abuse or diversion.
- If community standards for treating pain perpetuate or sanction inadequate pain relief, the board should upgrade the standard.
- Modern principles of opioid pharmacology, especially pharmaco-

kinetics, should be the foundation for judging practitioners' use of narcotics.

- Standards of practice should be established to judge repeated surgical attempts to correct causes of pain, especially back pain.

Action by Drug Enforcement Agencies

- Investigators for drug enforcement agencies should be aware of targeted symptoms and medical conditions for which opioids are indicated, especially the difference between nociceptive and neuropathic pain.
- Investigators should be taught modern opioid pharmacology, especially pharmacokinetics.
- Emphasis in enforcement of drug laws should be on illegal use and diversion for profit. Physicians who treat patients for chronic painful conditions in which a valid physician-patient relationship exists need little attention from law enforcement officials.

Action by State Legislative Bodies

- Legislative bodies should remove ambiguities in HPAs that would subject a practitioner to unjust discipline.
- Guidelines for practice standards should be clear and available to practitioners so that they will know how to conduct themselves in such a way as not to provoke charges by government authorities that are based on unsound knowledge about pain and opioids.
- Guidelines for practice standards should be crafted to consider outcome of treatment rather than merely initiation of a treatment process.
- State-controlled substances acts should recognize, and explicitly state, that controlled substances have legitimate medical uses.
- The acts should clearly define *drug abuser* to distinguish unequivocally such persons from patients who require opioids for pain relief. This will ensure physicians that every patient for whom they prescribe long-term opioids and who develops the expected physiological dependence on the drug will not be immediately labeled

an addict, thereby making the physician vulnerable to disciplinary action.

- If community standards of practice fall below adequate standards of pain relief because they are based on unscientific principles, myths, prejudices, and misinformation about narcotic use, they should be remedied by statute.

References

Cancer Pain Update: Wisconsin's 120 dosage unit limitation is repealed. Cancer Pain Update 22:1, 1991

Diamond S: Editorial. Headache Quarterly, Current Treatment and Research 2:165, 1991

Edwards WT: Optimizing opioid treatment of postoperative pain. Journal of Pain and Symptom Management 5:S24–S36, 1990

FLA STAT Chapter 458.331(1)(Q)

Foley KM: The treatment of cancer pain. N Engl J Med 313:84–95, 1985

Foley KM: The "decriminalization" of cancer pain, in Drug Treatment of Cancer Pain in a Drug-Oriented Society. Edited by Hill CS Jr, Fields WS. New York, Raven, 1989, pp 5–18

Goodman A: Addiction: definition and implications. Br J Addict 85:1403–1408, 1990

Haislip GR: Impact of drug abuse on legitimate drug use, in Drug Treatment of Cancer Pain in a Drug-Oriented Society. Edited by Hill CS Jr, Fields WS. New York, Raven, 1989, pp 213–233

Hill CS Jr: Clinical issues: achieving balance in national drug control policy: the use of analgesia, in Balancing the Response to Prescription Drug Abuse: Report of a National Symposium on Medicine and Public Policy. Edited by Wilford BB. Chicago, IL, American Medical Association, Department of Substance Abuse, 1990a, pp 37–48

Hill CS Jr: Relationship among cultural, educational, and regulatory agency influences on optimum cancer pain treatment. Journal of Pain and Symptom Management 5:S37–S45, 1990b

Hill CS Jr: Influence of regulatory agencies on the treatment of pain and standards of medical practice for the use of narcotics. Pain Digest 1:7–12, 1991

Jaffe JH: Trivializing dependence. Br J Addict 85:1425–1427, 1990

Joranson DE, Cleeland CS, Weissman DE, et al: Opioids for chronic cancer and non-cancer pain: survey of state medical board members. Federation Bulletin: The Journal of Medical Licensure and Discipline 79:15–49, 1992

Kaiko RF, Grandy RP, Oshlack B, et al: The United States experience with oral controlled-release morphine (MS Contin tablets); Parts I and II: review on nine dose titration studies and clinical pharmacology of 15 mg, 30 mg, 60 mg, and 100 mg tablet strengths in normal subjects. Cancer 63:2348–2354, 1989

Marks I: Behavioral (non-chemical) addictions (editorial). Br J Addict 85:1389–1394, 1990

Marks RM, Sachar EJ: Undertreatment of medical inpatients with narcotic analgesics. Ann Intern Med 78:173–181, 1973

Morgan JP: American opiophobia: customary under-utilization of opioid analgesics, in Controversies in Alcoholism and Substance Abuse, Vol 5. Edited by Stimmel B. New York, Haworth Press, 1986, pp 163–173

Peele S: Ain't misbehavin': addiction has become an all-purpose excuse. The Sciences July/August 1989, pp 14–21

Perry S, Heidrich G: Management of pain during debridement: a survey of U.S. burn units. Pain 13:267–280, 1982

Portenoy RK: Opioid therapy in the management of chronic back pain, in Interdisciplinary Rehabilitation of Low Back Pain. Edited by Tollison CD. Baltimore, MD, William & Wilkins, 1989, pp 137–157

Portenoy RK: Chronic opioid therapy for persistent non-cancer pain: can we get past the bias? APS Bulletin 1:1, 4–5, 1991

Porter J, Jick H: Addiction rare in patients treated with narcotics. N Engl J Med 302:123, 1980

Rinaldi RC, Steindler EM, Wilford BB, et al: Clarification and standardization of substance abuse terminology. JAMA 259:555–557, 1988

Robins LN, David DH, Nurco DN: How permanent was Vietnam drug addiction? Am J Public Health 64:38–43, 1974

Schuster CR: Does treatment of cancer pain with narcotics produce junkies?, in Drug Treatment of Cancer Pain in a Drug-Oriented Society. Edited by Hiss CS Jr, Fields WS. New York, Raven, 1989, pp 1–3

Sriwatanakul K, Weis OF, Alloza JL, et al: Analysis of narcotic usage in the treatment of postoperative pain. JAMA 250:926–929, 1983

Texas Medical Practice Act, Texas Revised Civil Statutes Annotated, Article 4495b (Vernon Supplement 1989) § 3.08(4)(E)(F)(18)

Turk DC, Brody MC: Chronic opioid therapy for persistent non-cancer pain: panacea or oxymoron? APS Bulletin 1:1, 4–7, 1991

Turk DC, Brody MC: What position do APS physician members take on chronic opioid therapy? APS Bulletin 2:1–5, 1992

Twycross RG: The management of pain in cancer: a guide to drugs and dosages. Oncology 2:35–47, 1988

CHAPTER TWELVE

Psychotropic Drug Development: The FDA and the Pharmaceutical Industry

Alex A. Cardoni, M.S. Pharm.

It is axiomatic that drug therapy represents a critical treatment modality for psychiatric illness in the 1990s. A patient's good response to medication can mean the difference between a satisfying and productive life and one of continuing misery. But life was not always like this—for the patient and the doctor. Most practicing psychiatrists have never treated schizophrenia without phenothiazines or haloperidol, and many cannot recall the prelithium treatment of manic-depressive illness. The value of various psychotherapies aside, how do you treat the major anxiety disorders without benzodiazepines or major depression without antidepressants? Clearly, the development and introduction of these medications have represented major advances in the treatment of psychiatric illness since the early 1950s. The momentum continued into the 1980s and 1990s with the development of triazolo benzodiazepines (alprazolam, triazolam, and adinazolam) and the selective serotonin reuptake inhibitor antidepressants (fluoxetine, sertraline, and paroxetine) and with the availability in the United States of clomipramine for obsessive-compulsive disorder and clozapine for schizophrenia.

It is clear that clinical psychiatric practice in the 1990s is very different from what it was in the 1950s and that the emergence of "biological psychiatry" in the 1970s and 1980s with its biochemical underpinnings is largely responsible for this change. Many of the advances in our understanding of neuropathophysiology have emerged as a result of basic and clinical psychopharmacology studies. In turn, increased knowledge and understanding of neuropath-

247

ophysiology drives the search for more effective and safer medications and provides a heuristic basis for future drug development.

To a great extent, psychiatrists and other prescribers of psychotropic medications are constrained by market availability of drugs and drug products. What are the industrial and regulatory factors that influence market availability? Why is it that many other countries have had easy availability of some psychotropic drugs for years and yet we in the United States have experienced delayed access or have been denied availability altogether? What role does the pharmaceutical industry play in developing and facilitating access to new drugs? How well does the Food and Drug Administration (FDA) strike a balance between responsible protection of the public and undue delay in approval of new drugs?

In this chapter, in an attempt to answer these questions, I review the evolution of drug law in the United States, describe the FDA drug approval process, comment on drug development and marketing from an industry perspective, and discuss two case studies that illustrate problems of significant delay in the availability of two important psychotropic drugs: clozapine and clomipramine. The process of approval of tacrine for treatment of Alzheimer's disease is also discussed.

Evolution of United States Drug Law

The FDA acts to protect the public health by ensuring that all drugs on the market in the United States are safe and effective. Statutory authority for this emanates from the Federal Food, Drug, and Cosmetic Act of 1938, a law that has undergone many changes over the years (Department of Health and Human Services 1990). When it was enacted, it changed drug regulations that had been in effect for nearly 30 years. To appreciate the current role and functions of the FDA, it is helpful to review some of the major milestones in the evolution of United States drug law.

The Food and Drugs Act of 1906 required only that drug products meet official standards of strength and purity. In order for a drug product to be removed from the market, the FDA was required to prove that a drug's labeling was fraudulent.

The Federal Food, Drug, and Cosmetic Act of 1938 was a complete revision of the 1906 law. The bill establishing this law was introduced into the Senate in 1933 but it took the infamous "elixir sulfanilamide tragedy" in 1937 to prompt passage of this bill. This deplorable therapeutic misadventure resulted in 107 deaths from diethylene glycol, a nephrotoxic solvent that served as the vehicle for sulfanilamide in this preparation. Under law in effect at that time, the manufacturer was charged only with "misbranding" because there was no alcohol present in the preparation (an elixir, by definition, contains alcohol). If the word *solution* had been used instead of *elixir*, there would have been no violation of the law! With the passage of the 1938 legislation, a manufacturer had to prove the safety of its product before it could be marketed (Department of Health and Human Services 1990).

In 1951, the Durham-Humphrey Amendments to the 1938 law (see amendments to Federal Food, Drug, and Cosmetic Act 1938) established the prescription "legend" and defined prescription drugs as those unsafe for self-medication and those that should therefore be used only under a doctor's supervision (prescription).

In 1960, the FDA prevented the marketing of thalidomide in this country, largely through the efforts of Dr. Frances Kelsey, who was an FDA medical officer (Mintz 1962). This highly effective hypnotic drug had caused nearly 400 cases of phocomelia, a major congenital malformation marked by seal-like flippers in place of arms and legs, in infants born in Germany from 1959–1961. Similar cases were noted in Australia, Japan, and other countries (Taussig 1962). Publicity surrounding the banning of thalidomide in the United States increased public interest in drug safety and generated new interest in the effectiveness of drugs.

In 1962, fallout from the thalidomide experience provided impetus for the congressional passage of the Kefauver-Harris Amendments to the Federal Food, Drug, and Cosmetic Act (see amendments to Federal Food, Drug, and Cosmetic Act 1938). With this legislation, manufacturers had to demonstrate not only that their product was safe for humans but also that it was effective for the intended use. This new requirement was applied retroactively to drug products marketed since

1938. To help implement these amendments, the FDA contracted with the National Academy of Sciences/National Research Council to review the efficacy of drugs approved solely on the basis of safety since 1938. Although panels of experts had been used by FDA since 1964, it was not until 1972, with the passage of the Federal Advisory Committee Act (1972), that the advisory committee structure became an integral part of the new drug approval process.

Other legislation of note includes the Orphan Drug Act of 1983. "Orphans" are drugs shown to be effective for the treatment of rare diseases. Examples of orphans are pimozide for Tourette syndrome and L-5-hydroxytryptophan for spastic myoclonus. These drugs offer little or no profit to the manufacturer, but may benefit people with these diseases. To encourage orphan drug development, this law allows drug companies to take tax deductions for about three-quarters of the cost of their clinical studies. Firms are also given exclusive marketing rights for 7 years for any orphan products that are approved (Department of Health and Human Services 1990). It is of note that despite the absence of these incentives, Merck, Sharp, and Dohme marketed Cuprimine (penicillamine) in the 1960s for the treatment of Wilson's disease (incidence: 1 case per million) long before orphan drugs were ever thought of.

Drug Development and the FDA Drug Approval Process

The FDA does not test drugs for safety and efficacy; the drug sponsor is responsible for this. Rather, the FDA performs inspections, conducts review of data by both in-house and extramural consultants, and makes final judgment of approval for all drug products in the United States. Figure 12–1 shows the time line for new drug development under the United States drug approval process. The FDA publishes regulations with which a sponsor must comply to bring a drug to market, using whatever time it takes to do this. Current patent protection time is 17 years from the date the patent is awarded, but much of this time elapses before the drug is brought to market. The ratio of premarketing drug development time to postmarketing patent life is a major economic determinant of a drug's market price: the smaller this ratio, the more time the manufacturer has to recoup research and development costs and the lower the price of the drug. Usually the converse is also true: the larger this index, the less time to recover costs and the higher the market price. The presence of generic drugs affects pricing as well.

The first phase of drug development begins with synthesis of compounds. Hundreds and sometimes thousands of chemicals must be synthesized to find one that will be safe and effective. Compounds are then evaluated in laboratory animals where basic pharmacology and toxicology testing is performed. Following the thalidomide trag-edy, safety evaluation data in pregnant mammals, including at least

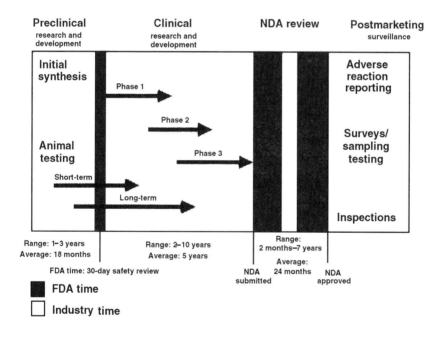

Figure 12–1. Time line for new drug development in the United States. Average of approximately 100 months from initial synthesis to approval of new drug application (NDA). From Department of Health and Human Services 1990.

one primate species, are required (Silverman and Lee 1974). This phase may take from 1 to 3 years, with an average time of 18 months.

If everything goes well in the preclinical phase, an application for an investigational new drug (IND) is submitted to the FDA. Review of safety data usually takes about 1 month, and, if accepted, the sponsor is awarded an IND and may initiate phase 1 clinical studies.

These "first-time-in-humans" studies involve evaluation of the drug in healthy volunteers to determine tolerability of the drug at various dosages and to identify its clinical pharmacokinetics. These studies are typically single dose and sometimes do not reflect kinetic parameters that characterize multiple-dose, long-term use of the drug seen in clinical practice. For example, the published half-life of elimination of fluoxetine (Prozac) is 48–72 hours and that of its active metabolite norfluoxetine is 7–9 days (Eli Lilly 1992). These values were determined in single-dose phase 1 studies. Subsequent postmarketing studies demonstrated that these parameters can increase significantly in patients who take the drug daily for up to 1 year. The half-life of fluoxetine increased to 8 days for parent compound and to 20 days for the active metabolite (Pato et al. 1991).

If the drug passes through phase 1 in good order, phase 2 studies are initiated. FDA review of phase 1 studies is not required before the onset of phase 2 studies. In this phase, the drug is evaluated in small numbers of patients with the illness for which the drug is intended. Much of the work done in this phase relates to "dose finding," the determination of optimal dosage to treat the illness effectively with an acceptable frequency and severity of side effects. Some pharmacokinetic studies may be performed also, especially blood-level–outcome correlations. If everything goes well in phase 2, the drug enters phase 3 testing.

In phase 3, the drug is evaluated in large numbers of patients with the illness. These studies are often performed in multiple sites to ensure that the numbers of patients evaluated will be large enough to satisfy the requirements for statistical evaluation. Dose-response relationships are further defined, blood-level–response relationships (if present) are strengthened, and additional side-effect and adverse-effect data are collected. Following completion of these studies, a new drug application (NDA) is submitted to the FDA. The clinical phase of development (phases 1–3) represents the bulk of time required to bring a drug to market. It may take as few as 2 years or as many as 10 years to complete clinical studies, with an average of 5 years.

Review of clinical data represents the largest block of FDA time in the drug approval process. This time may be as short as 2 months or as long as 7 years. The average length of FDA review is 2 years. There are some exceptions to this, however. Zidovudine (AZT, Retrovir) was approved for use in patients with acquired immunodeficiency syndrome (AIDS) in a record 107 days ("fast tracking") largely because of an increased budgetary allocation of approximately $600,000 for accelerated review (Young 1990). Unfortunately, the decision to employ an expedited review is clearly an example of the "politicalization" of the FDA review process in that FDA responded to the clamoring of AIDS advocacy groups for drug therapy for AIDS. Although, on the surface, accelerated review appears to respond to imminent need, especially with AIDS, it can backfire. Such review of zidovudine came under criticism because of the "surrogate marker" methodology used to prove efficacy of AZT (Altman 1993). Critics claimed that the CD_4 count in an AIDS patient was not a reliable indicator of clinical benefit of the drug and that studies should have been conducted for a longer time. The surrogate marker methodology has been used for years by the pharmaceutical industry and substitutes an easily measured parameter for disease or death—such as the use of blood pressure for risk of stroke, serum cholesterol for risk of heart attacks, and tumor enlargement for cancer. Not only can surrogate markers substitute for disease or death as a measuring point, they can significantly reduce the number of subjects needed in a drug efficacy study. Markers that can identify drug effects within a few weeks after starting treatment can shorten the time it takes to complete a study and significantly reduce research costs. These savings should allow companies to test a larger number of drugs in a shorter period of time.

Psychotropic drug evaluations typically do not use surrogate markers to determine drug efficacy. One could claim that extrapyramidal symptoms (EPS) are a surrogate for antipsychotic activity, especially with the early neuroleptics, but this correlation is simply not reliable. Typically, the index of response for psychotropic drugs is symptom reduction in the patient, whether one is treating psychosis, depression, or major anxiety disorders. The lack of reliable, easily measured markers for psychiatric illnesses undoubtedly has contributed to the longer times of drug approval for psychotropic agents in comparison with medical drugs.

If all goes well with the clinical efficacy review, the FDA will approve the NDA, clearing the way for the sponsor to market the drug in the United States. The time from NDA submission to eventual approval usually depends on whether the data were submitted to an advisory committee for review. In the neuropharmacologic division, for example, new chemical entities (NCEs) reviewed by an advisory committee spent 20 months longer in the NDA review phase than did unreviewed NCEs. In contrast, reviewed NCEs in the metabolic/endocrine and oncology/radiopharmaceutical divisions took, on average, 27.8 and 25.1 fewer months, respectively, than did unreviewed drugs in those divisions (Kaitin et al. 1989). Although the reasons for these remarkable disparities are not clear, they may be related to different philosophies among divisions toward the use of advisory committees. They may also be related to committees' requests for further FDA data analysis prior to approval as well as the need for upper management to review the application one last time before the final decision is made.

A different pattern emerged, however, when drugs were grouped by therapeutic rating: results showed a consistent increase in NDA phase length for reviewed drugs. Indeed 1-A drugs (important therapeutic gain) submitted for advisory committee review took longer to approve than did 1-B drugs (modest gain) not submitted for review. These findings suggest that advisory committee review may delay the approval of agents representing important therapeutic breakthroughs as well as those representing more modest gains. These findings strongly support the need for expedited review of drugs that offer significant therapeutic gains.

The issue of economic value of new drugs has surfaced as an additional factor to consider in the drug approval process (Leary 1993). The major impetus for this is from insurance companies and health maintenance organizations to minimize their costs. Thus, many drug companies are hiring "pharmaco-economists" to look at cost-effectiveness and quality-of-life issues related to new drugs. Of course, the industry is opposed to drug price regulation and warns that this will ultimately negatively impact on research and development of NCEs. In an absolutely extraordinary reflection of evolving FDA policy, some FDA advisory panels have already begun taking cost into consideration in their review of data provided in the NDA. Early in 1993, the FDA refused to approve another biotechnology drug for sepsis, nebacumab (Centoxin), manufactured by Centocor, Inc., primarily because the drug showed effectiveness only in a small subgroup of patients who could not be readily identified in advance. But the drug's high cost ($3,750 per dose) was also a factor. With other biotechnology agents (alglucerase [Ceredase], Genzyme) costing from $71,000 to $500,000 for a year's treatment of Gaucher's disease, a rare enzyme-deficiency disease, some critics argue that these drugs should not be made, as cost effectiveness is impossible (Office of Technology Assessment 1993). The professional and public outcry against the original cost of clozapine ($9,700 per year) seems unwarranted in view of the incredible cost of these biotechnology drugs, but of course the number of people affected by clozapine is far greater and the organized response by professional associations, the insurance industry, and patient and family advocacy groups was so intense that the distribution of clozapine was changed, resulting in a price reduction. This is discussed further under the case study of clozapine later in this chapter.

Postmarketing drug product surveillance is conducted by the FDA in several ways. First, via implementation of the Adverse Reaction Reporting program, the agency seeks to collect data on misadventures involving drug products. The intent of this system is to generate a data base of adverse reactions for a given drug, but there are problems. One problem is that the program is voluntary. For every adverse reaction reported, there are at least 10–20 similar reactions that are never reported. Clinicians simply do not have the time to do this. Also, critics argue that the frequency of adverse reaction reports seems to coincide with media attention focused on a particular drug. The best examples of this in psychiatry are sensational media coverage of alleged suicidal ideation and behavior associated with fluoxetine (Prozac) and aberrant behavior purportedly linked to triazolam (Halcion). This program may help to detect impending major adverse effects that might require a drug recall. A case in point for psychiatry involved the short-lived

Psychiatric Practice Under Fire

antidepressant nomifensine (Merital, Hoechst-Roussel), which was voluntarily withdrawn from the market in 1985 after reports of fatalities secondary to immune-mediated hemolytic reactions.

In addition to the above program, surveys, sampling, and testing of drug products are occasionally done. Last, regular inspections of manufacturing facilities are conducted to ensure ongoing high-quality production of drug products.

Problems With Psychotropic Drug Development

There are several reasons why psychotropic drug development has lagged behind other therapeutic categories. First, there is still the stigma associated with psychiatric illness, which affects public perceptions, attitudes, and policy. The federal government has been very slow to recognize the "legitimacy" of psychiatric illness as a "real" disease, in part because of the financial implications that would follow if government and private insurance for psychiatric illness were nondiscriminatory. Annual federal psychiatric disorder research budgets typically pale against similar expenditures for major medical diseases. In the president's 1993 fiscal year budget, federal research expenditures for mental disorder research (National Institute of Mental Health) totaled $0.56 billion ($1.90 per American afflicted with psychiatric illness, 40 million adults and children afflicted). In contrast, similar figures for heart, lung, and blood research reached $1.2 billion ($4.22 per capita, 10 million affected); the National Cancer Institute topped all National Institutes of Health agencies at $1.8 billion ($6.04 per capita, 1.5 million persons affected) (P. Seravedca, personal communication, May 27, 1993).

Second, the imprecision of psychiatric diagnosis, the heterogeneity of psychiatric disorders, and the lack of knowledge of precise mechanisms by which medications alleviate psychiatric illness all contribute to significant lengthening in time for psychotropic drug development. This is evident in both preclinical drug screening for activity and clinical drug evaluation for efficacy and safety. Diagnostic uncertainty creates heterogeneous patient groups that respond erratically to the drug under investigation. For example, amoxapine was thought to possess a significantly faster onset of action than older tricyclics (3 days) because of encouraging results in phase 3 trials. However, when used clinically in patients with major depression, the drug performed like old-line tricyclics with the usual 2- to 4-week delay in onset of effect. Closer examination of several studies that supported early onset of action revealed that patient populations contained a large proportion of "reactively" depressed patients, a proportion who favored early response (Dugas and Weber 1982). To avoid similar problems in the future, investigators must develop more precise diagnostic tools that will result in greater homogeneity in drug study groups.

Clozapine

Clozapine (Clozaril, Sandoz) was marketed in the United States on February 5, 1990, *a full 32 years after it was synthesized*. In fact, in 1990 clozapine had been available worldwide for clinical use for at least 20 years. This remarkable delay in clozapine's introduction to the United States market was primarily the result of the FDA's concerns about the incidence of agranulocytosis and the Sandoz marketing program, which intended to minimize legal liability related to this.

The indications for clozapine use include patients with "treatment-resistant" schizophrenia and those who develop intolerable EPS or tardive dyskinesia on typical agents. There are several excellent reviews of the pharmacologic and therapeutic profiles of this drug, and the reader is referred to these for a complete discussion of these topics (Baldessarini and Frankenburg 1991; Safferman et al. 1991).

Background

Clozapine was synthesized by Sandoz-Wander chemists in 1958 as one of more than 1,900 compounds (dibenzodiazepines) that were structurally similar to the then recently introduced imipramine (McKenna and Bailey 1993). Animal testing revealed marked effects on autonomic function as well as significant reduction in motor activity. Clozapine also showed potent anticholinergic and antiadrenergic activity. Since this profile was similar to that of chlorpromazine, clinical testing was begun in psychotic patients.

Clinical Studies

The first studies were carried out at the University Psychiatric Clinic in Bern in 1961–1962. Although early results with low dosage (maximum of 240 mg/day) were disappointing, later studies (Gross and Langner 1966) using doses of up to 700 mg/day for 6 months were more promising: 24 of 34 patients showed good to very good response. Subsequent studies confirmed these findings, and the drug was licensed for clinical use in Switzerland and subsequently in 34 other countries by 1972.

Agranulocytosis

By this time, 2,900 patients had received clozapine, of whom 4 had developed agranulocytosis, with one fatality (0.14%). This incidence was considered comparable to that of existing neuroleptics. But in 1975, following the approval of the drug in Finland, 16 cases of granulocytopenia occurred in patients taking clozapine, 13 of these became agranulocytic, and 8 died from secondary infections (Amsler et al. 1977; Anderman and Griffith 1977; Idäänpään and Heikkila et al. 1975, 1977). Why was there such a discrepancy between the Finnish experience and that of the rest of the world? Although the exact reason is not clear, it may lie in the fact that the Finnish postmarketing drug surveillance monitoring system was very "tight" and was able more accurately to attribute the adverse effect of agranulocytosis to the drug, in comparison with other countries. Approval of clozapine was therefore withdrawn in some countries that had previously made it available for general use. Its use was further restricted in other countries, including the United States, where some clinical investigations were in progress. This latter action may have reflected the emerging view that clozapine possessed exceptional clinical properties through clinical impression and in controlled evaluations against other neuroleptics, and because of its atypical properties, such as absence of acute EPS. In 1976, the FDA called for data substantiating the efficacy of clozapine in treatment-resistant patients, and, beginning in 1977, a number of carefully monitored investigations of clozapine were carried out (Gelenberg and Doller 1979; Shopsin et al. 1979). The most comprehensive of these was the multicenter retrospective and prospective clinical trial of clozapine versus chlorpromazine (Kane et al. 1988), which eventually became the landmark study supporting FDA approval of the drug in October 1989.

Clearly, the delay in eventual marketing of clozapine was directly related to the adverse Finnish experience with the drug in 1976, which resulted in a 62% mortality rate of patients who developed agranulocytosis. This devastating experience alone would have permanently killed any other drug. But clozapine remained alive because it demonstrated unique therapeutic activity: good efficacy, in some cases superior efficacy, with no EPS. But the FDA was foremost concerned with ensuring patient safety and therefore, on recommendation of the Psychopharmacology Advisory Panel, set the requirements for the multicenter efficacy study of Kane and colleagues (1988). This is the first time that the FDA required that a drug be shown to be *more effective* than the current standard of treatment, rather than "just as effective." All of this required significant time, and the study itself took 3 years to complete. The other factor responsible for the time delay in clozapine's availability is the manufacturer's insistence of weekly complete blood count (CBC) determinations, centralized record keeping, and weekly supply of medication, all provided in one "bundled" package for a "prix fixe," $172 per week. Planning, coordination, and implementation of this program also required a substantial time commitment, necessitating agreements with Caremark (phlebotomy) and Roche Laboratories (data management). It should be noted that the bundling of the system was *not* an FDA requirement for marketing, although the weekly CBC determination *was* a requirement.

Marketing in the United States

The FDA approved United States sale and labeling of clozapine in the fall of 1989. Neither the FDA nor the Psychopharmacology Advisory Panel required or recommended a monitoring system such as the Sandoz CPMS (Clozaril Patient Management System) in approving the drug. This name described the bundled system for the distribution, blood drawing, and safety monitoring of clozapine. However, Sandoz did include the CPMS in the labeling materials submitted to the FDA for approval, and the FDA approved the wording. Thus, any change in the labeling without FDA approval would constitute misbranding. However, Sandoz could have requested labeling changes. At a national meeting of state mental health program directors, an FDA representative was asked to explain how the FDA could approve Sandoz's CPMS in which a proprietary—yet not patentable—service process was being required and endorsed. However, no substantive response was given (Reid 1990). The FDA representative said that the labeling can be changed only on request of the manufacturer, but this was disputed by several persons in attendance. It is, he stated, "out of [the FDA's] jurisdiction" to respond to states' requests for labeling changes. Sandoz, of course, did not request labeling changes.

The CPMS required weekly CBC determinations before another week's supply of drug would be dispensed. The blunt phrase "no blood, no drug" was coined to describe this situation. Furthermore, the monitoring was performed only by employees of Caremark, a laboratory division of Baxter Laboratories. Caremark phlebotomists went into the patient's home or onto the hospital floor to draw weekly blood for white blood cell (WBC) testing. The samples were sent to Roche Laboratories in New Jersey for quantification and centralized record keeping.

During the first year of availability of clozapine, negative reaction to the unprecedented Sandoz practice of "bundling" a patented product (clozapine) with a requirement to purchase nonpatentable services (phlebotomy, CBC, and limited case management) was swift. Various constituencies and physician groups, pharmacists, state Medicaid agencies, private insurers, and mental health advocacy groups all spoke out against the "all-or-nothing" method of marketing of clozapine and the huge price attached to the bundled system (Goleman 1990; Lee 1990; Salzman 1990). There was also great concern that the linking of a drug product (clozapine) with a service (phlebotomy, case management) would set a precedent that could spread to other drugs and procedures. Several national groups petitioned Congress for a review of issues of antitrust and unfairness to severely ill and vulnerable patients (Freudenheim 1990).

The FDA approval of clozapine required weekly WBC monitoring because of the higher incidence of agranulocytosis (1%–2%). But the FDA never required that WBC monitoring and supply of the drug be made available *only* as a complete "bundled" package. This was a decision of Sandoz. Why was this decision made? Sandoz claims that their early experience with clozapine showed that although physicians were very good with CBC monitoring in the early weeks of treatment (about 90% compliance), compliance dropped to about 70% several months later. They felt that vulnerable patients needed reassurance that an early warning detection system would be in place. Sandoz was also concerned that the drug be available regardless of where patients lived. Thus, the decision was made to go with Caremark, who, according to Sandoz, was the only company to make a commitment to provide service to patients no matter where they lived. The "one price for all" was established again so that the drug would be available to all patients regardless of their location. Patients in remote areas would pay the same amount as patients in urban areas (Moran 1992).

It is reasonable to believe that concerns about liability for agranulocytic fatalities played a significant role in the decision by Sandoz. It is well established that the United States is more litigious than other countries where clozapine is available without weekly CBC monitoring. Therefore, from a medical liability viewpoint, Sandoz must ensure that weekly monitoring takes place, and this is best accomplished if *they* control the monitoring. Perhaps this posture is related to the past therapeutic misadventures that Sandoz experienced with pigmentation retinopathy and resultant irreversible blindness associated with thioridazine (Mellaril) in the late 1950s and early 1960s (de Margerie 1962; Hagopian et al. 1966; Kyaer 1968; Weekley et al. 1960). In addition, Sandoz argued that, in the interest of the nation's public safety, protection of patients from developing agranulocytosis required that they control the distribution and monitoring of this drug. This is a difficult point. We know that consistency of behavior is optimized when fewer "players" are involved; that is, the greater the number of people involved in a system, the greater the probability that more variability in operations will occur. So, from this point of view, Sandoz had a point. The question is, what are the limits of tolerance in such a system?

Eventually, Sandoz "de-bundled" their program in response to an antitrust lawsuit brought against Sandoz and Caremark. By December 1990, 33 states had joined the suit, and, in response, Sandoz agreed to separate the cost of the drug from the monitoring services. In place of CPMS, they instituted a requirement that physicians and pharmacists register with the company as designated "treatment systems" for clozapine. More states joined the suit, and Sandoz was charged by the Federal Trade Commission with unlawfully tying the sale of the product to purchase of patient-monitoring services. The distribution system was abandoned in May 1991, and Sandoz began charging wholesalers an average of $4,160 per year per patient for the medication alone. Under an agreement settling charges by the Federal Trade Commission, Sandoz was prohibited from requiring any purchaser of clozapine or patient taking clozapine sold by Sandoz to buy other goods or services from Sandoz or its designees. In September 1992, Sandoz and Baxter/Caremark agreed to pay $20 million to state governments and individuals that sued over patient-monitoring requirements for clozapine. About $10 million was paid to individuals and state mental hospitals and Medicaid programs that purchased the drug between February 1990 and May 1991. About $3 million was paid to patients who could not afford the drug and were not eligible for Medicaid, and about $3 million went to the National Organization for Rare Disorders for a drug program for indigent patients, according to Sandoz (*American Journal of Hospital Pharmacy* 1992).

Perhaps the lesson to be learned from the clozapine experience is that the industry needs to talk to those groups that will be affected by their marketing decisions and take the feedback into advisement in designing a system that will optimize response for the patient, be acceptable to the health professionals, and be economically sound for the company.

Some critics have unfairly blamed the FDA for the delay in availability of clozapine in the United States. In fact, the Finnish agranulocytosis experience delayed use of this drug in this country for at least 10 years because studies needed to be completed that showed that clozapine was superior (not just equivalent) to preexisting standard antipsychotic drug therapy. This higher standard was necessary to justify patient exposure to a potentially life-threatening adverse effect.

The FDA in consultation with its advisory committee and consultants and with Sandoz chose the correct, conservative course of action. With patient safety as the paramount concern, there was no other option.

Clomipramine

Clomipramine (Anafranil, Ciba-Geigy) was approved by the FDA in December 1989 for the treatment of obsessive-compulsive disorder (Peters et al. 1990). The reader is referred to several fine reviews of the clinical pharmacology of this agent (Peters et al. 1990; Trimble 1990). The approval of clomipramine in the United States ended almost 20 years of frustration for patients and clinicians who knew of the benefits of this agent for obsessive-compulsive disorder but could not obtain it through legitimate means in this country. Many physicians had their patients travel to Europe and later Canada or Mexico to obtain the drug, or purchased it by mail from foreign sources. Again, why did it take so long to have this drug approved by the FDA?

It appears that the major reason for the delay was the use of poorly designed early clinical trials, most likely developed by the drug's sponsor, Ciba-Geigy. Patients entered into these studies were not screened for comorbid depression, and differences between clomipramine and the standard tricyclic antidepressants were not evident (Rapoport et al. 1980; Thoren et al. 1980). Thus, the trials had to be repeated with subjects who had "pure" obsessive-compulsive disorder (Clomipramine Collaborative Study Group 1991; J. Rapoport, personal communication, April 27, 1993). All of this took additional time (years) and dollars. Once the subject selection problems were resolved, the unique properties of clomipramine (60%–70% response) versus standard tricyclic antidepressants (20%–30%) and placebo (3%–5%) were demonstrated (Leonard et al. 1989; Volavka et al. 1985; Zohar and Insel 1987). The drug was then made available in the United States under the "Anafranil Treatment Program for Obsessive-Compulsive Disorder." Under this program, "patients who are seriously ill can receive Anafranil prior to FDA's marketing approval under the guidelines of a controlled treatment program" (Ciba-Geigy 1989). Once the noncontroversial expedited review was completed by the

FDA, approval came on December 29, 1989.

In this case, the problem of significant delay appears to have rested with the manufacturer and not the FDA. Had the early studies been well designed to avoid comorbidity and had they been rigorous in subject selection, the time to market in this country could have been shortened considerably. Did Ciba-Geigy deliberately delay seeking FDA approval of clomipramine to avoid a competitive situation with its highly successful Tofranil (imipramine)? If anything, one would think the company would have pursued a depression indication for clomipramine in view of the patent expiration of imipramine that occurred in the mid-1970s. Although the answers to these questions are unclear, one is left with the impression of significant internal mismanagement of the overall clomipramine program by Ciba-Geigy.

Tacrine

On September 9, 1993, the FDA approved the use of tacrine (Cognex, Parke-Davis) for the treatment of Alzheimer's disease. Six months previously (March 18, 1993), the FDA Neurology Advisory Committee had recommended approval of tacrine in a surprising reversal of their previous negative recommendation (D. Rhodes, personal communication, May 5, 1993). This turn of events followed discussion of two new studies (Farlow et al. 1992; Parke-Davis, unpublished data, March 1993) and emotional testimony by patient advocacy groups. The new data apparently influenced committee members enough to change their opinion about the merits of the drug. Results of an earlier study (Davis et al. 1992) showed that after 6 weeks of treatment, the drug produced slight improvement in patients who were diagnosed with mild-to-moderate cases of the illness, but not enough to detect by physician global assessment of behaviors. Indeed, the study was designed to give the drug every chance of producing a positive outcome. Only patients who showed early positive response to tacrine were included in the placebo-controlled portion of the study. Results indicated that there was some improvement in patients who received the drug compared with placebo. But the improvement has been characterized as being "clinically trivial" (Growdon 1993), with the very modest short-term effects of tacrine being incapable of reversing the signs and symptoms of the disease. In addition, 10% of patients were withdrawn from the study because of side effects, including changes in hepatic enzyme values. But clinical response to tacrine may be related to duration of treatment at therapeutic dosage. In the study by Farlow and colleagues (1992), 51% of 37 patients receiving 80 mg/day showed a four-point or greater improvement in cognitive function (Alzheimer's Disease Assessment Scale) after 12 weeks of treatment, and 27% achieved an improvement of seven or more points. These differences from placebo were statistically significant (analysis of covariance, $P = .015$) and clinically significant, comparable with reversing 6 months of disease progression. Clinician-rated, interview-based assessments also revealed significant, dose-related improvement with tacrine over placebo at 12 weeks. Reversible asymptomatic transaminase elevations greater than three times normal occurred in 25% of patients along with nausea/vomiting (8%), diarrhea (5%), abdominal pain (4%), dyspepsia (3%), and rash (3%). The hepatic changes confirm the need to have patients obtain weekly transaminase determinations, a situation analogous to that with clozapine, and weekly CBC. A concern is the high dropout rate (41%), with 106 of 195 "dropouts" not included in the data analysis because of "insufficient efficacy data."

The company also provided the FDA with safety data collected in more than 4,000 patients who were provided the drug prior to marketing under an FDA-approved program.

Despite the favorable results with the study of Farlow and colleagues (1992), approval of tacrine suggests a double standard by the FDA when compared with the clozapine experience: tacrine, which has shown mixed results in placebo-controlled studies accompanied by a high incidence of hepatic enzyme changes that may lead to hepatotoxicity, was approved, at least in part, because of patient advocacy group pressure. In contrast, approval of clozapine required proof that the drug was superior to well-known standard antipsychotic drug therapy for an illness whose diagnosis is well defined. Although this was justified based on the risk of agranulocytosis, tacrine's frequently occurring hepatotoxicity has not prompted a similar requirement. There is no doubt that senior citizen advocacy groups have exerted tremendous pressure on the FDA to approve tacrine for the treatment of Alzheimer's disease, and this was successful. Why did this not happen with clozapine? Are senior citizen groups more influential than mental health advocacy groups? Does the stigma of psychiatric illness affect decisions at the governmental and industry levels that result in delay in needed treatments for psychiatric illness? It is worth noting that the potential market for the use of tacrine is enormous, and this certainly is a factor from the manufacturer's point of view in pushing for approval. This notwithstanding, tacrine currently represents the only treatment available for Alzheimer's disease, whereas clozapine was the latest of a host of "new improved" antipsychotic agents introduced over the past 40 years.

Summary

The modern history of psychopharmacology in this country has been exciting and largely successful—successful for the industry, for the clinician, and for the patient. The anguish of severe psychiatric illness has been alleviated for many patients as biological psychiatry has emerged and begun to flourish since the 1950s. But it is also evident that long delays have characterized psychotropic drug development, and these have placed constraints on our ability to treat patients in need effectively. Some of this delay is due to the FDA drug approval process, but not the vast majority. Indeed, the pharmaceutical industry is the key player in determining which agents eventually make it to market. Of all the players in this arena—industry, government, academia, and the public-at-large—the industry by far has the greatest financial means to finance drug research and development. Some critics of the pharmaceutical industry's favorable financial status have called for reform in drug pricing (Pear 1992). Others have called for a dramatic change in drug patent protection or for turning the pharmaceutical industry into a national public utility. Although the profits of this industry have been consistently among the best in the business world, we should think twice about placing a discriminatory cap on this industry's profits that may well curtail inventiveness, ingenuity, and creativity.

The specter of managed care and health care reform is with us, and we all feel the pressure to shorten length of inpatient stays and to make outpatient treatment as efficient as possible. In this environment, the need for pharmacotherapy that is effective, safe, and affordable takes on added import. Research should be directed to the expeditious development of faster-acting medications for mood disorders; for effective antipsychotic agents that will follow in the steps of clozapine, yet provide a much better safety profile; and for agents that can eliminate the pervasive anxiety that causes loss of productivity in millions of Americans. We need targeted drug research in populations previously ignored, such as women and children and the elderly; early signs suggest that this will be forthcoming (Hilts 1993). We need cooperation between industry, the public, and practitioners to avoid the missteps illustrated by the clozapine story. Finally, we need a drug approval regulatory process that balances the need for new effective therapies with the need to prevent harm, and a process that does so in a timely manner.

References

Altman LKK: AIDS study casts doubt of value of hastened drug approval in U.S. The New York Times, April 6, 1993, p C3

American Journal of Hospital Pharmacy: Clozapine suit settled against Sandoz and Caremark. Am J Hosp Pharm 49:2651, 1992

Amsler HA, Teerenhori L, Barth E, et al: Agnanulocytosis in patients treated with clozapine: a study of the Finnish epidemic. Acta Psychiatr Scand 56:241–248, 1977

Anderman B, Griffith RW: Clozapine-induced agranulocytosis: a situation report up to August 1976. Eur J Clin Pharmacol 11:199–201, 1977

Baldessarini RJ, Frankenburg FR: Clozapine: a novel anti-psychotic agent. N Engl J Med 324:746–754, 1991

Ciba-Geigy: Anafranil Treatment Program Brochure. Ciba-Geigy, 1989

Clomipramine Collaborative Study Group: Clomipramine in the treatment of patients with obsessive-compulsive disorder. Arch Gen Psychiatry 48:730–738, 1991

Davis KL, Thal LJ, Gamzu ER, et al: Double-blind placebo-controlled multicenter study of tacrine for Alzheimer's disease. N Engl J Med 327:1253–1259, 1992

de Margerie J: Ocular changes produced by a phenothiazine drug: thioridazine. Transactions of the Canadian Ophthalmological Society 25:160–175, 1962

Department of Health and Human Services: From test tube to patient: new drug development in the United States (FDA Consumer Special Report) (DHHS Publ No 90-3168). Washington, DC, Department of Health and Human Services, 1990

Dugas JE, Weber SS: Amoxapine. Drug Intelligence and Clinical Pharmacy 16:199–204, 1982

Eli Lilly: Prozac product information. Indianapolis, IN, Dista Products Company, Division of Eli Lilly & Co, 1992

Farlow M, Gracon SI, Hershey LA, et al: A controlled trial of tacrine in Alzheimer's disease. JAMA 268:2523–2529, 1992

Federal Advisory Committee Act of 1972, Pub L No 92-463 (1972)

Federal Food, Drug, and Cosmetic Act of 1938, 21 USC § 321 (1938) (Durham-Humphrey Amendments 21 USC § 353 [1951]) (Kefauver-Harris Amendments 76 Stat 780 [1962])

Food and Drugs Act of 1906, 34 Stat 768 (1906)

Freudenheim M: Method of pricing drug is assailed. The New York Times, August 28, 1990, p D2

Gelenberg AJ, Doller JC: Clozapine versus chlorpromazine for the treatment of schizophrenia. Preliminary results from a double-blind study. J Clin Psychiatry 40:238–240, 1979

Goleman D: Schizophrenia drug hailed, except for cost. The New York Times, May 15, 1990, p C2

Gross H, Langner E: Das Wirkungsprofil eines Chemisch Neuartigan Breitband-Neuroleptikums der Dibenzodiazepingruppe. Wien Med Wochenschr 116:814–816, 1966

Growdon J: Tacrine in Alzheimer's disease (letter). N Engl J Med 328:810, 1993

Hagopian V, Stratton DB, Busiek RD: Five cases of pigmentary retinopathy associated with thioridazine administration. Am J Psychiatry 123:97–100, 1966

Hilts PJ: FDA ends ban on women in drug testing. The New York Times, March 24, 1993

Idäänpään-Heikkila J, Alhava E, Olkinvora M, et al: Clozapine and agranulocytosis. Lancet 2:611, 1975

Idäänpään-Heikkila J, Alhava E, Olkinvora M, et al: Agranulocytosis during treatment with Clozapine. Eur J Clin Pharmacol 11:193–198, 1977

Kaitin KI, Melville A, Morris B: FDA advisory committee and the new drug approval process. J Clin Pharmacol 28:886–890, 1989

Kane J, Honigfeld G, Singer J, et al: Clozapine for the treatment-resistant schizophrenic: a double-blind comparison with chlorpromazine. Arch Gen Psychiatry 45:789–796, 1988

Kyaer GCD: Retinopathy associated with phenothiazine administration. Diseases of the Nervous System 29:316–319, 1968

Leary W: New drug standard: economic value. The New York Times, January 18, 1993

Lee H: Pharmacists outraged by Clozaril system. Journal of Pharmacy Practice 3:6–8, 1990

Leonard HL, Swedo SE, Koby EV, et al: Treatment of obsessive-compulsive disorder with clomipramine and desmethylimipramine in children and adolescents: a double-blind, crossover comparison. Arch Gen Psychiatry 46:1088–1092, 1989

McKenna PJ, Bailey PE: The strange story of clozapine. Br J Psychiatry 162:32–37, 1993

Mintz M: "Heroine" of FDA keeps bad drug off market. Washington Post, July 15, 1962

Moran M: Ethical, legal, political dilemmas greet states trying to widen access to Clozaril. Psychiatric News, August 7, 1992

Office of Technology Assessment: Ceredase assessment report. Washington, DC, Office of Technology Assessment, United States Congress, 1993

Orphan Drug Act of 1983, Pub L No 97-414 (1983)

Pato MT, Murphy DL, DeVane CL: Sustained plasma concentrations of fluoxetine and/or norfluoxetine four and eight weeks after fluoxetine discontinuation. J Clin Psychopharmacol 11:224–225, 1991

Pear R: Clinton team to tackle drug pricing. The New York Times, December 4, 1992

Peters MD II, Davis SK, Austin LS: Clomipramine: an anti-obsessional tricyclic antidepressant. Clin Pharm 9:165–178, 1990

Rapoport J, Elkins R, Mikkelsen E: Clinical controlled trial of chlorimipramine in adolescents with obsessive-compulsive disorder. Psychopharmacol Bull 16:61–65, 1980

Reid WH: Summary report of meeting of National Association of State
    Mental Health Program Directors on Clozaril, Arlington, VA, February
    8–9, 1990

Safferman A, Lieberman JA, Jane JM, et al: Update on the clinical efficacy
    and side effects of clozapine. Schizophr Bull 17:247–261, 1991

Salzman C: Notes from a state mental health directors' meeting on Clozapine.
    Hosp Community Psychiatry 41:838–842, 1990

Shopsin B, Klein H, Aaronson M, et al. Clozapine, chlorpromazine, and
    placebo in newly hospitalized, acutely schizophrenic patients: a con-
    trolled double-blind comparison. Arch Gen Psychiatry 36:657–664,
    1979

Silverman M, Lee PR: Pills, Profits and Politics. Berkeley, CA, University of
    California Press, 1974

Taussig HB: A study of the German outbreak of phocomelia: the thalidomide
    syndrome. JAMA 180:1106–1114, 1962

Thorén P, Åsberg M, Cronholm B, et al: Clomipramine treatment of obses-
    sive-compulsive disorder; 1: a controlled clinical trial. Arch Gen Psychi-
    atry 37:1281–1285, 1980

Trimble MR: Worldwide use of clomipramine. J Clin Psychiatry 51
    (suppl):51–54, 1990

Volavka J, Neziroglu F, Yaryura-Tobias JA: Clomipramine and imipramine
    in obsessive-compulsive disorder. Psychiatric Research 14:85–93, 1985

Weekley RD, Potts AM, Reboton J, et al: Pigmentary retinopathy in patients
    receiving high doses of a new phenothiazine. Arch Ophthalmol 64:65–
    76, 1960

Young FE: Experimental drugs for the desperately ill (FDA Consumer Special
    Report). Rockville, MD, Department of Health and Human Services,
    1990

Zohar J, Insel T: Obsessive-compulsive disorder: psychobiological ap-
    proaches to diagnosis, treatment, and pathophysiology. Biol Psychiatry
    22:667–687, 1987

Index

Page numbers printed in **boldface** *type refer to tables or figures.*